THE SPORTS INDUSTRY'S WAR ON ATHLETES

THE SPORTS INDUSTRY'S WAR ON ATHLETES

PETER FINLEY AND LAURA FINLEY

Westport, Connecticut
London

Library of Congress Cataloging-in-Publication Data

Finley, Peter.
    The sports industry's war on athletes / Peter Finley and Laura Finley.
        p.   cm.
    Includes bibliographical references and index.
    ISBN 0–275–99172–5 (alk. paper)
    1. Sports—Economic aspects—United States.   2. Sports—Social aspects—United
States.   3. Sports—Corrupt practices—United States.   4. Racism in sports—United
States.   I. Finley, Peter S.   II. Title.
    GV716.F56   2006
    306.4′830973–dc22   2006014144

British Library Cataloguing in Publication Data is available

Library of Congress Catalog Card Number: 2006014144
ISBN: 0–275–99172–5

First published in 2006

Praeger Security International, 88 Post Road West, Westport, CT 06881
An imprint of Greenwood Publishing Group, Inc.
www.praeger.com

Printed in the United States of America

The paper used in this book complies with the
Permanent Paper Standard issued by the National
Information Standards Organization (Z39.48–1984).

10 9 8 7 6 5 4 3 2 1

Contents

Preface

Anyone who would write a book that challenges the status quo of big-time sports must be a sports-hating geek, right? Perhaps an out-of-shape slob who couldn't care less about physical fitness? Actually, nothing could be farther from the truth. We want to assure the reader from the outset that we wrote this book not because we hate sports, but because we love sports. We are lifetime athletes, competing on scholarship at the collegiate level and having engaged in numerous sports challenges as adults (Laura has run several marathons while Peter completed a grueling bicycle race across the state of Indiana). We also love to watch sports, both in person and on television. And because we are dedicated fans of sports at all levels and of all types, we feel compelled to explore some of the problems in the industry—problems that we feel are most threatening because they are systemic in nature. That is, they are built into the very structure of modern sports and thus are increasingly difficult to resist. The following sections highlight our personal stories regarding when we realized big-time sports are dedicated to profit and spectacle above all else.

LAURA'S STORY

My moment of realization occurred when I was on the cross country and track teams at Western Michigan University in the early 1990s. As athletes, we were generally in the know about things going on with other teams at the university. When word hit that the school was working on ways to increase the likelihood they would get big-time recruits for their football team, none of us were surprised. Even though other teams at the university were far more successful in regard to wins and losses, football, as at most D-I institutions, received the bulk of the attention. But the day we were told at practice that the university was considering employing female escorts, "the Bronco Belles," in order to entice prospective football players was the day I realized sports was about making money, not necessarily developing character or any of those other sound-good goals we're told. I truly believed this sexist ploy was one only Hollywood could produce, and was taken aghast when I discovered my error. Thankfully, the Belles never happened at Western Michigan but sadly it is a practice utilized at numerous other institutions. I now realize this was merely a minor byproduct, the sports machine just getting started. In their zeal to win in big-time sports, universities have tried virtually everything to attract highly rated athletes, including the exploitation of young women to appeal to the supposedly unscrupulous young men.

PETER'S STORY

Sports have helped define me through my life. From youth soccer teams and karate lessons as a boy to cross country and track and field teams in high school and college to bicycle racing and golf tournaments as an adult, I've always dabbled in sports. And I love every minute of it. So much so that I started coaching while still an undergraduate, volunteering at first and soon becoming a head coach. Frankly, I had loved distance running so much that as injury drove me to the sidelines I felt compelled to move into coaching. I just couldn't leave sports behind. To this day, some of the most rewarding relationships I have had were with teammates and athletes I coached.

Prior to February 28, 1998, I had likely never questioned the importance of sports. But then it became clear to me that "the games" were sometimes assigned a curious degree of importance. On that day, Miami of Ohio basketball coach Charlie Coles suffered a heart attack as his team played Western Michigan University in a Mid-American Conference tournament game. A proud Bronco, I was there to root on the home team in their drive to the NCAA tournament. To me, the game lost all meaning as I watched five doctors fight to save Coles' life on the side of the court. A packed house has likely never been so quiet.

The shocker, to me at least, was that after Coles was rushed to the hospital, the game resumed. There was an hour break, and the story circulated that the Miami of Ohio players had voted to continue, but it just didn't sit well with me or many other fans. In fact, when it was announced that the game would continue a murmur ran through the crowd. I heard several people whisper things like, "Ya gotta be kidding me . . . they're going to play this thing?"

I remember wondering how a game could be so important. Miami of Ohio standout Wally Szczerbiak was quoted in the paper the next day, saying, "All we could do was what we thought our leader would want us to do." And I'm sure that Szczerbiak was right. Coles almost certainly would have told his team to fight on. Many coaches would likely urge their team to continue. But is any of this rational?

Or have we assigned completely irrational importance to these contests? If a coach's courtside heart attack cannot even stand in the way of an event, it certainly seems as though a strong element of irrationality has pervaded the sports environment. But if this is the case, then the question becomes "How?" How have we allowed sports to get so out-of-control?

Perhaps we've been blind to the gradual development of irrational tendencies and practices because the big business of sports is simply so efficient at grinding out a compelling product. Such blindness would certainly be understandable, as a phenomenon; but it would also beg the question: At what cost is this entertainment provided? What else have we been missing?

Introduction:
The Big, Bad, World
of Sports

To the religiously devout, God is everything; to the American athlete, it would
seem, winning is everything.

—Arnold Beisser, *The Madness of Sport*

Sports in the United States is big business. This is true from the professional and collegiate levels to your local recreation center and youth sports
program. But the sports industry is not just about the games; rather, it
encompasses everything from the sales of sporting goods, to athletes endorsing
all kinds of products, to sports related tourism. Few Americans likely are aware
of the actual volume of money involved in the world of sports. The total volumes dwarf even the priciest contracts for the top professional athletes, which
receive most of the media coverage on the topic. The business of sports is at worst
the eleventh largest industry in the United States, with estimates ranging from
$152 billion to nearly $300 billion changing hands every year for sports related
reasons.[1] The *Sports Business Journal* even claimed that by 1999 the sports industry
was the sixth largest industry in the United States, trailing only real estate, retail
trade, health care, banking, and transportation.[2] While sports have been used as
public entertainment throughout history, sports today are commercial products as
much as they are anything else.[3]

A primary reason for huge volumes of money circulating around sports is that
businesses have realized the power of forming symbiotic relationships with teams,
events, and athletes. Sports need funds to exist and businesses need platforms
to market their products to potential customers. As sports continue to grow in
popularity and reach ever more clearly defined niches, businesses can put their

money to work by sponsoring events that will be watched by their target market. Sports far surpass other industries in its ability to attract corporate sponsorship: in 1997, $4.6 billion was spent on sports-related corporate sponsorship, compared to $675 million for sponsorship in the entertainment industry.[4] Some studies have shown steady growth in the size of the sports business industry, with typical annual increases of at least 13 percent and an amazing 141 percent increase between 1988 and 1995.[5]

Another way the sports industry has grown is in the construction of new full-service sports facilities. Spending on development of new arenas and stadiums for major league professional teams neared $16 billion in the period between 1995 and 2003. Further, over 160 new major league and minor league ballparks, arenas, and racetracks were constructed in the United States and Canada in the 1990s.[6] The 1990s also saw almost 180 new professional teams born, coupled with thirteen new leagues (for instance, the XFL, which unsuccessfully attempted to offer a radical alternative to the NFL) for a total of over 800 professional teams.[7] Between 1989 and 2001 the "Big Four" major leagues (NFL, NBA, MLB, and NHL) had expanded from 103 franchises to 123.[8] Even more spectacular has been the growth of minor league teams. Hockey alone had over 140 minor league teams in action in the United States and Canada by 2000.[9]

College athletics are also about big bucks. By 2000, college athletics had become a $4 billion enterprise.[10] In 2000, the average budget for athletic departments with major football and basketball programs was $20 million.[11] Some college athletic budgets have ballooned to an amazing $73 million.[12] Even at institutions with traditionally strong academic reputations, athletics take priority when it comes to distribution of resources. For example, Duke University gave $4 million in scholarship money to 550 intercollegiate athletes, while giving only $400,000 in academic aid to 5900 other undergraduates in a recent academic year. Similarly, the University of North Carolina at Chapel Hill gives an average of $3.2 million per year to 690 athletes. The almost 15,000 other students? They received a sum total of $636,000.[13]

Nor is the amateur level of sports immune from chasing down sponsorship contracts. In 2001, the University of North Carolina signed an 8-year agreement with Nike worth an astronomical $3.54 million annually. Over 200 other schools have similar but less lucrative gigs with Nike.[14] Television contracts are also pricey at this level. Notre Dame has a $45 million contract with NBC to televise its football games. Merchandise sales brings the school another million in royalties annually.[15] Schools have increased their revenue by licensing their name and logo everywhere imaginable.[16] Hence a fan (or fanatic?) can purchase such important items as Clemson toilet paper, shower curtains, and toothbrushes.[17]

THE MEDIA'S ROLE

Sports consume ever-greater amounts of media coverage. One-fourth of *USA Today*, the most widely read newspaper in the United States, is devoted to coverage of sports, and almost one-fifth of major network television time is devoted to sports.[18] The most watched television event is the Super Bowl.[19] Many sociologists have asserted that sports today is made for the media, a topic we take up at greater length later in this chapter as well as in subsequent ones. Control of the media is increasingly held in the hands of a few prominent companies. Disney owns numerous media outlets as well as teams (100% of the Mighty Ducks and 25% of the Anaheim Angels). Their broadcasting portfolio also includes ESPN and ABC. ABC has the rights to over $6 billion of college football coverage as well as the rights to PGA Golf, the NHL, the NFL, and Major League Soccer.[20] So, while viewers see more and more sports, they are seeing them from an increasingly narrow perspective.

WHO'S PROFITING?

If you're involved in sports, these numbers sure sound good. But, does everyone share in the monetary gain of the sports industry? Decidedly not. In fact, in our capitalist culture it is inevitable that some will benefit at the expense of others. Interestingly, despite the huge sums of money being exchanged in the sports industry, few major league teams or NCAA programs manage to avoid budget deficits. Only 48 of the 900 plus NCAA programs operated without a deficit in the late 1990s.[21] To help generate revenue, the "have-not" teams will often schedule games with elite teams, typically getting pummeled in exchange for a big payout that dwarfs the revenue they could generate from hosting an appropriately competitive foe.[22]

Generally the early season landscapes in football and basketball are littered with such second tier teams suffering at the hands of Powerhouse U. For example, early in the 2004 NCAA football season, Texas pounded North Texas 65–0, Miami crushed Louisiana Tech 48–0, Oklahoma scored 63 against an overmatched Houston team, and the University of Michigan spanked Miami of Ohio 43–10 in front of 110,815 adoring fans. In each case Powerhouse U. got a win at home and a tune up for tougher games ahead, while the loser limped home with pockets full of revenue.

In spite of the occasional windfall from such games, college programs on the whole lose money. Football programs at the NCAA Divisions IAA and IAAA levels average annual operating deficits of more than $2 million.[23] This deficit doesn't just disappear; it is siphoned from other funds, including those of other athletic teams and from academic areas. According to a *US News & World Report* article from 2002, almost one half of Ohio State University's capital budget went into building athletic facilities between 1998 and 2002. The library, in major need of renovation, might get an update by 2008, if funds are available.[24] Often a large portion of student fees is automatically turned over to the athletic department. At Colorado State University, not necessarily known for its big-time football, more than a third of the athletic budget comes from within the university, including student fees and other types of university support.[25] While the university as a whole loses money, those involved at the top level of athletics certainly do not. The coaches and athletic directors surely aren't struggling to pay the bills.

Nor do the spectators much benefit from the lucrative sports business. While accepting the Theodore Roosevelt Award, the highest honor bestowed by the NCAA, former President Ronald Reagan proclaimed in 1990, "When men and women compete on the athletic field, socioeconomic status disappears. African American or white, Christian or Jew, rich or poor... all that matters is that you're out there on the field giving your all. It's the same way in the stands, where corporate presidents sit next to janitors... and they high-five each other when their team scores..."[26] Not exactly. Working-class and middle-class families are finding it difficult to afford seeing major league sporting events live. The Fan Cost Index created by *Team Marketing Report*, an estimate of the average cost for a family of four with an average monthly income to attend a professional sporting event, clearly demonstrates a rapid cost increase among the Big Four leagues since 1990. A family of four would have to spend 30 percent of its weekly earnings to attend an NHL or NFL game in 2002.[27] Living in Colorado at the outset of writing, we were stunned by figures reported for a family of four to attend local sports in Denver in 2001: $426.64 to watch the Denver Broncos, $339.344 to watch the Colorado Avalanche, $235.44 to attend a Denver Nuggets game, and $130.50 at a Colorado Rockies game.[28] In addition, those who dole out almost one-third of their average weekly income to attend these events are not viewing the game from luxury seating. Rather, while the very rich enjoy the game from well-equipped suites, the plebians are seated in what was once called "the cheap seats." In today's market, these seats might be far from the action but they are anything but cheap.

Rather than take measures to return to the days of sports attendance for the workingman and woman, teams are devoting more of their seating to corporate ticket buyers.[29] This exacerbates the problem, as now not only can the less-than-affluent not afford to attend, but even when they are willing to spend their cash for tickets they often cannot purchase them because they have been earmarked for more wealthy patrons. Never fear, the Average Joe can simply get his sports fix on television, right? Certainly many do, but Sports sociologist Jay Coakley points out it even takes money to view sports on television, as many events now appear on cable channels.[30]

Ultimately, it is the fan that always pays for the commercialization of sports. While commercial sponsors pay, initially, in the end they raise prices to recoup their costs.[31]

The athletes must be the recipients of the payola, right? Certainly this is true to an extent, but while the public hears a lot about certain highly paid athletes, we hear very little about those who are not so heftily rewarded for their efforts in the sports arena. Some football players do earn fifty times that of the average American worker, with the average salary in the NFL in 2002–2003 standing at $1.26 million.[32] Yet other NFL players earn $200,000 a year and many professional athletic careers are short-lived.[33] Athletes in other sports are not nearly so well compensated, and the average professional career lasts only 5 years.[34] The median yearly salary for professional athletes is a far better measure, as averages outliers, or extremes, skew averages. The median salary for all professional athletes in all sports in the United States is only \$26,102. Not exactly an off-the-charts figure.[35] For the many players who never make the big leagues, pay at the minor levels is not exactly mind-boggling. Players at baseball's highest minor league level, Triple-A, for the Colorado Rockies minor league system make \$2,150 per month. At the Single-A level they receive \$1,200 per month. Professional football does not even have a minor league program, instead relying on so-called "amateur" collegiate athletes.[36] Arena League football players make about \$30,000 per year and have no health benefits.[37]

EXPLOITATION IN COLLEGE ATHLETICS

Nowhere is the difference between the laborers and the owners more clear than in college sports. At the collegiate level, many have asserted that so-called "student" athletes are little more than slaves. Sociologist D. Stanley Eitzen refers to big-time college sports as a plantation. First, he argues the NCAA preserves the plantation system by making and enforcing rules that protect the interests of the plantation owners, the "football and basketball factories." Coaches who extract the labor from their slaves/athletes are the overseers.[38] So why do these collegiate athletes let themselves be exploited? We'll devote much more attention to this in future chapters, but let us just say that, as did some slaves, many identify with the system that confines them. Sports sociologist George H. Sage argues similarly when he says most athletes have been conditioned to obey athletic authorities and to be politically passive, lest protest jeopardize their chances to play.[39]

NCAA rules require athletes commit to 4 years at a school and binds them by forcing them to sit out a year if they transfer to another school. Yet schools make their commitments to the athletes in yearly increments (scholarships must be renewed yearly at the coach's discretion), and coaches who job-hop in hopes of greater pay and visibility typically suffer no penalty. And, though these athletes bring attention to their colleges and universities, and their coaches make hundreds of thousands of dollars off their labor, they receive, at most, tuition, room and board, and books.[40] Nick Saban made \$1.6 million as football coach at Louisiana State in 2002, Rick Pitino, the highest paid college basketball coach, signed a contract to make \$12.15 million over 6 years, and can receive a "loyalty bonus" of \$5 million if he simply honors that agreement. It's like offering students extra credit for class attendance.

DISNEY AND MCDONALD'S IN SPORTS

So, sports is a billion dollar industry, yet the payoff is not always going to the athletes, whose sweat is sold as the product. Why? Because sports today is more like a machine, selling entertainment for profit. Fairly compensating all of the laborers is cost prohibitive. Precisely who is cashing in, and at what expense, is rarely questioned because, like any efficient machine, if the product is compelling enough, few will question the nasty effects.

In an attempt to explain why sports have become so focused on the ends versus the means, we can look to the field of sociology. That the sports business is now about creating products for consumption is not exclusive to the United States or to the world of sports. Indeed, it can be viewed as a part of the rationalization of society, observed in the late eighteenth and nineteenth centuries by German sociologist Max Weber. Rationalization refers to the focus on science, rather than religion or tradition, as a source of understanding. It involves a faith that numbers can accurately describe observable phenomena, and treats a numerically calculable progress as an important goal. Weber asserted that this rationalization was centered in the western world and generally corresponds with capitalism.

Sociologists George Ritzer and Todd Stillman explain that, in a competitive economy, rational systems, also known as bureaucratic systems, outperform alternative arrangements, at least when profit is the primary measure of performance.[41] When other measures are used, however—such as the quality of human relationships—rational systems tend to fall short. More recently, Ritzer has maintained that, rather than a pure bureaucracy, the model for rationalization in the United States has been McDonaldization. That is, as a culture, we have come to look more and more like the infamous burger chain. For Ritzer, McDonaldization is characterized by five qualities: efficiency, predictability, calculability, substitution of nonhuman for human technology, and control over uncertainty. All of these qualities are exemplified in sports in the United States.

Ritzer maintains that even areas of life that seemingly would not benefit from being bureaucratic nonetheless become that way.[42] This seems to be the case with sports, as we will demonstrate. The next sections describe more specifically the concept of McDonaldization, as well as demonstrate how sports fit this model. This description is intended to set the tone for later chapters, as it should explain to readers how and why the various problems described have originated and why they continue.

According to Ritzer, rationalization leads to an emphasis on finding the best means to reach the desired end: efficiency. While certainly some degree of efficiency is welcome, Ritzer maintains there are consequences of the drive for efficiency. For one, quality may be jeopardized. Oftentimes, the public is not aware of this consequence, as they become gradually accustomed to a reduction in quality. Further, Ritzer explains that the ends often come to justify the means.[43]

Applied to the sports world, an example of efficiency is obvious in the multiuse ballparks of the 1980s. Rather than being used exclusively for baseball, many are configured to accommodate the greater playing area of football. And, more than this, the real goal of the multiuse stadiums is to bring in more people. The reconfiguring of stadiums might seem to be a good thing—how can more attendees be bad? It can, however, be negative, too. Today's fans sit farther from the diamond than is necessary for sake of the efficiency of the stadium. In effect, as we show in a later chapter, this move lines someone's pockets but does little for the quality of the game.[44] The primary goal is that more people will spend more money on the various gadgets, grub, and gear, a topic taken up later in this chapter as well as in Chapter 8.

Football may appear to fans as somewhat anarchic, but in reality, it too is a carefully plotted exercise in efficiency. Planning is so geared toward effective and efficient ends that even the most absurd means seem plausible if they might bring results. For example, in their practices prior to a game with the Detroit Lions, led by star running back Barry Sanders, Los Angeles Rams defensive line coach John Teerlinck suggested the team simulate Sanders' running style and ability by chasing a live chicken.[45] During the game, quarterbacks do not typically call the plays; to allow them this power would be to reduce the efficiency of the game. Plays are called by coaches and communicated to players on field via headphones, thus the decision making is taken away from those "in the heat of the battle" and given over to the "hands of strategists."[46] While none of these examples are terribly grievous, the point remains that efficiency may reduce player control and, consequently, player enjoyment of the sports.

Part of the focus on efficiency involves marketing your ability; that is, it is critical that others be made aware of precisely how efficient you are. Hence, as Ritzer explains, "McDonald's expends far more effort telling us how many billions of hamburgers it has sold than it does telling us about the quality of those burgers."[47] It also touts the size of its burgers to the exclusion of their quality, that is, the "Big Mac," not the "Good Mac." In addition to touting their product all over the United States, McDonald's has taken their food across borders, a global phenomenon we have seen in the sports world as well.

The sports industry also excels at telling others their success stories and omitting the problems. Like McDonald's, sports emphasizes that its product are created efficiently, and tries to hide that the quality is suspect. Many seem incapable of admitting there are even a few problems with sports, let alone that the problems are systemic. Esteemed Duke Basketball coach Mike Krzyzewski lauded college sports after Duke was eliminated from the NCAA Division I finals one year. "All this stuff where people talk about college sports and things as bad, you have no idea. I want to whack everybody who says that. College sports are great. They're O.K. when you yell at each other, when you hug each other, when you live."[48] It is great Coach K is so positive, but to praise college sports as nonproblematic is as delusional as touting the benefits of Big Mac consumption.

The second component of McDonaldization is predictability. In a rationalized society, people want to know what to expect upon entering certain settings or purchasing certain products. In addition, people want to know that the product or service they receive will be virtually the same as that they received in an earlier time. Ensuring predictability requires discipline and order.[49] Predictable end products can typically be ensured when similar raw materials, technologies, and preparation techniques are used.

Regarding sports, rule development and changes in sports have served to make the action more predictable. This is not to say that spectators will know the final outcome of the event, as that certainly is not desired (unpredictable outcomes are actually highly desired to drive ticket sales). Spectators do want to be ensured, however, that the game will meet certain criteria. Rule changes are often designed to balance competition so games are close, so there is more action at a faster pace, so as to emphasize dramatic moments, and to allow for commercial breaks.[50] Further, the entire spectating experience is increasingly predictable; one can expect loud music, video displays, scantily clad cheerleaders, antic mascots, and announcers who tell spectators precisely how they are to feel through the content, tone, and volume of their comments.[51]

At the collegiate level, big-time college programs all seek to emulate those with a history of success, a form of predictability. To do so, many mid-size institutions have decided to upgrade their athletic programs to NCAA Division I, while some institutions already competing in Division I have moved their football teams to the highest level, Division I-A.[52] Often these moves are entirely inappropriate and are detrimental in myriad ways, but are part of the "upward drift" Murray Sperber describes in *Beer and Circus*.[53] *Sports Illustrated* explained in 1994 that the University of Alabama at Birmingham, located in a town where 25 percent of the population lives in poverty and 11 percent has less than an eighth-grade education, was to receive $2.2 million in public funds to start a Division I football team.[54]

Coverage of collegiate football is highly predictable as well. Games are highly charged battles between brilliant coaches.[55] If sports announcers are to be believed, it sounds like any old athletes can be plugged into the machine without noticeable effects on the end product.

As Ritzer explained, a great way to ensure a predictable product is to use similar raw materials. In the case of sports, we see this happening as recruiters search "certain" communities for athletes that will fit their model. Nike Corporation presents itself as benevolent for sponsoring high school basketball camps. Yet, according to Dennis Perrin, "The camps were not an exercise in corporate generosity, a place where the talented few may test one another's skills in a safe and supportive environment. The camps were designed as upscale slave markets, an auction space for America's hardwood plantations."[56]

An emphasis on numerical proof, or quantification, may be the most important component of McDonaldization.[57] Instead of trying to evaluate quality, a notoriously tricky endeavor, a rational society may develop quantifiable measures that substitute for measures of quality.[58] A great example of this quantification of quality can be seen in education. Since a students' quality of knowledge is difficult to measure, we have increasingly used quantifiable means to do so, generally taking the form of a standardized test. In the work world, the assembly line exemplifies the push toward efficiency and predictability.

Sports today are evaluated based on quantifiable measures. As sociologist Jay Coakley explains, "Games and events are evaluated in terms of market shares, rating points, and advertising potential. Athletes are evaluated in terms of endorsement potential and on-camera image . . . "[59] Today, quantity is what matters in sports. The number of wins is more important for many programs than "winning the right way," and trouncing your opponent is seen as a legitimate goal. Especially if doing so can score your team some time on *SportsCenter*.

We know that the drive for tallying wins has superceded playing for the love of the game when we see the steps taken to espouse the virtues of winning in youth sports. In a high school football game in Albuquerque, New Mexico, in 1996, players left the field oozing blood, with one senior requiring twelve stitches. The source? A player, willing to do anything to win, had jimmy-rigged a razor-sharp buckle on his helmet to slash up the opponents. He didn't act alone, however, but was assisted in his handiwork by his father, a local dentist.[60] Members of a Florida fifth-grade football team that lost their first game all season in a close state final received a plaque inscribed with a quote from the famed Green Bay Packers coach Vince Lombardi at the team banquet. The plaque reads:

There is no room for second place. I have finished second twice at Green Bay and I never want to finish second again. There is a second place bowl game but it is a game for losers played by losers. It is and always has been an American zeal to be first in anything we do and to win and to win and to win.[61]

Humans are limited in their capacity to perform certain tasks no matter how hard they may try. And, despite all efforts to make humans more efficient, predictable sorts, some still buck the trend and act in unforeseen ways. Thus a rationalized society increasingly turns to nonhuman means of production. This may occur in reality, or through a process of making humans virtually robotic. Ritzer explains that, while McDonald's does not yet have robot servers, the teenagers most often employed are virtual robots, as they are merely asked to follow established procedures and routines.[62] Consequently, people often feel as though they are dealing with robots when they encounter these personnel. This was the guiding principle behind Frederick Taylor's scientific management: workers would know rules and regulations and blindly obey them, not to evaluate for themselves the best way to do the work. Skills required to perform are carefully delineated so as to be easily learned, thus a worker can master his or her own piece and do it efficiently, without concern for the overall product.

Today we see football players specialize in their position to the point of being automata. They spend little time with teammates that play on the other side of the ball. It was this type of work that Karl Marx deplored, calling it "alienated labor." Far from "renaissance men," these athletes become so highly specialized that, if they sustain an injury or a change in the lineup occurs, their services can quickly be rendered obsolete.

In regard to sports, modern ballparks have exemplified this reliance on technology. Fans are able to wait for their nachos and beer without missing any of the action, due to video monitoring at concession stands. In some locations, fans may soon be able to order snacks during the game by using a credit card scanning device located on their seat.[63] Football teams are in constant communication with their coaches throughout a game, and coaches now have advanced technology that allows them to communicate with offensive and defensive coordinators, who are generally sitting in booths high above the field. These coaches then take camera shots of the opposing team's formations and alignments, which are sent down a wire to the team's bench, where the players can talk by headphone to the coach who sent them.[64]

Ultimately, nonhuman (or human but alienated) means of production are about the ability of those "in charge" to exercise greater control and to ensure conformity.[65] Generally, there are two mechanisms to ensure conformity: ideological control and direct intervention. Ideological control manipulates the ideas and perceptions of individuals so that they accept the ruling ideology as common sense, never questioning it or thinking of competing views.[66] New members are socialized into the ideology and typically accept it without question. Sports are a conservative institution promoting traditional values and social arrangements: it reinforces male superiority to females; defines heterosexuality as the norm; and fuels existing racism.

Athletes are also subject to numerous types of direct social control. Control may come from sports organizations, like the National Collegiate Athletic Association (NCAA), from coaches or other administrative officials, and from teammates. The NCAA demands athletes take drug tests. Athletic department personnel may monitor the behavior of athletes in dorms, or some schools even use closed-circuit television to do so. Sometimes, there are "spies" who watch and report on the behavior of athletes in local bars.[67] College athletes have no control over the position they will play, or often whether they will be allowed to play at all or will be red-shirted. They can be told to gain or lose weight with serious consequences for noncompliance, and can be "asked" to attend "voluntary" practice sessions.[68] We have lived this. As collegiate cross country runners, we both had voluntary-but-you-better-be-there practices at 6:00 a.m. Because the W-L record is all that matters, coaches find whatever means necessary to get around this kind of regulation.

Revisiting the college-athlete-as-slave notion, Eitzen explains religion can be used as a form of control. Team chaplains, chapel services, Bible study, and team prayers are fairly common in college sports today.[69] At the University of Colorado, basketball coach Richard Patton ends each practice with a Kumbaya circle, where players' exchange turns leading the team in prayer. Many are skeptical of the claim that these religious activities are truly voluntary.[70]

NFL training camp is an exercise in control; in fact, it can be likened to a total institution, like prisons, the military, and mental facilities.[71] The remoteness of the location of most training camps is intended to bolster solidarity and commitment to the team's mission in the absence of other distractions. The deliberate isolation serves to foster the individual athlete's commitment to the team and his or her obedience to the coach.[72]

In college football, team rules are intended to control the athletes. At the University of Texas, basketball coach Rick Barnes prohibits facial hair, earrings, the wearing of hats in buildings, and headphones on campus. Arriving late to a team meeting or workout would cause the entire team to run.[73]

In addition to controlling the means of production, rational systems also seek to control the consumer. New ballparks employ legions of ushers and security guards who ensure fans are behaving and *certainly* not attempting to move up to better seats.[74] Televised football follows a carefully plotted script to control the emotions and purchasing behavior of spectators. When the audience tired of game accounts emphasizing the technical aspects of the game, commentators began to present the game as a drama with a cast of heroes and villains. A key strategy to this end is to use nicknames for players and teams, hence the Minnesota Vikings' defense became the "Purple People Eaters," the Los Angeles Rams' defense was the "Fearsome Foursome," and O. J. Simpson running through holes in the defense was "the juice getting loose."[75] New technology has expanded the televised presentation of games. ABC's Roone Arledge spearheaded the changes by focusing on bringing the game to the fan's living room through the use of close ups, the use of directional and remote microphones, and hand-held cameras.[76] To attract "less sophisticated viewers," Arledge recommended the use of more cameras stationed off field to capture scantily clad cheerleaders. Monday Night Football, another Arledge invention (with the help of NFL Commissioner Peter Roselle), was "an extension of the football weekend . . . yet another holiday for the hard-core football fan."[77] John Gerdy explains, "The NBA has gotten so far away from being about sport, that the league does not feel the game is interesting enough to entertain fans without help of an organist or taped snippets of deafening 'rev up the fan' music blaring incessantly in the background."[78]

In sum, the characteristics described above create very effective and financially lucrative "selling machines."[79] So why is McDonaldization so bad?

Disenchantment is a common effect of McDonaldization. Ritzer and Stillman argue that, at one time, baseball stadiums were enchanted, magical settings.[80] They were enchanting because they were small, quirky, had some type of iconic feature, were situated in urban settings, and were historical, both in the sports moments that occurred within them as well as in their architecture.[81] In the mid-1960s and through the 1980s, the trend was to create more rationalized, multiuse stadiums. These typically featured synthetic grass, fixed roofs to accommodate inclement weather, and huge seating capacities. Parks fitting this model include the Houston Astrodome, Cinergy Field in Cincinnati, Veteran's Stadium in Philadelphia, and Seattle's Kingdome.[82]

Disenchantment can and often does lead to disengagement. In the sports world, that typically takes the form of loss of interest in the sport, mostly by the spectators. Indeed, declining attendance rates at major league events have troubled team owners in recent years. In baseball, declining attendance in the late 1980s through early 1990s was a result of fan disenchantment with huge player salaries and a lack of team loyalty. The greed of owners who railroaded municipalities into building bigger and more expensive stadiums (generally at public's expense) with threats of relocation was also a factor, as was the "disenchanted homeliness" of the ballparks.[83] It is not just the spectators who lose interest, though. Statistics show that more and more kids are dropping out of youth and high school sports because they are disenchanted with several of its McDonaldized features—they hate the rigidity of rules, the stress on competition and winning, and the way coaches treat them in order to rack up a good record.

The response, rather than to completely alter their focus, has often been to use some form of "simulated enchantment." Thus, on the surface, the sports experience may appear less rationalized, or "de-McDonaldized," but in reality, little has changed but the packaging. Ritzer and Stillman cite ten examples of ballparks that are still McDonaldized, only in a better package, including Camden Yards in Baltimore, Jacob's Field in Cleveland, Comerica Park in Detroit, and Coors Field in Denver. An example of the simulation of the traditional ballparks can be seen in Baltimore's Camden Yards, where the remains of an old warehouse are part of the backdrop of the stadium. This warehouse is not used, of course, but is intended to simulate the thriving warehouse industry of an earlier time.[84]

CREATING A SPORTS SPECTACLE

In attempting to make the experience of spectating seem more pleasurable, teams have made stadiums and arenas more spectacular. They have also used a variety of spectacles in the process. Ritzer and Stillman explain that the newest ballparks purposely create extravaganzas that often have little or nothing to do with baseball itself, with the intention of attracting and entertaining fans who may have little interest in or knowledge of the game.[85] For instance, most of the new parks have ultra high-tech score boards that are mammoth in size. Topping the list is the scoreboard at Detroit's Comerica Park, which is 40 feet long, 27 feet high, weighs 5,000 pounds, and is replete with twin tigers with flashing eyes.[86] And to help bring families out, some ballparks are now including play areas for children with swing sets and slides. In December 2004, the NFL unveiled plans for "The NFL Experience," a new football-themed fan park where visitors can partake in fifty interactive games. "It's all about moms, dads, grandparents, and kids coming together for a family outing. That's what the NFL Experience is about," said Mary Pat Augenthaler, the senior director for special events for the NFL.[87]

Televised sports also utilize the spectacle, with football leading the way. ABC was the first station to disseminate the notion of sports as spectacles to the masses. The hope was to get viewers who might not be "die-hard" fans, but who might tune in for the fun and frivolity. Their new model also catered to those most interested in seeing the scantily clad cheerleaders. The announcers became personalities, not just commentators.[88]

Even exploitation of tragedy is not considered taboo in the sports world, as long as it puts butts in the seats and draws in viewers. Eitzen illustrates how tragedy served to unite fans at the 2002 Super Bowl, the first one after September 11. Fox's 3-hour pregame coverage was called *"Hope, Heroes, and Homeland."* It featured a reenactment of the signing of the Declaration of Independence, former presidents reading passages of speeches by Abraham Lincoln, and singing of *"Let Freedom Ring."* Paul McCartney also sang, and many of the performers and their entourage were decked out in Statue of Liberty costumes, holding flags.[89] That they had reached all new levels of cheese didn't seem to bother the gung-ho American patriots who tuned in en masse.

The Arena Football League distributed 10,000 U.S. flags at the April 6, 2003, game between Dallas and San Jose. Military families were invited to see the home-town Desperados for free, and some family members were interviewed and the interviews were beamed overseas. Desperados' owner Jerry Jones described the effort as a collaborative one with NBC in order to show support for the troops. Jones said their goal was not to exploit public sentiment for sales and ratings. *Business Week Online* author Mark Hyman remarked, "Sure, Delta Force bobbleheads weren't for sale, but can that be far behind?"[90] *SportsCenter* even broadcast a week's worth of pro-U.S. military shows from Kuwait in September 2004. Some were skeptical of parent company Disney's motives. Sports columnist Dave Zirin argued, "At a time when we should have been bringing the troops home, Disney brought them Stuart Scott. Tragedy became a farce. Hold the booyah."[91]

Interestingly, when athletes demonstrate some type of value system contrary to the majority, they are not so well received. When Muslim Mahmoud Abdul-Rauf said standing at attention for the national anthem prior to his NBA games would violate his religious beliefs, he was roundly denounced as a traitor.[92] According to Dennis Perrin in *American Fan,* the worst of it took place on March 15, 1996, the night the Nuggets played the Bulls in Chicago. Insults and, of course, American flags, flew throughout the stadium. "What better way to honor freedom than to harass someone who has a minority opinion and virtually no power to enforce it?"[93]

Further, the sports industry has imploded the boundaries between leisure and consumption, making sports attendance an exercise in buying as much as possible. Ballparks increasingly include shopping malls and concourses, usually with chain stores, food courts (of course with chain restaurants like McDonald's and Little Caesar's), breweries and bars, video arcades, museums offering team memorabilia and simulations, and even amusement parks. At Comerica Park there is a 50-foot Ferris wheel with cars shaped like baseballs and a carousel featuring thirty hand-painted tigers.[94] Of course, the new ballparks also include the most important element: lots of conveniently placed ATMs. In other words, a visit to the ballpark is more and more like a visit to the mall or to a theme park.[95]

THE CLASS IMPLICATIONS

The more sports become a vehicle for consumption, the more it further excludes the traditional working-class, urban baseball, basketball, or football fan.[96] Yet, as we show in a later chapter, taxpayers are more often than not footing the bill for these stadium monstrosities.[97] In the 1990s, about $8 billion of public money was used to build stadiums and arenas that made a lot of money for team owners and a few others, while offering little benefit for the taxpayer.[98] In fact, wealthy investors generally purchased the tax-free municipal bonds used to build these facilities. So, in essence, city and even state taxes were collected from the general population to pay off bonds, the bonds were bought by wealthy investors tax-free, and team owners make exorbitant amounts of money for themselves and their corporations. One U.S. senator called this method "little more than a public housing program for millionaire team owners and their millionaire employees."[99] These projects are often sold to the public under the guise that they will produce an economic windfall for the community. That has proven true on limited occasions, but more often than not has little to no pay off to the average Joe. Dennis Perrin describes the attitude of team owners in his book *American Fan*: "They're so accustomed to screwing fans that they no longer bother zipping their flies, and in certain cases forgo wearing pants altogether. When they've had their fill of fan tail, they waddle off to a 'friendlier' city where their special 'needs' are met: a new stadium, more sky boxes, tax breaks so outrageous that even the IRS is rendered dumb."[100]

THE IMPACT

We contend that, in addition to disenchantment of fans, the making of American sports into a profit-driven machine has led to a variety of negative consequences. The focus on efficiency, the need for predictability, the quest for greater control, and the numbers game have created a situation whereby all the major players in the sports business have "me-first goals regardless of the means."[101] Yet, too frequently the consequences of this market-oriented sports world are overlooked or simply ignored. Eitzen explains that, too often, any problems in sports are chalked up to "bad people." We contend, as do others, that the win-at-all-costs climate created by the McDonaldized world of sports is a more appropriate explanation for many of the problems in sports.[102]

Sporting spectacles divert the public's attention from the major problems in sports today.[103] The problems with this machine mentality are generally referred to in the sociology world as positive and negative deviance. In reality, as the following chapters will elucidate, deviance is perhaps not the best word, as clearly cheating, on-field violence, and the other examples we explore are part and parcel of sports success today.

chapter 1

The Sports Ethic

No man is entirely worthless, he can always serve as a bad example.
—Shotputter Brian Oldfield, while smoking
cigarettes between throwing shots.

When people fail to adhere to societal norms, they are often referred to as deviants. In the field of sports, those who fail to adhere to norms are often classified into two types: positive deviants and negative deviants. According to sports sociologist Jay Coakley, most deviance in sports is not due to a rejection of norms, as it is in the world at large.[1] For instance, people who speed on the highway are rejecting the norm that all drivers should obey traffic laws. In contrast, deviance in sports is more likely the result of an overacceptance of norms. This is positive deviance. Positive deviance may be self-injurious, such as when elite gymnasts shovel in the ex-lax and colace to maintain the weight of 10-year-olds as they advance into their teens, or when a football player slams a steroid-filled syringe into his rear-end to get bigger, faster, and meaner. Positive deviance often injures others, as is the case with the football player who hammers the opposing quarterback to the ground after the ball has been passed, or the basketball player who purposely elbows an opposing player in the face when making a rebound. While those outside the world of high-level sports might see these actions as a rejection of norms, it must be understood that within the sports culture norms are redefined to create an atmosphere in which winning is everything. As we will show in subsequent chapters, deviance in sports even harms entire communities and the society at large. Positive deviance typically involves uncritical acceptance of norms, what Coakley calls "the sports ethic."[2]

THE SPORTS ETHIC AND ATHLETES

According to Coakley, there are four beliefs that constitute the sports ethic.[3] First, it is believed that an athlete must make sacrifices for "the game." Following this belief, "real athletes" love the game, and consequently put it before anything else. Those who appear not to put their love of the game before other pursuits are deemed slackers and are not considered to be serious athletes. Second, athletes must always strive for distinction. Following this, "real athletes" are often trying to improve their performance through whatever means possible. Winning is the sign of improvement, and therefore losing is not tolerable. Third, athletes must accept risks and play through pain. Athletes do not give in to pain, pressure, stress, or fear. They must voluntarily accept the risks of sports engagement, including facing crippling injuries. Fourth, athletes must accept no limits in their pursuit of success. "Real athletes" believe anything is possible in sports, but only to those who are dedicated enough. This philosophy makes invisible structural conditions of inequality that limit sports opportunity, sports success, and that also create sports problems. As bell hooks so eloquently explains, "An almost religious belief in the power of competition to bring success permeates American life."[4]

In opposition, negative deviance refers to underconformity to the sports ethic. It is behavior that doesn't measure up, either due to lack of awareness or a rejection of the norm. In sports, negative deviants are those slackers who don't work hard enough on the court or field. This type of behavior is far less common among collegiate and professional athletes, as it is simply not tolerated. The athlete who skips practice or the one who constantly complains of side cramps while running wind sprints is likely to take a lot of guff from teammates and coaches. Those displaying negative deviance are typically weeded out of sports long before they reach the most elite levels.

Studying deviance in sports is complicated by the fact that what is "normal" may be significantly different in the world of sports than outside of it.[5] This is obviously true in certain sports: For example, boxing would be considered felonious assault if it was outside the ring, but inside the ring it is called "the sweet science." Likewise, the intense hatred often fostered on the field or court or in the ring would be considered unhealthy outside of sports. Yet breeding contempt for a rival is considered by many to be the best way to motivate an athlete. Studying sports deviance is also difficult because the players themselves often do not see their behavior as deviant or problematic—they have bought into the sports ethic.[6]

Building on the Introduction, we are not so sure the term deviance should even be used to describe athletes' overconformity or underconformity to norms. The term itself suggests some behavior out of the norm. Sports sociologists recognize that in sports these behaviors may not be viewed as deviant by those committing them, or even those watching them or commentating about them, yet still we use terminology that suggests the behavior is "abnormal." We contend these behaviors are simply part of the business of sports today. This book is focused on incidents of positive deviance, or the problems in sports that come from the need to succeed. These problems impact individuals, relationships, and society as a whole, which are the topics of subsequent chapters.

While all athletes are likely familiar with the sports ethic, not all athletes are equally likely to adhere. Research has demonstrated athletes involved in "power and performance" sports are more likely to overconform. Power and performance sports include those that are highly organized and competitive. These sports typically emphasize: speed, strength, and power as a means to dominate the opponent; the idea that competitive success is a measure of excellence; the importance of setting records; defining the body as a machine and using technology to control and monitor it; exclusive participation based on physical skills and success in competition; hierarchical authority structures; and antagonism between opponents, who are viewed as enemies. Examples of power and performance sports are football, basketball, and ice hockey. Hence it is in these sports that we see the most frequent, and typically most egregious, problems.[7]

Because men more commonly play these sports, it is suggested that male athletes are more likely to overconform to the sports ethic. This is changing, however, as more women are getting involved in football, boxing, hockey, and other sports that feature collisions and extreme physical aggression. In 2002 there were 1,000 girls playing football in more than seventy high school football programs, more than 700 females registered as pro-boxers, and over 2,000 female amateur boxers.[8] Similarly, minorities from low-income backgrounds are overrepresented in the power and performance sports, with the exception of ice hockey. In addition, those who are getting toward the end of their careers, those with low self esteem who wish to be accepted by peers, and those who see sports success as their only way to get ahead, are more likely to overconform to the sports ethic.[9]

The sports ethic is a powerful ideology. It has helped make sports a religion to many. According to Charles Prebish, Professor of Religious Studies at Penn State University, "Sport is religion, in the full sacred sense of the term. . . . It may well be America's . . . most powerful religion."[10] Sociologist Michael Novak explains that while sports are entertaining, they take on different elements than, say, prime time television sitcoms, as most viewers do not just passively watch.[11]

Dennis Perrin suggests that Christianity reinforces the sports ethic nicely; " . . . nothing beats Jesus nailed to a cross. That crown of thorns, that blood trickling from palms and feet, that look of celestial anguish—what better image to inspire players and coaches to victory? If Jesus can take that kind of punishment, what's a broken rib or collarbone, a cracked femur, torn cartilage?"[12] Some companies making sports-related gear have capitalized on the connection between religion and the sports ethic. T-shirts declaring, "Lord, give me the guts . . . and I'll give you the glory" are merely one example among many. In fact, while coaching high school cross country at a Christian school, Peter was alarmed to see runners from a rival

Catholic school wearing T-shirts claiming, "God is on Our Side." Jeez . . . with God on the other team, why bother to run the event?

Calling on God's favor in sports is widespread. Former University of Colorado football coach Bill McCartney founded a Christian fundamentalist group for men, *The Promise Keepers*, while he was still coaching at CU. McCartney claimed, "A Godly man is a manly man" and Jesus is his "Master Coach."[13] Boxer Evander Holyfield claimed in 1996 that it was not he but God who beat Mike Tyson in a fight in Los Angeles, and if God wanted him to he'd certainly fight again.[14] God must have wanted Holyfield to have a partial ear as well. Increasing numbers of athletes are "doing what Jesus would do" on the field, at least in their own minds. Randy Johnson, Major League Baseball player, said in 1996: "The greatest feeling I get playing baseball right now is knowing that I can go out and be a warrior for the Lord. I can go out . . . and say my prayer and then be a very aggressive, warriorlike pitcher, glorifying Him . . ."[15] Another "warrior for God," football player Gill Byrd, said in 1991, "If somebody comes into my territory, my zone, I want to hit him hard. I don't ever want to take a cheap shot, but I'll hit him with all the love of Jesus I can muster."[16]

In fact, many athletes have explicitly stated that their religion does not diminish their adherence to the sports ethic. It may even exacerbate the likelihood that they overconform. Major League Baseball player Danny Scheafer stressed that his Christianity made him more intense and no less aggressive than other players. "I'll be the first person to knock a Christian shortstop into left field on a play at second. I've been hit before by Christian players. I've charged Christian players (who have thrown pitches at me)."[17] Ultimate fighting participant Kimo Loepoldo, who has carried a cross on his back as he heads into a no-holds-barred fight, claimed that while he's "not yet worthy to walk with the cross," his athletic endeavors for God are "not a gimmick" either. Kimo pummeling in the face of an opponent while personally covered in Jesus tattoos isn't a gimmick either. It just leaves us wondering, "Who would Jesus pummel?" That these self-proclaimed religious advocates have no trouble reconciling the Christian emphasis on peace and respect with their violent behavior demonstrates how ingrained the sports ethic has become.

It is not difficult to see that athletes internalize the sports ethic, as it is all around them in a culture that loves its sports and worships its athletes. Ralph Cindrich, former NFL linebacker, explained in 1996, " . . . it was just a case of loving to play. . . . We all just took shots or painkillers or whatever they offered you and went right back out there, because we wanted to play football."[18] Once they've internalized the sports ethic, it is a relatively easy step for athletes to justify cheating, violence, and other egregious behaviors as merely what was required for success. And they often are right; winning in big time sports often hinges on questionable conduct by players, and this is certainly the focus of television airtime. Former football player Don Sabo explains how he learned the sports ethic through grade school, high school, and his time as a linebacker for an NCAA Division I team. "I learned to be an animal. Coaches took notice of animals. Animals made first team. Being an animal meant being fanatically aggressive and ruthlessly competitive. If I saw an arm in front of me, I trampled it."[19] Many pros have made similar claims; that they are expected to be violent, not to care about their opponents, nor to worry about the consequences of their actions. And, many perceive that if they were to refuse to jump into a bench-clearing brawl, for instance, they would lose playing time, at minimum, and may even be cut from the team.[20] Elwood Reid recounted his experience as a Big Ten football player in 1997. He said, "In the world of Big Ten football, you feast on inflicting pain—on and off the field. You do it because you can . . . because it's what's expected of you."[21]

In criminology there is a theory to explain crime called "Techniques of Neutralization." It posits that there are a number of mechanisms people use to rationalize committing crimes or becoming deviant. For instance, some will deny that anyone was victimized by their actions, while others will claim their behavior was justified because someone or some thing had wronged them first. This seems a good explanation for what happens in the minds of athletes who overconform to the sports ethic. Rationalizing poor behavior in sports is not a new phenomenon, just one that occurs more frequently and has taken on an all-new importance. In ancient Greece and Rome, "It is notorious that no player of any game ever starts dirty play. When guilty of the most blatant foul he always claims that he acts in retaliation. So no Greek pankratist ever gouged; he only 'gouged back' or gave 'dig for dig.'"[22]

Former pro-football player Tim Green explains, "You cheat to win and because you can. Most illegal blocks, pass interference, holding and hands-to-the-face penalties go uncalled. In football, you're not wrong unless you're caught."[23] Warren Sapp offered a similar view: "If you aren't cheating, you aren't trying to win." John Underwood argues that the problems in sports are often hard to detect because they begin small. Minor incidents of brutality, for instance, are deemed "part of the game," and provide a ripe breeding ground for escalating acts of brutality.[24] Adherence to the sports ethic often means disrespecting opponents, sometimes by annihilating them in a game situation. The system is structured in such a way that, in big time college football, running up the score is virtually required as it affects ranking and consequently helps determine potentially lucrative bowl selections. In 1992, the Colorado State football team beat Louisiana State in an upset. On the winning drive there was a fumble. While an LSU player fell on the ball, a CSU player ended up with it. The player was later quoted in the newspaper saying he elbowed and kicked an opponent in the pileup in order to grab the ball, but the referees did not see it. Rather than condemn his athlete's use of illegal and immoral tactics, the CSU coach credited Geoff Grenier's tough play as integral to the win.[25]

The Killer Instinct

Sadly, humiliation of the opposition occurs at all levels. A Laramie, Wyoming Junior High Girls' Basketball Team won a game 81–1. An integral part of their tactic was use of the full-court press for the entire game. A high school team in

Camden, New Jersey, did the same thing, winning 157–67 with one player alone scoring 100 points.[26]

In a Michigan high school girl's basketball playoff game, Walkerville trounced Lakeshore 115–2. When questioned about whether that might have been a wee bit excessive, the coach responded, "What do you tell our girls? Not to play?" Perhaps not exactly, but almost countless means of limiting scoring do leap to the mind. As an assistant director from Michigan's athletic association suggested, coaching tactics and strategies can be used to prevent these results. Apparently it never dawned on the coach to instruct his girls to only pass the ball and kill the clock when the score reached, say, 80–2? After the game, the "winning" coach explained that the game "had the potential to be really, really bad." Gee, good thing it wasn't really, really bad. Then people would write books about it.

Trash Talk

Another way to debase opponents is the use of trash talk. While it is the specialty of certain athletes, such as former NBA star Dennis Rodman, trash talk is even sold to young athletes as *the* way to play basketball. Nike's 1998 advertisement called "The Fun Police" utilized NBA players to allegedly show young girls how much fun sports can be. Gary Payton tells two young ladies, "We're goin' try trash talking,' kay?" One yells, "Come strong or don't come at all." Payton points at the other girl and says, "In your face!" which the girl then repeats. Malone comments, "That's some fine trash."[27]

Athletes can justify their behavior by claiming, as did former NBA player Charles Barkley, they are not and should not be role models. Barkley tells parents, "Just because I can dunk a basketball doesn't mean I should raise your kids."[28] Obviously Barkley's argument makes some sense, in that it would be lovely if parents or teachers were kids' role models, but it's also a load of garbage. Like it or not, we live in a culture where sports matter to people immensely, and consequently athletes will be looked up to by the young and the old. As Lawrence Wenner points out, "Charles may say, 'Don't do as I do' out of one side of his mouth, but out of the other comes 'buy these shoes' and be like Charles, the meanest, toughest, fly-high guy to jam one in your face. Don't be like me, but buy so you can be like me."[29]

Taking One for the Team

Teammates constantly reinforce the sports ethic in many sports and at all levels. Athletes may ridicule those who are injured and must take time off, as both of the authors have experienced. Unless a bone fragment is bulging out of his or her skin or blood is spewing left and right, an athlete who claims an injury requiring time off may not be taken seriously by teammates. While some considered their actions admirable, many fans and fellow players criticized NBA players who passed up on the chance to play for the 2004 U.S. Olympic Basketball Team in Athens out of fear for their own safety, dubbing them unpatriotic and cowardly. Even in times when athletes have missed games for the birth of their children they have been viewed as less committed. David Williams chose to miss a 1993 NFL game to be with his wife, Debi, as she gave birth to their first child. He made the mistake of saying, "I love football. But I have more in my life, and my family comes first."[30] His team, the Houston Oilers, fined him $111,111, the equivalent of 1 week's pay, for having such nerve. His offensive line coach offered the team's rationale: Missing the game was like missing action in World War II.[31] It's not clear how he concluded this game had the same stakes as that of a World War, but the coach's logic is certainly interesting. In his analysis of locker room conversations among college athletes, Curry found teammates contributed to a climate of disrespect, which they do as part of their bonding to each other and their acceptance of the sports ethic. Striving for academic excellence was ridiculed, women were discussed as objects and as inferior to men in all respects, and homophobic comments, including stories of gay bashing, were common.[32]

The "Mama's Girl" Motivator

Athletes also sling the sissy comments. NHL player Bryan Marchment said in 1995: "I've never, ever, sent a 'Get Well' card (to a player I've injured)... Hey, it's a man's game. If you can't play, get out and play tennis."[33] Sociologist Michael Messner tells the story of Bill, who injured his knee just before the state championship game. "I was hurt. I couldn't play, and I got a lot of flack from everybody. The coach said, 'Are you faking it?' And I was in the whirlpool and a teammate said, 'You fucking pussy.' That hurt more than the injury. Later, people told me it was my fault that we lost... not just other players and coaches, but people in the whole town."[34] When the NHL passed rules in an attempt to limit fighting, Tie Domi responded: "If you take out fighting, what comes next? Do we eliminate checking? Pretty soon, we will all be out there in dresses and skirts."[35]

Sometimes athletes internalize the abuse. Jackson Katz tells the story of a 250-pound American arm-wrestling champion who lost his first match to a petite woman in a bar in Tijuana, Mexico, in 1994. When the woman won in less than 20 seconds, the champ seemed to take it in his stride, buying a round of beer for all in the bar, as the two had agreed the loser would do. After his friends mocked him for the loss, he walked out of the bar, kicking some chairs along the way. They thought he had left to drink some more beer. He had not. The former champ went to his trailer, drank two six-packs, and blew his head off. Everyone who knew him knew the reason: He was too macho to face the shame of having lost to a woman.[36]

THE SPORTS ETHIC AND THE PUBLIC

The sports ethic is marketed to everyone. So, not only do the athletes internalize it, but fans do so as well. They too come to expect that their idols will achieve at all costs, that they will play through pain and make sacrifices for the game. As John Underwood explains in *Spoiled Sport,* fans are so anesthetized they don't realize how "unsporting our spectator sports have become."[37] Underwood goes on to explain that fans simply expect cheating, violence, and unsportsmanlike behavior from athletes.[38] Jack McCallum reported a frightening example of this expectation in his *Sports Illustrated* article, "Way Out of Control." On the way to a baseball game a boy said to his dad, "Jeez, dad, I hope we see one today. I've never seen one." "A homer?" inquires dad. "No, a brawl," responds the son.[39]

Fans sometimes heckle athletes so much that they blow up. Texas Rangers relief pitcher Frank Francisco was arrested and is being sued for throwing a chair at a heckling fan and his wife. The wife suffered a broken nose.[40] Apparently there's even a hierarchy of "good" heckling. One experienced heckler claimed that, "bad heckling" is to yell, "You suck," because "You don't know why he sucks."[41] Some work hard to read up on players so as to incorporate the most inflammatory pieces. These fans see it as their right to verbally assault players, and feel players must simply take it. Said one heckler, "If they don't like what fans are saying they should go and buy a set of ear plugs for three bucks."[42]

Fans debase the opposing team and their fans, often through appalling means. Basketball player Patrick Ewing, when playing for Georgetown, was subject to fans wearing shirts reading "Ewing Kant Read 'Dis,'" and banners stating, "Ewing Can't Read" and "Ewing is an Ape."[43] Since the goal of sports today is to beat Ewing's team, not to affirm the worth of the opponent, such signs are rarely removed from stadiums and, in fact, sometimes get coverage on the next *Sports Center*. Fan behavior like this also occurs at the high school level. Sociologist Mike Messner recounts his days as a basketball player for a poor, blue-collar school. When they were beating their wealthier rival in his senior year, he recalls their fans yelling, "That's all right, that's OK, you'll be working for us some day."[44]

Although not the specific focus of this book, fans who get overly immersed in their sports idolatry have also resorted to heinous acts of violence. This often seems to be a result of the modern sports mantra of profit-above-all. David Thomas of the *Fort-Worth Telegram* connects the increasing number of violent fans in baseball to disconnect with highly paid athletes and a feeling among fans that they acquire more rights because they now pay more for game tickets.[45] But violent fans are not a new phenomenon. In 1974 The Cleveland Indians had a 10-cent beer promotion. Thousands of fans stormed the field in the ninth inning (after sales reached approximately 60,000 cups of beer), attacking players and umpires.[46] At a New York Giants game in 1996, fans pelted the visiting San Diego Chargers with snow and ice balls. Fifteen people were arrested, including a retired police officer. Robert Mulcahy, head of the group that operates Giants stadium, said, "I'm concerned about the lack of personal responsibility people seem to feel when they come to a sports event. There seems to be an increased sense that when you buy a ticket you have the right to behave any way you want."[47] Dennis Perrin described the fan behavior outside of Wrigley Field when Sammy Sosa hit home run number 61 out of the park and into the street: a mob plowed over a man in a wheelchair while chasing the ball. And home run number 62? "The poor bastard who grabbed the ball was slammed to the pavement by two thugs, one of whom bit into the hand clutching the treasures."[48] This type of behavior is shocking, yet not surprising, given the hype surrounding the home run race.[49]

Some fans, typically men, get so "into" the game that they become abusive to girlfriends or spouses. Jennifer, a 44-year-old African American who has lived with her partner, Charles, for 7 years, tells how he started beating her after his favorite team, the Buffalo Bills, lost their first Super Bowl game. She explained, "It was horrible, crazy. He punched me in the mouth, split my lip. I had bruises on my body and on the side of my face. This was the worst. Now I have to get out of the house when he starts throwing things. As soon as he starts yelling, my eldest daughter (6 years old) goes for help. The police have come often. Now it happens weekly during football season, then there's a break, and the weekly attacks start up again with basketball (season). If he understood hockey, it would be even worse."[50] Charles' behavior is exacerbated by the fact that he drinks and smokes marijuana throughout the games, and he typically bets on the game. As a graduate student at the University of Florida, Charles Hillman found some disturbing things about fan behavior. He measured the heart rate and brain activity of low-, moderate-, and high-interest fans of Florida Gator Football, while showing them a variety of scenes, including clips from Gator games, neutral objects, romantic embraces, and violent images. All three groups measured similar responses to every scene except when the Gator clips came on. The most interested fans measured near the top of the scales. One professor explained the results this way: "There were fewer brain resources available" when the fans viewed their favorite team.[51] When we see fans going bare-chested and painted in team colors at outdoor football games during treacherous winter storms, we wonder, can these fans spare any additional brain resources?

Even children are not protected from the wrath of an overzealous fan. Peter recalls this scene from a college hockey game: A young boy who was dressed as a hockey puck was sent onto the ice to excite the crowd. He would skate around holding up a hockey puck that would be thrown into the stands for the section that cheered the loudest. After making a few trips around the ice, he launched the puck into the rowdiest section. Instantly the rest of the arena, in unison, yelled, "F . . . you, puck boy." Apparently this was a staple occurrence at the team's home games. As the boy skated off and into the arms of his mother, Peter had to wonder how many puck boys the team went through in a season.

THE SPORTS ETHIC AND THE MEDIA

The media clearly plays a major role in marketing the sports ethic. One way they do this is by glorifying athletes who overconform. John Underwood refers to television as an "aerial pollutant" in his book *Spoiled Sport*.[52] The media praises athletes who play hurt, especially when they play hurt *and* do it well. Athletes who make comebacks from injury are also lauded by the media, as are those who return to a game after an injury appears to have stymied them. Few fans can forget Kerri Strug, hoisted in the arms of her coach,[53] after competing while seriously injured. The Nagano Winter Olympics in 1998 featured a similar comeback kid when the media emphasized Picabo Street's return from several serious injuries to win the downhill skiing gold.[54] The media also emphasizes the most vicious violent actions taken on the field or court, often re-airing them *ad nauseum*. This is generally done absent any type of commentary on the appropriateness of the action.[55] Because a major goal of the teams today is to get airtime, coaches and teammates may encourage athletes to play hurt or return too soon from injury. Then the media adores them, and the cycle continues.

Feature films also stress the sports ethic. *Varsity Blues,* a cheesy rendition of high school football, shows a coach administering cortisone to an ailing athlete so he can suck it up and keep playing, despite the risk that the shot will merely numb the pain so he does not notice as he does further, potentially irreparable, damage to his body. The recently released film *Friday Night Lights,* from H. G. Bissinger's analysis of football at Permian High School in Odessa, Texas, shows a son who seems only to be able to win his father's praise by playing with a broken collarbone.

The media also hypes sports scandals, especially when they can be cast in terms of good versus evil or the like. Coverage of Tanya Harding and crew's attack on oh-so-sweet Nancy Kerrigan prior to the winter Olympics demonstrated the ways the media helps to create winners and losers. The media then tore down Kerrigan as quickly as they had pumped her up. Kerrigan, seated next to Mickey Mouse in a car driving through Disneyland, proclaimed, "This is so corny. This is so dumb. I hate it. This is the most corny thing I've ever done,"[56] which gave the media ample ammunition to destroy her image. It seems in America we love nothing better than to build up a celebrity to watch him or her fall, despite Kerrigan's obvious insight that a parade with Mickey Mouse is indeed corny and boring.

In yet another example of our feasting on other people's failure, the authors were appalled at the coverage of the 2004 Olympic women's gymnastics team. While not being selected would be devastating enough, the media felt it appropriate to cut to the scene of selection (at the Karolyi ranch), zooming in on the tortured faces of the girls who were learning they would not be going to Athens. The gobs of makeup on their faces did little to mask the horror.

Fomenting hatred and even racism is another area in which the media excel. This may be done overtly, or it may be subtler. Radio broadcasts and commentary typically use denigrating language to describe opponents. One commentator in Philadelphia explained that he typically, "checks his conscience at the door."[57] In *Beyond the Cheers,* C. Richard King and Charles Fruehling-Springwood illustrate how the local college radio station near Oklahoma State University provided listeners with appalling images of black athletes in order to get them fired up for upcoming football or basketball games with rival University of Oklahoma. Here is one fictitious interview conducted with black athlete Wayman Tisdale:

Interviewer: Well, Mr. Tisdale, what are your thoughts on the upcoming game?

Tisdale: Ugah bugah hoogaloo ugh ugh.

Interviewer: Really—would you share your thoughts on your coach, Billy Tubbs?

Tisdale: I be, yo be, we be, yo' mama![58]

In an example of more subtle racism, Don Sabo and Sue Curry Jansen report that NFL game coverage clearly favors white players. They were praised more frequently than black players, while the past failures of black players were far more likely to be mentioned.[59] Viewers are left with negative images of black athletes, while they have nothing but respect and admiration for their white counterparts. Funny how, while the media drones on about Brett Favre starting at quarterback for over 200 consecutive games, there is no mention of the painkiller addiction that kept him on the field for part of the streak.

Continuing the focus on the media, athletes and fans also learn the importance of adherence to the sports ethic from advertisements. Nike's ad in the 1996 *Sports Illustrated* Olympic Preview Issue is a great example. The ad said, in part: "Who the hell do you think you are? Are you an athlete? Because if you are, then you know what it means to want to be better, to want to be the best. And if you are, then you understand it's not enough to just want to be the best. You can't just sit around and BS about how much you want it."[60] The "Fun Police" ad mentioned earlier also reinforces that there are particular ways basketball should be played, and trash talk is required. In another effort directed at girls, the inaugural issue of *Sport's Illustrated for Women* featured a picture of girls at a camp with T-shirts reading, "If it's too tough for you, it's just right for me."[61] Nike's most famous ad campaign, "Just Do It," certainly tells athletes they should adhere to the sports ethic. No one interprets the ad to say, "Just Do It," unless your body is worn out or injured, or you have a big test tomorrow. Then "Do It In Part" or "Do It Another Day."

THE SPORTS ETHIC IN THE LOCKER ROOM

Obviously, many coaches promote adherence to the sports ethic, often leading to multiple problems for individual athletes and for relationships between athletes. Even signs that coaches hang up in locker rooms, according to Sociologist Eldon Snyder, stress the sports ethic. "Never be willing to be second best," "Winners never quit and quitters never win," and "Win by as many points as possible," all stress to athletes that to err is not human but the mark of a loser.[62] Coaches teach the sports ethic when they give pre-game speeches such as those infamous Green Bay Packers coach Vince Lombardi was known for. "To play this game you must have fire in you, and there is nothing that stokes fire like hate" is a great Lombardiism to show how athletes learn from their coaches to disrespect and hate the opposition.[63]

Coaches have long used a variety of tactics to intimidate athletes, and have encouraged their athletes' do the same to opponents. These range from the relatively mild glare or yell, to cursing, kicking, and even spitting in someone's face.[64] In their book on sports ethics, Lumpkin et al. tell of a baseball coach who swore at his team twenty-seven times during the seventh inning stretch alone. When asked why, and whether he really thought that it was necessary to curse more than say, ten times, the coach responded, "A coach doesn't have the time or energy to be worried about who needs what form of motivation, positive or negative. Cursing and screaming get the job done quickly so I can spend my time concentrating on strategy."[65] He then explained that he had borrowed his specific form of berating those in his charge from the military, where it was known to work marvelously.

The authors know of a high school coach who tried to fuel his football team's anger and hatred of their rival by trashing his own team locker room and making it appear the opponent had done it. Another high school coach bit off a toad's head to model aggressive behavior for his athletes.[66] A coach in a youth hockey league in Minnesota launched his "get the girl" strategy, where he demanded his 13-year-old players slam the lone girl playing for the opposing team into the boards so viciously she collapsed and was rushed to the hospital.[67] Pat Riley, when coaching the NBA's Miami Heat, fined his players $1,500 if they helped an opposing player off the floor.[68]

Coaches encourage male athletes in particular to overconform to the sports ethic by appealing to their hegemonic definitions of masculinity. Players may be called "sissies," "mama's boys," and "faggots" if they are not aggressive enough. This type of message is so common in sports that we have even heard women make comments about "taking off their skirts" and "hitting like a girl" when their performances are subpar. Homophobic comments both reflect and feed on an antigay culture. Don Sabo tells the story of a teammate, Brian, who was a bit flabby during their sophomore year and didn't seem to have the "killer instinct." Their coach made him block for the entire defensive team during a practice, all the while berating him by saying, "How many sisters you got at home, Brian? Is it six or seven? How long did it take your mother to find out you were a boy, Brian? When did you stop wearing dresses like your sisters, Brian? Maybe Brian would like to bake cookies for us tomorrow, boys. You're soft Brian, maybe too soft for this team. What do you think, boys, is Brian too soft for the team?"[69]

Bobby Knight, always an exemplar of best practices in coaching, once put a tampon in a player's locker to let him know he was considered a wimp.[70] Here's another brilliant motivational strategy by Knight during his Indiana teams' viewing of a videotaped game: While berating an athlete for not running down the court hard enough, he said, "Look at that! You never push yourself. You know what you are, Daryl? You are the worst f. . . pussy I've ever seen play basketball at this school. The absolute worst pussy ever."[71]

The organization "Out Sports" provides a list of the most flagrant antigay comments. Here's a good one: In discussing how glad he is he doesn't play for New York, baseball player John Rocker utilized a bevy of antieveryone gems. "Imagine having to take the 7 train to (Shea Stadium in New York) looking like you're (in) Beirut next to some kid with purple hair, next to some queer with AIDS, right next to some dude who got out of jail for the fourth time, right next to some 20-year-old mom with four kids. It's depressing."[72]

Sometimes athletes have had all they can take of a coaches' abuse and erupt, as was the case with Latrell Sprewell. Golden State Warriors coach P. J. Carlesimo was demanding and never happy with his team's performance. He had perfected the craft of "motivating" his team through obscenities and confrontation, often spewing profanity directly in the face of a player during a game. Sprewell lost it after repeated haranguing, attacking Carlesimo twice. The NBA suspended Sprewell for a year, and the Warriors voided the rest of his contract, worth approximately $25 million. The NBA defended its action, citing the Uniform Player Contract's moral clause, demanding all players "conform to the standards of citizenship and good standards." Sprewell also lost his contract with Converse. An arbitrator later reduced Sprewell's punishment to a 7-month suspension and reinstated the last 2 years of his contract, but Sprewell still lost an estimated $6.4 million over the incident.[73] While certainly no person, coach or not, should ever be subject to a physical assault and Sprewell deserved some punishment, we are concerned that the NBA failed to reprimand Carlesimo for repeated behavior that likely was not even close to demonstrating "good citizenship and good moral character." In general, this type of behavior is accepted among coaches as it is simply chalked up as their intense drive to win.

College coaches will recruit virtually any athlete, as long as he or she buys into the sports ethic. This often includes recruiting athletes who have little chance of academic success at the college level. One athlete who was recruited by Boston College in 1995 (but had his ACT score invalidated because he had raised it from a 14 to 22) admitted to cheating on his own, but claims getting help from a coach or someone else would not have been difficult. He said, "I talked to a few Division I coaches who said they'd have it taken care of. Schools you'd recognize. It doesn't take a brain scientist to find out what they're talking about."[74] Former Clemson basketball coach, Tates Locke, admitted that, in trying to attract black players to the virtually all-white university, blacks were paid to pretend to be members of a fictitious fraternity when black recruits visited campus.[75] Recently, the University of Colorado football team has been under investigation for possible use of sex and alcohol to recruit athletes. Surely CU is not alone.

If they can play, even those with prior criminal convictions may be recruited, under the guise that coaches are benevolently offering them a second chance. Five big time programs recruited New York City star Richie Parker, despite his conviction in high school for felony sex abuse. Cleveland State offered a scholarship to Roy Williams despite his murder conviction. Williams repaid the university with a rape arrest.[76] University of Nebraska football player Christian Peter is a scary example of an athlete being offered a second, third, fourth, etc., chance. In *Public Heroes, Private Felons,* Jeff Benedict's study of athletes and crimes against women, readers can learn that Peter had flunked out of Christian Brothers Academy in New Jersey, and performed poorly at Tilton School in New Hampshire. Coach Tom Osborne offered Peter a scholarship, but he had to sit out his first year because he did not meet the NCAA's minimum eligibility standards. Peter was red-shirted his second year, so he spent his first 2 years at the University of Nebraska breaking the law it seems, racking up six arrests in that time, including one for threatening to kill a parking attendant. He also used his time to sexually assault a number of women, including Miss Nebraska, Natalie Kuijvenhoven. When Kuijvenhoven complained to a friend who was also a football team captain, he responded that they hear things about him all the time, but warned, "I don't know what you think you're going to do about it, but whatever it is, you'll never get it over the football team."[77] Natalie found just how difficult it is to challenge anything to do with Husker football, as coach Tom Osborne repeatedly backed Peter. Indeed, Osborne "excused a litany of highly public felony charges against his players."[78] Of course, some of Osborne's athletes were actually punished: After being convicted, Christian Peter was required to attend all his university classes. Strangely, in some circles this is considered a privilege. Peter also had to miss a spring scrimmage, which must have devastated him. In explaining his recruiting strategy, Osborne told the *Omaha-World Herald*, "You don't win football games with choirboys. You've got to be tough to play."[79]

Sexual misconduct problems among players are certainly not limited to a few campuses or the failing watch of rogue coaches. Although an independent report found University of Minnesota administrators did not deliberately interfere with investigations regarding sexual misconduct by their athletes, they did show favoritism toward athletes. In several of the more than forty cases over a 6-year time span, athletic officials were found to have tried talking victims into changing their stories or dropping charges.[80] Similarly, University of Colorado football coach Gary Barnett was allowed to keep his job after declaring he would "back his players 100%" in light of allegations of sexual assaults occurring during recruiting visits. When kicker Katie Hnida spoke out about her ill treatment while a member of the team, Barnett demonstrated absolutely zero tact, as he took jabs at her playing ability despite having allowed her on the team. But alas, by the end of the tumultuous season, Barnett would be honored as Big 12 Coach of the Year.

Likewise, professional teams will take anybody (including Christian Peter), regardless of the baggage they may bring. As Jim Bouton, former New York Yankees pitcher, explained, "They'd find room for Charles Manson if he could hit .300."[81] After all his legal troubles at the University of Nebraska (including violent assault of his former girlfriend), running back Lawrence Phillips was still drafted by the St. Louis Rams and offered a $5 million contract. Other teams considered drafting Phillips. One factor they looked at was U of N coach, Tom Osborne's personal letter to every NFL coach complimenting Phillips' character. John Butler, General Manager of the Buffalo Bills, said, "When you get someone as respected as Tom Osborne vouching for a player's character, you have to put a lot of stock in that."[82] Wouldn't it be nice if the coaches put as much stock in a criminal conviction as a statement of character?

Nor are coaches in the pro leagues quick to cut a great player, no matter how much trouble he may be in. Benedict chronicles the case of Lewis Billups. Over the course of his 7-year NFL career, Billups "raped, beat, and terrorized many women."[83] Despite multiple arrests, lawsuits, and a plethora of graphic evidence of his violence toward women, neither his team, the Cincinnati Bengals, nor the NFL saw fit to assign Billups any formal punishment. Nor did any of his teammates confront him, ignoring his off-the-field behavior because "he never had a problem with other players."[84] Eventually Billups self-destructed, dying in a car accident in which he was traveling over 100 miles per hour.

Jeff Benedict demonstrates that 40 percent of the 177 NBA players he investigated during the 2001–2002 season had a police record for a serious crime. Sadly, because the teams have invested so much into the players (including valued draft picks) it becomes more palatable to move a player to another team rather than to cut him.[85] In the end, there is a revolving door on the front of most NBA franchises with questionable characters constantly cycling through. They are only pushed out of the league's exit door when they can no longer score and rebound.

There have even been several cases where coaches will begin their careers with a lie. It was discovered that George O'Leary had lied to the University of Notre Dame about having a Master's Degree. O'Leary scored the job for 5 days in December 2001 before his falsifications were discovered. Of course, O'Leary had a habit of lying to employers. He also lied to the athletic director at Liverpool High School, where he was a coach. When asked about the inconsistencies in his resume, O'Leary saw no problem, saying, "A lot of people do that."[86] Of course, none of this hurt him too badly; O'Leary received another lucrative gig as an assistant coach for the Minnesota Vikings in 2002, and then on to a head coaching position at Central Florida.

Blaming coaches, however, may lead us to overlook how the structure of sports today creates this situation. Coaches are under immense pressure to win or they will lose their jobs, and thus can find it pretty difficult if not impossible not to look the other way when certain byproducts occur, or not to encourage them from the get-go. College coaches have complained of receiving hate mail, not just if they lose, but also if their team doesn't cover the betting spread.[87] And the sports ethic is sold to many athletes well before they reach the professional or even collegiate levels, hence coaches at these levels may have to do little to foster adherence; it's already ingrained.

EARLY INDOCTRINATION TO THE SPORTS ETHIC

Kids become familiar with the sports ethic early on, often in their first experiences with organized sports. At some public schools football takes on as much importance, not just to the athletes and their families but also to the entire community, as it does at the collegiate and professional levels. This phenomenon was clearly illustrated in H. G. Bissinger's *Friday Night Lights*. The book and film portray how education often takes a back seat to football at Permian, and in many Texas schools. Star players are idolized by the town and allowed to do pretty much whatever they want; that is, until they no longer win or they get injured. This is football in Texas.[88]

Former pro basketball player turned announcer Bill Walsh explains how the process begins with the youth league coach who tells a kid he or she could be a "great player." To do so, however, the kid must specialize. No more dabbling in a variety of sports leagues or learning the guitar. It is sports only, all the time. Because the kid likely still enjoys sports at this phase, he or she is typically eager to please the coach and has aspirations of being a big star. Once in a high school, the coach notices his or her potential, and "whether he realizes it or not, the coach starts directing his life—telling him what courses to take, giving him a study program that does not challenge him in the classroom or develop the disciplines of the mind that will best serve him in society."[89] By then the parents have fallen into the trap, and sometimes even the local townspeople rally on board. Often special things are done for him, as no one wants to be the one that jeopardize his chances. And then the college recruiters come, and even more strings are pulled and much more special treatment ensues. As one highly sought after college basketball player explains, "Coaches would come up to me offering the moon and stars. They would flatter you and flatter their program. Coaches would come up and tell you, 'I can see the NBA written on your forehead' and stuff like that."[90]

Parents can be some of the most vocal, and most dangerous, purveyors of the sports ethic. D. Stanley Eitzen recounts the story of Todd Marinovich in *Fair and Foul*. Todd's father Marv started his training to be a star athlete while Todd was in the womb, when his mother ate nothing but natural foods. Marv started Todd on a daily stretching and flexibility regimen at 2 weeks. Todd was never allowed to eat white sugar, white flour, or any processed food while young, and was only given fruit juices, bottled water, and skimmed milk to drink. Experts were hired to work with young Todd on speed, agility, endurance, strength, and peripheral vision. Todd worked out 7 days a week for most of his youth. On his fourth birthday Todd ran 4 miles at an 8-minute mile pace. Todd's parents had him switch schools three times in high school because Marv felt his coaches were inept. Todd became a high school and collegiate quarterback star, and was drafted from USC to play for the Oakland Raiders. It was then that Marv's stress on the sports ethic caught up with them; Todd lasted only 2 years with the Raiders and has been busted several times for possession of illegal drugs.[91]

Parents have, sadly, been known to model aggressive behaviors toward coaches or officials when their kids' sporting events don't go as they wish. The National Association of Sports officials reported an increase in parents and coaches assaulting officials and began to offer assault insurance in 1998.[92] As Douglas Putnam explains in *Controversies of the Sports World*, "Nothing can put a damper on a soccer game between 7-year-olds like an irate father bounding onto the field to deliver an obscenity-laced tirade in the face of a referee who has made a bad call. The only thing that might be worse is a hyperventilating coach heaping abuse on a 9-year-old who hasn't put on his 'game face.'"[93] Former Major League Baseball player and manager of the Cincinnati Reds Ray Knight was charged with disorderly conduct after punching a parent while coaching his daughter's softball team in Albany, Georgia. The parent had heckled Knight from the stands, telling him he "couldn't play with the big boys."[94] Of course Knight had to defend his masculinity. A mob in Kissimmee, Florida, in the 1980s "acknowledged the efforts of the four coaches of a winning team of 12-year-old football players by attacking them with clubs and pipes. One coach wound up in the hospital. A cry from the crowd ('He's dead!') apparently sated the mob and it withdrew just before the constables arrived."[95] A principal in Teton, Idaho, angered that his football coach was being penalized for unsportsmanlike behavior during a playoff game, called the referee to the sidelines and punched him in the stomach. He clearly felt vindicated, despite his $500 fine, because the league suspended the referee.[96]

Even when parents don't control their kids as directly as Marv did Todd, their attitudes and behavior may tell children their worth is related solely to their athletic success. In *Little Girls in Pretty Boxes*, Joan Ryan explains how many of the parents who subjected their daughters to the abuse of gymnastics coach Bela Karolyi did so because they felt they were providing them with the chance of a lifetime. Because they firmly believed in the mission, they were able to ignore or minimize the abuse they obviously knew about.[97] But when mothers and fathers are willing to live in separate cities and to work multiple jobs in order to pay for their child's gymnastics coaching and assorted paraphernalia like costumes and hairstyling, the message to the young lady is she had *better* succeed and never complain. "Look at all that we have done for you," is a lot of pressure for anyone to handle. And while the athlete may appear outwardly to handle it, the stress may manifest itself in less visible ways, such as through self-mutilation and eating disorders. Lack of praise for effort and improvement reinforces to kids that winning is all that matters.[98]

CONCLUSION

We have created a sports business that tells all involved it is okay to do whatever is necessary to win, and we have so successfully marketed a specific image of success that few stop to question whether it is detrimental. Sports are defined in warlike terms, and in a war there are no-holds-barred. As many have explained, the language of sports is the language of violence. We would add that it is also the language of excess and extremes. Teams are not exhorted to merely win a game or match, they are told they must stomp, rout, trounce, kill, murder, or destroy the opponent. George Orwell summed it up nicely: "Serious sport has nothing to do with fair play. It is bound up with hatred, jealousy, boastfulness, disregard for all rules, and sadistic pleasure in witnessing violence: in other words, it is war minus the shooting." The government has also used sports metaphors, reinforcing the connection between war and football, in particular. Richard Nixon referred to himself as "the quarterback," and the elder Bush called the Gulf War "his Super Bowl."[99] Jackson Katz explains that many coaches actually have a military or police background. His own was an ex-Marine with a buzz cut, who constantly used war metaphors in his coaching. After a key player was declared ineligible one season, the coach declared, "When you're trying to take the hill, you're gonna lose some men on the way up."[100]

So, are we saying athletes, fans, and coaches have no free will, no ability to reject overconformity to the sports ethic? The answer is no. What we are saying is that athletes often perceive that there are only certain avenues to sports success. Likewise, coaches and fans are sold this same model. Alternative models are generally not offered. Following the sports ethic, competition is virtually always conceived as beating another, not bettering yourself. Jon Leizman explains in *Let's Kill 'Em* how this is due to the mind-body dichotomy of the Western world, as well as the fact that sports have long been conceived of as preparation for the military.[101] President Theodore Roosevelt applauded sports as a means of developing masculinity and preparing males for service.[102] Resistance to competition is often decried as anti-American.[103]

Yet there are indeed alternative models. Drew Hyland, in the *Journal of Philosophy of Sport*, suggested, "Competitive play should be one of those occasions where our encounters, intense, immediate, and total, are those of friendship, in which we attain fulfillment, however momentary, together."[104] In his book *No Contest*, Alfie Kohn refutes the arguments that competition is "human nature," and that it builds character, and that there are no alternatives. He provides extensive evidence to support that cooperative endeavors are better for building self-esteem and developing empathy. And, despite the claims of die-hard capitalists, Kohn shows that people are more productive when they work cooperatively.[105] In *Fair and Foul*, D. Stanley Eitzen describes the attitude between premier distance runners Todd Williams and Bob Kennedy. After a tough 2-mile race in the 1995 Prefontaine Classic, the two hugged and jogged a lap together. Kennedy, the winner, said, "We're friends but we were both racing to win, and we wound up taking each other to a higher level."[106]

Traditionally, it has been those most marginalized in society that are best able to debunk, or question the status of things. In the United States that has often been racial and/or ethnic minorities. Examples of black athletes pushing for social change throughout history provide a model: Muhammad Ali stood up to the white establishment and refused to fight in Vietnam; John Carlos and Tommie Smith raised their fists for black power at the 1968 Mexico City Olympics, to the ire of many. Yet today's black athlete seems far more likely to accept the sports ethic. Sports Sociologist Richard Lapchick contends that today's black athlete, unless he is a superstar, cannot speak out or he will be let go. He cites the example of Craig Hodges, a peripheral player for the 1992 NBA Champion Chicago Bulls. Hodges was critical of how the police handled the Rodney King situation, and was cut by the Bulls and not picked up by another team.[107] Some maintain this is merely evidence of a greater paradox in America: while we claim to love individuality and expression, we really only tolerate it when it is nonthreatening. In most cases, conformity is required, even from athletes.[108]

Coaches are also unlikely to speak out about sports-related problems, lest they lose their jobs. Tommy Harper's contract with the Boston Red Sox was not renewed in 1985, even though he was doing a good job as special assistant to the general manager. Harper's mistake? Pointing out racist policies of the Red Sox, such as providing white players free passes to the white's only Elks Club in Winter Haven, Florida, during the team's spring training. Harper sued the team for their discriminatory firing and won, but it took him some time to get back into the world of baseball.[109]

King and Springwood explain that today's black athlete generally avoids politics, looking more like Bill Cosby's Heath Huxtable, the wholesome, responsible, and time span decidedly middle class construct of the 1980s whitewashing of racism than they do Ali.[110] Michael Jordan was the "good black" who successfully marketed the game and its products, and refused to take an active stance against his sponsor's use of sweatshop labor. Even Dennis Rodman, the "bad black" was merely a symbolic threat to the status quo, as his commodified image was about making money as well.[111] Rodman may have offered a unique look, but was never a vocal advocate of any political change. In general, athletes are not encouraged to offer any critique of the sports industry, or social commentary in general. Charles McNair, former student-athlete, said in 1993, "Overall, athletes are loved by everybody until their consciousness is raised and they start to speak out on social issues."[112]

Perhaps Bob Dylan's song about the 1963 Featherweight boxing match between Davey Moore and Sugar Ramos best sums up the American approach to sports deviance. Ramos beat Moore so harshly that he died 75 hours after the fight. Within a week of Moore's death, three other boxers were killed in the ring. In "Who Killed Davey Moore?" Dylan demonstrates how the finger gets pointed in a lot of directions, but no one admits they are responsible because, ultimately, they are *all* responsible. The referee is not at fault, he says, because if he had stopped the match early the crowd would have booed at not getting their money's worth. The crowd claims no responsibility, as all they wanted to do was see some sweat and blood. His manager was also not at fault, even though, perhaps, he should have talked an already under the weather Moore out of the match. The gambler? Also not at fault—he never touched anyone, and besides, he bet on Moore to win. The sports writer also denies responsibility, claiming he's not supporting boxing, just doing his job. And most of all, his opponent does not take the blame. "I hit him, I hit him, yes, it's true. But that's what I'm paid to do. Don't say "murder," don't say "kill," it was destiny, it was God's will." Such is sports today. Athletes suffer and the responsibility is passed like a hot potato from one interested party to another.

chapter 2

Doping

I dunno. I never smoked any Astroturf.
—Pitcher Tug McGraw, when asked if he preferred grass or Astroturf.

The national past time is juiced.

—Jose Canseco

To the uninitiated, doping appears to be the ultimate threat to the success and profitability of big time sports. In fact, many experts claim there is no greater threat to the integrity of the games, and that the specter of an unleveled playing field will kill fan interest. But there is an alternative truth. As we see it, doping that leads to unprecedented achievements from superhuman athletes is the very fuel that makes sports such a popular spectacle for the die-hard fans. The sports industry yearns to produce ever bigger, faster, and stronger athletes. Behemoths, who look less and less like the fans in the stands and more and more like the comic book heroes of our youths. When athletes set records or take a beating and keep on competing, the fans cheer ever louder without really wondering how it all is achieved. And the sports industry profits. When athletes fail drug tests and are suspended, they are treated as one-offs, pariahs of the game, forever branded as cheats. But there is no attention paid to the systemic problems that drove them to it. Meanwhile, team owners, representatives, and league officials can claim, "See! We keep our yard clean. We caught this guy and suspended him. No need to worry. Now, watch this beer commercial." And the profits continue to grow. For instance, when Rafael Palmeiro was suspended for testing positive for steroids, Baltimore Orioles manager, Peter Angelos, maintained the problem was solved, saying he knew Palmeiro would return from the suspension reformed and ready to be a "productive member of the Orioles."[1] Clearly the emphasis is on the "productive member" part.

For many sports, such as track and field and swimming, fan interest is closely tied to the pursuit and breaking of records. Long periods without new records threaten to render the sports "dull" or "boring" to fans. In the intense competition between sports for the interests and loyalty of sports fans, being seen as boring is unacceptable.

A prime example comes from track and field's long jump competition. Entering the 1968 Olympics, the world record stood at 27'4 ¾" and the world awaited the first 28' leap. Bob Beamon leapt into history by skipping over the 28' range altogether, landing 29'2 ½" from the board, capturing both the gold medal and the world's imagination. It was an outrageously important moment for track and field. Unfortunately, the record stood for nearly 23 years. Finally, at the World Championships in 1991, Mike Powell soared farther, pushing the record to 29'4 ½". His record still stands. In over 37 years the world record has been improved once. As former track and field athletes and coaches, we guarantee few fans can name a significant moment in the long jump that occurred in the 1970s or 1980s. Without record-breaking performances, the attention of fans simply turns elsewhere. Thus, we suggest that for the sports industry, long periods without new records, and the waning fan interest that results is a far greater threat to profitability than is a failed drug test here and there.

Baseball provides another sterling example. Roger Maris attracted tremendous fan interest in 1961 when he smacked 61 home runs, breaking (by 1) Babe Ruth's record, set in 1927. This record stood until Mark McGwire outlasted and outblasted Sammy Sosa in their famed Homer race in 1998. Their battle couldn't have come at a better time, as it reinvigorated fan interest, which had been in decline ever since the 1994 strike. It also gave baseball top billing on the nightly news and in the morning papers and dominated sports broadcasting, as ESPN cut away from any and every event to bring us live coverage of the two sluggers' every at-bat. And nobody seemed to blink when it was revealed that androstenedione, a muscle-building performance enhancer, aided our new home run king. And nobody seriously suggested stripping his record. Major League Baseball simply played it down as a nonissue because they had not banned his drug of choice, even though it was banned by every other respected sports organization. In the end, the fans were happy, as they had seen a spectacular home run race. The coaches, athletes, and MLB were happy, as profits rolled in. Never mind that the record had been set under questionable circumstances or that it would stand only until broken by Barry Bonds under even more dubious circumstances.

American sports, with their emphasis on adherence to the sports ethic, often command athletes to enhance their performance by whatever means possible. We cheer on the injured player who hobbles back into the game, glorify the most reckless players who deliver bone-crushing hits, and weep for the malnourished gymnast as the medals are draped around her neck. To get to the top, athletes have special diets, intense training regimens and, for some, a training table replete with illegal performance enhancing substances. The primary motive for taking performance-enhancing drugs is winning. Psychologists say elite athletes often have compulsive personalities and often gauge their sense of self-worth on their athletic success. Societal fixations on appearance, competition, and, above all, winning, are all contributors.[2] While the trend in the United States is to blame individuals for their problems and not to address the role of systems or structures, sports sociologists recognize that doping is the responsibility of many, as the entire society is involved in creating and sustaining the sports ethic to which these athletes are adhering.[3]

Athletes growing up in the current American sports environment often feel compelled to do whatever they can do, to take whatever substances are necessary, regardless of the consequences, to help them win or maintain their role on their team and in their sports. In explaining the motivation to dope, the International Olympic Committee's Medical Commission stated the following in their Manual on Doping: "The merciless rigor of modern competitive sports, especially at the international level, the glory of victory, and the growing social and economical reward of sporting success (in no way any longer related to reality) increasingly forces athletes to improve their performance by any means possible."[4] Many athletes ignore the risks of performance-enhancing drugs, because they know that they can use them under the advisement of medical doctors or trainers.[5] Whether these doctors are ethical is a different question. As more information became public about the BALCO scandal (described later), it was clear that these athletes trusted leader Victor Conte to provide them useful drugs in "safe" quantities. As a Division I athlete, Laura never questioned what substances were provided by the trainers for her injuries. None were illegal, but the point remains that athletes put their trust in these experts.

In addition to athletes pursuing victory at any cost, athletes described as "fading-has-beens" are also shockingly vulnerable to the temptation of drug use.[6] This group has often been so role engulfed that they are unprepared for life beyond sports, and seek to extend their participation as long as possible. American middle-distance runner Regina Jacobs is a prime example. Rumors had circulated for some time that Jacobs must be doped to be able to perform at the highest level in middle age. At the age of 40, Jacobs won her 12th national 1500-meter title, unheard of in distance running. Sadly, it was later announced that Jacobs had failed a test for THG on the day of that achievement and was sanctioned with a 4-year ban. Jacobs had announced her retirement 1 week earlier—strange timing, to say the least.[7]

Barry Bonds offers another case study of the issue of aging athletes, incredible achievements, and potential abuse of performance enhancements. Many have been skeptical that a person of his age—40 years—can still put up the numbers he does.[8] Further, Bonds admitted to a grand jury that he unknowingly used a performance enhancing substance. Despite these admissions, Giants manager Felipe Alou defended Bonds when a Senate Commerce, Science, and Transportation committee member proclaimed him a cheat. Rather than address the charges, Alou attacked the charger, saying, "These are people who aren't spending time with him in the trenches . . . I hope he's judged by the real baseball players when he's finished—people who know a baseball player when they see one."[9]

A fascinating and scary poll sums up how many athletes feel about doping. The poll of sprinters, swimmers, power lifters, and other U.S. Olympians or aspiring Olympians in 1995 asked the athletes if they would take a banned performance-enhancing substance with two guarantees: (1) you will not be caught; and (2) you will win. One hundred and ninety-five athletes said "yes." Only three said "no." Given a second scenario in which they would win and would be guaranteed not to be caught but would die from the side effects of the substance in 5 years, more than 50 percent still said they would take the substance.[10] While this is likely shocking to the reader (it certainly shocks us), this only demonstrates that winning holds an importance in the minds of many athletes that most of us cannot relate to. Perhaps it is the years of hard work and single-minded focus that causes many athletes to value winning over life itself. As we discuss in the chapter on cheating, high stakes competition seems to inevitably lead to increased cheating.

COACHES AND PERFORMANCE-ENHANCING DRUGS

Richard Davies, author of *America's Obsession*, contends the door to drug use by athletes was opened when coaches either "openly condoned or winked" at the use of painkillers and amphetamines.[11] Renate Vogel Heinrich was an East German swimmer in the 1970s who claims she had no idea her coach was doping her up. She says when she looks at pictures of herself from that time period she feels sick. At the time, she says, "We never really noticed what we looked like, because swimmers were always kept together. It didn't hit me until an old friend said, 'Wow Renate, you speak like a man, and you've got those unbelievably broad shoulders.'"[12]

The problem of doctors and other "behind-the-scenes" experts doping athletes has changed little over the years. Dr. Daniel F. Hanley, a professor at Bowdoin College in the 1980s, described the problem this way: "Quackery. That is the bane of sports medicine. We've rid ourselves of some of the worst, but there are still many people handing out get-good-quick pills, touting machines that send blue sparks and make big muscles, or advising athletes to drink superduper seaweed extracts."[13] Twenty years later the problem persists, as demonstrated by Victor Conte and his Bay Area Laboratory Co-Operative (BALCO). He and three others have been indicted by a federal grand jury for distributing designer steroids to athletes and their trainers. These special "'roids" were completely undetectable because the testers had no idea they existed. Finally, an anonymous source in track and field snatched a used vial from a trash can and the residue it contained was used to create a test for the drugs. The resulting fallout has shaken the world of sports. But the question remains: How many more unscrupulous doctors and chemists are hard at work creating and distributing designer steroids? Conte suggests that the next generation of undetectable steroid is already in use by big-time athletes.[14]

Doctors are sports fans, and some simply take their love for a team or player way too far. Dr. John Finley, a team physician for the Detroit Red Wings in the 1980s, said, "Exuberance, our own exuberance, is something we physicians in sports have to guard against. Most of us work with teams as a sort of labor of love, because we are fans. I know I am. I root hard for the Wings. I'm trying to think of what I can do to help them win. Maybe there is a drug that will help. I try to watch myself, not let my emotions influence my medical judgment, but it is something to keep in mind."[15] Another doctor summed up the problem by acknowledging that most doctors are men of action who seek immediate results, rather than "wait around for a double-blind control study to find out the drug is effective or what it will do to the liver three years later."[16] Doctors know, and sometimes tell their athletes, that side effects generally only occur in a small percentage of people.[17] Athletes may figure, as do many Americans, that if a doctor says something is not too risky, it must be a-okay.

Some doctors take a more pragmatic approach to drug use, arguing that athletes will get them anyway, so they might as well help make the process as safe as possible. Dr. Robert Kerr is one who felt he was providing a service.[18] Kerr also justified administering drugs to athletes by pointing to other innovations that help athletes improve their performance.[19] That Kerr and others fail to see the distinction between flexible pole vault poles and anabolic steroids is frightening, at best.

If a team doctor or an athlete's primary physician refuses to dole out the dope, an athlete may elect to doctor shop. Victor Conte contended that NFL player Bill Romanowski did just this, adding new tricks and trinkets to his juice cocktail from a plethora of sources.[20] Romanowski's 1996–2001 teammates nicknamed him "Rx" for the medications he took, which were, according to sports columnist Woody Paige, "not always prescribed . . . to him, at least."[21]

Of course, if team doctors won't provide athletes with pills or injections, team trainers might. Trainers are under immense pressure to keep players healthy and are dependent on the team for their livelihood. They may decide, "Athletes don't win sitting on the bench with injuries. Some athletes don't win unless they are fired up enough to go out and tear into their opponents with total disregard for the possibility of injury to themselves" and thus become dope dispensers.[22] Joe Kuczo, a former trainer for the Washington Redskins, explained that, at one time, such actions were reserved for the "big games," but now almost everything is a big game.[23] Trainers work under the difficult expectations of having players healthy and competing, with an emphasis on competing. So when a player is borderline in preparedness, the pressure on the trainers to get the player back in action can be intense.

WHEN ATHLETES INITIATE

Although there have been some cases of athletes being given substances against their will, often they feel coerced in other ways. Because the professionals' livelihoods depend on playing at the highest level, they may feel compelled to do whatever it takes to stay in the sports and improve performance. One author, cited in Simon, says, "The onus is on the athlete to continue playing and to consent to things he or she would not otherwise consent to . . . Coercion, however subtle, makes the athlete vulnerable. It also takes away the athlete's ability to act and choose freely with regard to informed consent."[24] The athletes are acutely aware that, as the sports machine grinds on, new, young, and willing athletes are always coming along to replace the aging stars. When performance enhancers represent a means to hang on for another year, or to get a lucrative contract extension, it can be no surprise that many athletes capitulate to pressure from teammates and doctors.

Athletes who have admitted doping often claim they did so because they thought all their competitors were. Bob Goldman explains the doping cycle in *Death in the Locker Room: Steroids and Sports:* "Each takes drugs because he believes his competitor is doing so. Each takes more than he believes his competitor takes so that he can have the advantage over his competitor."[25] Sadly, at the top levels of sports, the athletes are almost certainly right. Their competitors likely are juiced to the gills! As Jose Canseco told Mike Wallace in a *60 Minutes Interview,* "The national pastime is juiced." He also claimed that 80 percent of Major Leaguers had used steroids at some point.[26] And it is shortsighted to believe that competitors are always the guys on the other team. Almost all teams include both the stars and the newcomers who are anxious to push out the stars in their own quest for glory. Each group, then, has a motive for using performance enhancers.

Use of performance enhancing substances by high profile professional athletes has set a poor example for young athletes, who wish to emulate their idols. After Mark McGwire set the home run record in 1998 and admitted using androstenedione, a steroid substitute, sales of "andro" jumped 1,000 percent and steroid use by teens rose.[27] Charles Yesalis, professor of exercise and sports science at Penn State, said, "If you really believe in winning at all costs, and that's how you raise your kids, drug use is not illogical."[28] According to orthopedic surgeon James Andrews, the problem is that parents think they can make professional athletes out of their children, if they simply start the training early enough. Kids may then internalize this, doing whatever it takes to make Ma and Pa proud.[29]

Although there is enticement to use performance enhancers at ever-younger ages, it generally begins later, as the player climbs the ladder nearer the top and is more likely to be a role model for others. With each advancement—from high school to college, to minor leagues, to professional ranks—separating oneself from the pack becomes more difficult. This is particularly true if the dream of riches is just a step away. Baseball star Fred McGriff said, "A career minor leaguer, he might see this as a way to pull it off and get to the major leagues and take care of his family."[30]

A BRIEF HISTORY OF DOPING IN THE MODERN WORLD

Use of performance enhancing substances in sports is by no means a new phenomenon. The first recorded drug-related death in sports was in 1886, when a cyclist collapsed during a distance race in Europe after taking a "speedball," a combination of cocaine and heroin intended to boost his strength and endurance.[31] In the 1870s cyclists often competed in events that lasted 6 days, 144 straight hours of competition. While the athletes rotated racing and recovery, the events were brutally difficult. To endure the events they would often take sugar soaked in ether, nitroglycerine, caffeine, peppermint and cocaine mixtures, as well as cocaine-heroin combinations.[32] Similarly, prizefighters were known to consume alcohol, strychnine, and a variety of concoctions before entering the ring to help them handle fatigue and to dull pain.[33] 1904 Olympic marathon champion Tom Hicks of the United States admitted sipping brandy and consuming small amounts of strychnine to keep up his stamina.[34]

Use of performance enhancing substances grew more frequent and more sophisticated in the twentieth century as sports became more popular, the competition more intense, and greater scientific knowledge had been developed.[35] Anabolic steroids were discovered in the 1930s, initially for medical use. Anabolic steroids are hormones that may be either naturally or synthetically produced. They may be taken in pill, powder, or liquid form, and are typically used in sports requiring intense and exhausting training.[36]

Use of anabolic steroids by athletes in the United States escalated as use of performance enhancers became obvious in other countries. Athletes in the former Soviet Union and other communist nations used steroids with great frequency in the 1950s and 1960s, often unknowingly, as their countries' sports machines doped them up. Because neither the Olympic Games nor any other international competition conducted drug testing, none were punished at the time.[37] In 1954, the U.S. Olympic Team's physician, Dr. John B. Zeigler, gave steroids to his team, hoping to help them compete with the Soviets.[38] As Goldman explains, "Getting beaten on the playing fields, as well as in outer space and the cold war, was a hard-to-swallow pill for American doctors who had been raised on American virtue-will-out based supremacy."[39]

The IOC first developed a list of banned substances in 1967 and then instituted the first tests for doping at the 1968 Mexico City games.[40] In 1975 the IOC banned anabolic steroids.[41] Two American swimmers voiced some of the early concerns about their competitors' use of steroids in 1976. At the time, Shirley Babashoff and Wendy Boglioli were dismissed as whiners, but in 1991, after the fall of the Communist regime in East Germany, many of the swimming coaches suspected that every female medal winner in the Montreal games was doped. Even the East German secret police, the Stasi, were involved in the doping of some 10,000 athletes.[42] The IOC gradually added substances to their banned list, including caffeine and testosterone in 1983, and diuretics and some corticosteroids in 1985.[43]

Steroid use on the international sports scene gained unprecedented attention in 1988, when Canadian sprinter Ben Johnson tested positive for stanozolol, a synthetic form of testosterone. Johnson's medal was stripped and given to the second place finisher, American Carl Lewis, who many have also accused of doping. Johnson's manager claimed someone spiked the sprinter's Gatorade prior to the event, an argument Olympic officials rightly rejected as ludicrous. Johnson evidently did not learn his lesson, as he tested positive for steroids again in 1993.[44]

AN ESCALATING PROBLEM

The concern over steroid use among track athletes has only escalated. The 2004 Olympic Track and Field trials featured virtually nonstop coverage of the breaking BALCO scandal, which seemed to spawn media attention of other earlier doping allegations. U.S. Sprinter Jerome Young received a lifetime ban by the U.S. Anti-Doping Agency in November 2004 for his second positive test, one for nandrolone and the second for EPO (discussed later in the chapter). Young was a member of the gold-medal winning 1600-meter relay team from the Sydney games, and his ban could cost the other members their medals. Of course, team member Alvin Harrison accepted a 4-year suspension a month earlier for violations discovered during the BALCO investigations, while his twin, Calvin, also on the relay team, is serving a 2-year suspension.[45] These cases are likely only the tip of the iceberg, as it is difficult to believe that only those few athletes who were caught were using the BALCO wonder drugs.

The problem is certainly not confined to track and field. Now whenever an athlete delivers a record-breaking or otherwise outstanding performance in any sports, many levy the doping allegations. Hence the nonstop buzz that seven-time Tour de France champ Lance Armstrong was junked up and the allegations that baseball single-season home run record holder, Barry Bonds, didn't do it on his talent alone. While some record setters are almost certainly doped, others may not be. But so widespread is drug use that a culture exists in which sports fans have to question every apparently great success.

On the U.S. front, the NCAA has tried to curb the use of performance enhancing substances at the college level, initiating drug testing in 1986. That same year, the public was captivated when Brian Bosworth, all-American defensive back for the University of Oklahoma, was banned from postseason play for steroid use.[46] The NFL began checking for steroids the following year, maintaining they would give a 30-day suspension to anyone who tested positive. The NBA currently bans thirty-two kinds of steroids.[47]

Major League baseball has perhaps taken the most heat for their shoddy policies and even shoddier testing. Under the testing rules introduced after the BALCO scandal broke, players could only be tested once during the season for steroids, as well as marijuana, cocaine, LSD, heroin, and ecstasy. The first time a player was caught, he was to submit to a treatment program. A second violation resulted in a suspension of 15 days. It took a fifth positive test to receive a 1 year suspension, so given the once yearly testing policy, a player had 5 years of doped playing before he would face a year off.[48] After MLB was roundly criticized for this shockingly weak policy, they amended the penalties several times in the following year. Some also assert the new policy was put in place because no one in professional sports wanted the federal government involved. At the time, Congress, lead by Senator John McCain, was threatening to add federal legislation directing steroid testing and applying uniform punishments for professional baseball, basketball, football, and hockey. Major League Baseball players now face a 50-day suspension for a first offense, a 100-day suspension for a second offense, and a lifetime ban after failing three tests. Through just the first season of testing, twelve players were penalized for violations of the doping policy. Certainly this was a major step, but critics assert there are still many loopholes and that more consistent enforcement of the policy is needed. One commentator from the *San Jose Mercury News* remarked, "The new steroid policy will allow owners and players to tell the public that the hammer has come down hard. But here's the dirty little secret: the hammer is still made of Swiss cheese."[49]

The most noteworthy player suspended was Rafael Palmeiro of the Baltimore Orioles. Noteworthy because on March 17, 2005, he had the audacity to wave his finger at a congressional committee looking into drug use in sports and declare, "I have never used steroids. Period."[50] He would later amend that statement to, "I have never intentionally taken steroids."[51] How reassuring. When he returned to the field, the boos and chants of "steroids!" drowned out the cheers, especially in Toronto, where Palmeiro went to the plate wearing earplugs. They didn't help as he went 0–4 in the loss. His batting average was the least of his worries at the time, however, as lawmakers considered pursuing perjury charges against him for his finger-waving grandstanding.

THE SUBSTANCES OF CHOICE

Which drug is the substance of choice varies somewhat depending on the sports. One study found one-third of bodybuilders had used steroids.[52] By the mid 1970s an estimated 50 percent of professional football players had experimented with steroids, with up to 75 percent of linemen and linebackers being dedicated users.[53] One of the most high profile examples of steroid abuse was two-time All-Pro, Lyle Alzado. Upon retirement Alzado admitted he would not have achieved at the same level had he not taken Dianabol, which he began using as a collegiate athlete at Yankton College in South Dakota. Within 2 years he had ballooned from 190 to almost 300 pounds, with impressive speed and strength to boot. When the NFL began testing, Alzado simply began using masking agents. Alzado claimed his trainers and coaches knew about his use and never reprimanded him because they liked the results. Alzado estimated 90 percent of those he knew in professional football used some type of muscle-enhancing drugs.[54] Another athlete actually claimed his coach introduced him to steroids. Steve Courson, offensive linemen for the Pittsburgh Steelers and Tampa Bay Buccaneers, blamed an assistant coach at the University of South Carolina for his use.[55]

In the summer of 2002, retired Major League Baseball MVPs Jose Canseco and Ken Caminiti admitted using steroids, while a *USA Today* poll of 556 Major League players found 89 percent believed there was some steroid use in the game. Ten percent believed more than half their peers are using steroids. Close to one half (44%) felt there was great pressure to use steroids in order to stay competitive.[56] Allegedly Barry Bonds testified to a grand jury in 2003 that he might have "unknowingly" taken steroids. How did that happen? Supposedly Bonds was using "flaxseed oil cream" to treat arthritis. Creative story. It seems far more likely that the cream he was seen rubbing into his muscles in the locker room was "The Cream," a designer steroid that Bonds' personal trainer was buying from Victor Conte and BALCO. Hall of Fame Pitcher Bob Feller, while maintaining Bonds should keep his home run record, stressed, "for him to say he didn't know what he was taking is like a player who got caught with a corked bat saying he didn't know the bat was corked."[57]

In an interview with CNN's Wolf Blitzer on December 3, 2004, former baseball commissioner Fay Vincent said that a few years ago tests revealed only 7 percent of MLB players used steroids, although he guessed it was much higher.[58] In fact, this test was given essentially to get a baseline for the depth of the problem and to determine if a random testing plan was needed. Shockingly, the players knew the test was coming, and at least 7 percent of them still failed it!

New York Yankees' player, Jason Giambi, testified to a grand jury in December 2004 that he had used human growth hormone (HGH) in 2003 and had used steroids for at least three seasons. Human growth hormone is not specifically banned by Major League Baseball and, until very recently, there was no test for it. Giambi claimed he obtained several different steroids from Barry Bonds' personal trainer, Greg Anderson (one of the four people who were indicted by the grand jury in the BALCO investigation).[59]

According to Victor Conte, founder of BALCO, Olympic star Marion Jones injected herself in the leg with human growth hormone in front of him on at least one occasion. Conte claimed he began providing a number of performance enhancing substances to Jones in the weeks leading up to the 2000 Sydney games. Jones has vehemently denied the allegations. Jones' partner Tim Montgomery, current 100-meter world record holder, was also implicated by Conte. He would later be suspended for 2 years and stripped of the world record. In contrast, sprinter Kelli White, who went from virtual obscurity to superstar sprinter status, admits taking a variety of substances from Conte. White tested positive for steroids and was stripped of several world championship medals.[60]

Blood Boosting

The hormone erythropoietin (EPO) has become the drug of choice in endurance events like cycling and distance running. EPO stimulates the production of red blood cells, which allows the blood to carry more oxygen. This risky procedure can spike hematocrit levels (percentage of red blood cells) to the point of heart failure, pulmonary edema, and even death.[61] Dr. Gary Wadler, professor of clinical medicine at New York University, says using too much EPO creates an excess of red blood cells, where "the blood becomes viscous—it's like sludge."[62] Between 1986 and 1991, the deaths of eighteen European cyclists were linked with EPO use.[63] Rumors persist that many elite cyclists sleep with heart rate monitors on, set to alert them if their heart rates drop to dangerous levels. They then apparently spring out of bed and do jumping jacks to get their thickened blood pumping.

As tests have been developed to detect EPO use, athletes are looking for other means to enrich their blood. The new trend, rather than finding creative ways to deliver EPO, is to utilize modified versions of hemoglobin, a.k.a., artificial blood. It's not just the stuff of Halloween; two hemoglobin-based blood products have allegedly made the rounds in the track and field world already.[64] Further, athletes appear to be returning to older methods of blood doping, including boosting their blood with their own blood, withdrawn and stored earlier, or with the blood of a friend with a matching blood type.

In the most peculiar story of suspected doping in recent years, American cycling stands to see the downfall of a man that is a hero to many. Professional cyclist Tyler Hamilton was almost stripped of his Olympic Time Trial medal because his blood tests from the Athens games revealed *someone else's blood coursing through his veins.* Hamilton vehemently denies that he has ever transfused blood, but the jury is still out.

So, why would an athlete have someone else's blood in his veins? By increasing the amount of oxygen that can be carried to the muscles, performance can be improved significantly. Typically athletes would do this with their own blood so as to minimize the risk of AIDS and other blood-borne diseases. The advantage to borrowing blood, however, is that he would not have to ease up on training. Using the athlete's blood causes fatigue and thus missed training time. No expensive equipment is required; athletes simply need an IV line to drip the blood into the body[65] and a friend with the matching blood type. In all, it is a relatively easy way to cheat that has been escaping detection. Until now that is.

In every way Hamilton is seen as the epitome of class in sports: a hard worker, brave, quiet, and polite, and, above all, unquestionably dedicated to his sport. In fact, Hamilton has even been called the Boy Scout of pro cycling.[66] While he had been a "big name" to die-hard American fans for years, he truly captured the attention of fans around the globe by completing the grueling 2003 Tour de France after crashing and breaking his clavicle during an early stage of the race. He even went on a long solo breakaway to win a stage in spite of difficulty holding the handlebars and pained breathing from the broken bone. So impressive was Hamilton's position against doping and so strong his character that it seemed impossible he would cheat. In fact, if Hamilton is a cheat, all bets should be off regarding any other pro cyclist.

Ultimately, Hamilton was allowed to keep his gold medal, as a lab technician mistakenly froze his "B" sample rather than refrigerating it, rendering it useless for verification of the first test. But his troubles were far from over. He failed the same type of test twice more, during the famed Spanish Vuelta and, after initially being suspended, was fired from team Phonak. He has been banned for 2 years and his career is almost certainly over, as cyclists generally pass their peak before their mid-thirties. To make matters worse, Hamilton's teammate Santi Perez, who won three stages and finished second overall in Spain, also failed the same type of test. Critics now contend there was likely a doctor involved with the team who helped "prepare" the athletes for competition; because they used the same means to cheat, and they both were caught. Within a month of the positive test results the team doctor, Inaki Arratibel, had resigned.[67]

Although Hamilton has his supporters who believe the test to be fallible, many others disagree. Dr. Jacques Rogge, International Olympic Committee president, and Dick Pound, chairman of the World Anti-Doping Agency, have both expressed their belief that Hamilton is guilty and have suggested he return the Olympic medal.[68] Fellow American cyclist Bobby Julich, who finished third in the Olympic Time Trial and roomed with Hamilton in Athens said, "The rest of us at the Olympics passed the test. Why didn't he? I'm sick of people who cheat, sick of cleaning up their mess and trying to explain it."[69] Hamilton appealed his suspension before the North American Court of Arbitration for Sports but lost a 2–1 decision. And sadly, it looks like the career is over for the bicycling Boy Scout.

Stimulants

Athletes often take some type of stimulant, including amphetamines (speed), and ephedrine, which is the primary ingredient in cold medicines, nicotine, and caffeine. Amphetamines are stimulants that lower a player's sensitivity to pain and provide a surge of energy. Of course, they are also highly addictive and can cause serious bodily damage and personality changes. Even moderate regular use can increase blood pressure, create abnormal heart rhythm, and cause irritability, insomnia, and anxiety. Aggression, however, is the primary effect. Continued use can even lead to paranoid psychoses with delusions and hallucinations.[70]

Several Washington Redskins players told a reporter for the *Washington Post* in 1979 that up to one-third of NFL players used amphetamines every time they played.[71] Said one player at the time, "What you've got to be concerned about is the amphetamine gap between you and the opposition. . . . If their pupils are dilated, and they're jabbering away in paragraphs, fidgeting and ranting and licking their lips, those are pretty good clues there's an amphetamine gap. It's disconcerting to look across the line and see that."[72]

Researchers conducting a two and a half year study titled "The Sunday Syndrome," noticed uncharacteristic obscenity, violent diarrhea, vomiting, temper tantrums, and repetitive pacing by players before NFL games. Oakland Raiders owner Al Davis told the researchers amphetamines were used to counteract fear.[73] A more recent survey of ninety-three NFL athletes found 60 percent admitted to using amphetamines to improve their performance.[74]

Prior to writing this book we spent considerable time with an employee for a minor league baseball team. The stories he told us were astounding. According to him, players are so focused on making the Majors that many will do whatever drugs necessary to get there and those who will not are considered "heartless." Beyond steroids, he often told us that "uppers" were used to get players hyper-focused so they would be better at the plate. In fact, use of uppers was so widespread that playing without them was called "playing naked" and, when a player had a hitless day while "playing naked," he faced considerable scorn from teammates.

Perhaps the most commonly used stimulant is caffeine. In addition to the obvious sources of coffee and soft drinks, caffeine can also be present in flu remedies and painkillers.[75] Moderate caffeine use is allowed by the IOC, but consumption of approximately six cups of coffee 2 hours prior to a test would likely result in a positive response.[76] Research has suggested caffeine enhances the utilization of fats, thus sparing glycogen stores. In other words, caffeine reduces the amount of sugar needed from other sources in our body. It may also increase alertness and decrease an athlete's perception of fatigue.[77]

Of course, at the local levels of sports competition there generally are no tests but participants still value their results. Thus, it has been no surprise to us to see athletes at bicycle races and local 5-kilometer running races downing obscene amounts of energy drinks, such as Red Bull, prior to competing. And isn't it interesting that Red Bull has been a major advertiser during Outdoor Life Network's coverage of the Tour de France? We wonder how they are defining their product and their target market? Perhaps they are carving out a niche as the poor man's performance enhancer.

Street Drugs

Even so-called "street drugs," such as cocaine, have been used to provide a boost. Former Major League Baseball player Daryl Strawberry regularly used cocaine and other drugs. He said, "It became a lifestyle for me. Drink, do coke, get women, do something freaky . . . all that stuff. I did it for so long. I played games when I was drunk, or just getting off a drunk or all-night partying or coming down off amphetamines."[78] Surely his drug habits infuriated his teammates, right? Wrong. Keith Hernandez gave Strawberry advice on how to break out of a batting slump, telling him to "Go out and get smashed."[79] While certainly this advice might be psychological in nature—cut loose, have a few, and you'll play better—it is clear his teammates were not making any effort to keep Strawberry clean and sober. Because his habit got him "up" for games, few cared about its legality or about Strawberry's health.

Of course, cocaine has also been the source of terrible tragedy in the sports world. The sports world did not take cocaine use seriously until the 1986 death of would-be Boston Celtic, Len Bias. Bias was both talented and popular when he played for the University of Maryland, and was the Celtics top draft pick. Bias suffered a heart seizure induced by cocaine after an all-night party in his dorm. Bias was not the victim of a brief temptation of the stimulant; family and friends attested to his long-term use.[80] And, while the nation reeled over Bias' death, Cleveland Browns' defensive back Donald Rogers died under similar circumstances.[81]

Those who are familiar with the effects of cannabis may find it hard to believe it could enhance performance, yet the IOC added cannabis products to its restricted substances list in 1989.[82] The goal of taking cannabinoids is likely escape from pressure and relief of anxiety.[83] Skier Ross Rebagliati was suspended but later reinstated for testing positive for cannabinoids at the 1998 Winter Olympics in Nagano, Japan. A *New York Times* study in 1997 implicated between 60 and 70 percent of NBA players as smoking marijuana and drinking excessively. The

NBA Players Association has lobbied against testing for these substances, so the league does not.[84] It seems illogical to ingest anything but air into your lungs as a runner, yet it seems some do. U.S. sprinter John Capel, the 200-meter world champion, was dropped from the 400-meter relay team at the Athens Olympics after a positive test for marijuana at a pre-Olympics meet in Munich. Capel is a "first time offender," according to official Olympic track and field rules, but he would be suspended if he tests positive again.[85]

Beta Blockers

Beta-blockers dilate the blood cells, which reduces the heart rate and lowers blood pressure. Archers, rifle-sports participants, pool players, and golfers are most likely to use beta-blockers to keep a steady hand and thus improve aim.[86] One example is propranolol, used by ski jumpers to prevent heart palpitations that occur in anticipation of the jumps. Trap shooters, golfers, and archers have also used alcohol, lithium, valium, and serax to steady their hands and promote sleep before competitions.[87]

Over-the-Counter Doping

Not all performance-enhancing substances are illegal. In the NHL, Sudafed has become a drug of choice. Players purchase the cold medicine legally and even over-the-counter not because there's an epidemic of colds in hockey, but because it provides a surge of energy.[88] A runner we knew was banned from USA Track and Field-sponsored events because he downed cold medicine before competing. One of the most commonly detected substances by the IOC is sympathomimetic amine, or stimulants commonly found in over-the-counter treatments for upper respiratory tract infections.[89] Some athletes have become dependent on dexedrine, benzedrine, and methedrine, sometimes legally obtained and sometimes illegally obtained. These substances mask fatigue, so some endurance athletes have died of exhaustion because their bodies were unable to detect their natural signals.[90] Asthma treatments are also a drug *du jour*. While approximately 10 percent of the population has asthma, 60 percent of Olympic athletes use a prescription drug for asthma, presumably to increase their lung capacity.[91] Rick de Mont was stripped of his 1976 Olympic medal because he tested positive for a stimulant taken through his asthma inhaler.[92]

It seems bodybuilders are now using albuterol, a popular asthma drug. The bodybuilders "learned about the drug's effect from combing the journals of agricultural science, in which veterinarians frequently reported on the bulging muscles they saw in cattle after injecting them with albuterol. It turns out that the drug blocks an enzyme that chews away at muscle. Beef begat beefcake."[93]

Another legal substance that is widely used in athletics is creatine. According to supporters, creatine has the same effect as steroids without the negative side effects. It is said to delay fatigue, facilitate recovery from high intensity exercise, and increase body mass and muscular strength without adding fat.[94] Yet we know people who have tried using creatine only to be disturbed by their racing heartbeat. Side effects of creatine may include increased risk of dehydration, stomach cramps, nausea, flatulence, and diarrhea. In the long-term, creatine use may inhibit the liver's ability to produce naturally made creatine. Other studies have found that creatine users are more likely to suffer from muscle, tendon, and ligament strains. Because creatine makes the muscles more explosive, athletes may push harder. But creatine does nothing to make those muscles mechanically strong, so rapid contractions may result in tears of these nonreinforced muscle cells and connective tissues.[95] Research has suggested athletes using creatine may maintain strength gains for up to 3 weeks after the cessation of use.[96] Creatine is available for over-the-counter purchase at stores like the General Nutrition Center (GNC). Anecdotally, athletes we know from several Division I schools have admitted at least dabbling with creatine, and have estimated that most, if not all, of their teammates have done the same.

ALWAYS A STEP AHEAD OF THE MONITORS

Athletes are typically far ahead of their monitors in regard to the types of substances they may consume. Only recently have athletic organizations found a way to test for human growth hormone (HGH), which has simply led the athletes to move on to explore new types of performance enhancement. Gene-based compounds may be the wave of the future, and are difficult to detect because compounds delivered directly to the muscles typically remain there, rather than reaching the bloodstream or urine where they could be analyzed. Muscular dystrophy labs provide a ready pipeline of these potential doping agents. The disease "mimics an exaggerated form of the stress that highly trained athletes inflict on their muscles," so labs are constantly researching and developing compounds for muscle making.[97] In an admittedly rare instance, the World Anti-Doping Agency was actually ahead of the cheats in early 2005. Canadian scientists announced in February that they had uncovered a new steroid, desoxy-methyl-testosterone (DMT), which was designed to avoid detection. They believe they found the drug, similar to THG, prior to any use by athletes.[98]

Athletes are now practicing stacking, where they look for the most effective combination of drugs.[99] Some take only two drugs at a time, while others have taken up to sixteen.[100] This is the allegation against the sprinters implicated in the BALCO scandal. Victor Conte created elaborate doping schedules for his athletes, including injections of his own "nondetectable" substance called "the Clear" as well as insulin, EPO, and HGH. A look at these calendars on ABC's *20/20* highlighted the frequency of use; most athletes were taking some type of substance almost every day, and sometimes more than one on a day. Conte implicated NFL player Bill Romanowski as using a number of steroid products he had supplied, as well as a cocktail of other substances provided by other doctors.[101] Sometimes athletes take one drug to counteract the side effects of another. For instance, athletes who take anabolic steroids may take amphetamines to reduce the bloated and sluggish feeling, thus the "upper-downer merry-go-round."[102]

SIDE EFFECTS

Of course, there are numerous negative effects of all of these substances, as there are of every drug, both legal and illegal. It is well documented that steroids increase blood pressure, result in hair loss, may either dramatically increase or decrease sex drive, and can lead to impotence, insomnia, and liver malfunction.[103] According to Anshel and Russell, the effects of steroids are both acute (including dehydration, heat stroke, and cardiac arrest) as well as chronic (such as liver cancer and lymphoma). Other physical and psychological maladies have been reported, including kidney stones, irregular heartbeat, sterility, hypertension, anxiety, suicidal tendencies, shortened attention span, depression, and schizophrenia have been reported.[104] In addition, steroid use may contribute to athletic injuries, as athletes are using overdeveloped muscles. Orthopedic surgeon James Andrews has seen an increase in the incidence of rotator cuff injuries and injuries to elbow ligaments from throwing.[105] Among young athletes, steroids can stunt growth.[106] Steroid use by young people is also linked with other risk-taking behaviors. Yesalis et al. found that 80 percent of 12–17-year-olds who had used steroids in the past year had also acted aggressively against other people or committed a property crime.[107]

Although males are more likely to use steroids, females do as well. They typically do so in lower doses and for shorter periods of time, but the effects may be even more significant.[108] In women, excess levels of testosterone may lead to the growth of facial hair, deepened voices, shrunken breasts, and either interruption or complete cessation of menstrual cycles. These effects are irreversible.[109] If a woman takes steroids while pregnant, the masculinizing effects will be passed to the developing child.[110] Many women who admit to having used anabolic steroids are afraid to have children. Renate Vogel Heinrich, the former champion East German swimmer who was nurtured on steroids, said, "I would love to have children, but I am afraid that I would bring them into the world handicapped."[111]

The most widely publicized effect of steroid use is increased hostility and aggression, dubbed "roid rage." University of South Carolina lineman Tommy Chaiken explained when he used anabolic steroids,

Besides the muscle growth, there were other things happening to me. I got real bad acne on my back, my hair started to come out. I was having trouble sleeping, and my testicles began to shrink—all the side effects you hear about. But my mind was set. I didn't care about the other stuff. . . In fact, my sex drive during the cycle was phenomenal, especially when I was all charged up from the testosterone I was taking. . . (yet) in certain ways I was becoming an animal. And I was developing an aggressiveness that was scary.[112]

Anecdotally, dozens of steroid users have been linked with arsons, rape, traffic altercations, assaults, bar fights, and domestic violence.[113] Lubell (1989) documented two murder cases where anabolic steroids were likely a factor. Both Horace Williams and Glenn Wolstrum were considered psychologically normal until they began taking steroids. Both pleaded not guilty, arguing their steroid use caused insanity. Both were convicted anyways.[114] Choi and Pope's (1994) research has suggested a link between steroid use and aggression toward women. A group of steroid users were far more aggressive toward their female partners than were nonsteroid users.[115]

Some argue that the use of performance enhancing substances has become so common and so difficult to detect that it is simply not worth the bother to try. Like the old *Saturday Night Live* skit, perhaps we should just accept the use of performance enhancing substances in sports and commence with the "all drug" Olympics or other events. Regardless of one's personal view on that subject, it is clear the specter of widespread drug abuse by athletes "has done physical and psychological damage to athletes of both sexes, of all nationalities, and at all levels of competition—from the highly paid professional to the beginning amateur . . . It has damaged the very nature of sports, twisting many of the world's best-loved games and events into anything but the healthful, exciting and fair contests of skill and prowess that they were intended to be."[116] There is still some disagreement among medical professionals regarding whether steroids are physically addicting, but few fail to recognize their psychologically addicting nature.

THE PUBLIC REACTION

Sadly, as noted earlier, perhaps those who need to care the most, the fans, simply do not. *Sports Illustrated* columnist Tim Layden argues that few fans care that the recent BALCO scandal may put the reputation of superstars and their records at risk.[117] Even if investigations into the company reveal that Barry Bonds was indeed provided steroids, his single-season home-run record of 73, set in 2001, will not likely be in jeopardy, as steroids were not banned by MLB until 2004.[118] Layden states, "If four members of the Oakland Raiders who tested positive for THG last fall, including robo-linebacker Bill Romanowski, were given their drugs by BALCO, the Sunday ritual of the NFL, with it's cartoon violence and religious fan fervor, is little more than a lab experiment gone wild."[119] Yet he argues that fans have simply gone on as before, shrugging off the news (Okay—confirmation—who *really* questioned whether some of these athletes were doping?) and rationalizing, "What's the difference between THG and Vitamin C? What is the difference between the juice in a slugger's biceps and the silicone in a starlet's bosom? Both are entertainers. Gimme the remote and pass the nachos."[120]

Obviously the leaders of major sports organizations are aware of the problem. President Bush called on "team owners, union representatives, coaches and players to take the lead, to send the right signal, to get tough, and to get rid of steroids now" in his 2004 State of the Union address. This all begs the question, "Why does it persist? Why don't they crack down on those athletes they suspect are using performance-enhancing substances?"

THE OWNERS' REACTION

Professional team owners, according to Pound, are often loath to support greater testing, as they worry about their bottom line. They pay huge salaries to some of their athletes and want peak performance. That is often too much to ask an athlete to do naturally. "In the final analysis, owners do not care what the athletes do, or have to do, to meet such demands. What is important is that they be on the field on game days. If they need drugs to do so, so be it."[121] Likewise, corporate sponsorship may decrease if more athletes test positive. Kathryn Jay, of the *Washington Post,* writes, "The real profiteers in the steroid wars are inside the sports industry itself. Performance-enhancing drugs help leagues maintain an electrifying on-the-field product, which fuels ticket sales, television revenues, endorsement deals, Web site hits, and merchandising."[122]

DRUG TESTING

Every major athletic organization bans steroids, including the NFL, NCAA, and the U.S. Olympic Committee (USOC). In fact, in order to be considered an Olympic sport, some type of control of drug use is required. Hence the world's chess federation has announced it will begin testing—despite any evidence of juiced up chess players—because they would like to receive Olympic status.[123] Yet steroids are still notoriously easy to obtain, either by mail order, through friends, acquaintances, or even coaches, and even by receiving a prescription from a doctor. *The Underground Steroid Handbook* advises young people they should look for a "kind, honest, humanitarian-type doctor" to provide their junk, preferably one newly out of medical school.[124] Most major sports organizations claim they are curtailing drug abuse through drug testing policies. Often, however, these tests do not include all the types of drugs athletes are using. In fact, not all substances that athletes are using are even known about, as BALCO demonstrates.

Further, punishments for drug violations are often so minimal as to be laughable. Steve Howe, a left-handed Major League Baseball pitcher, was arrested seven times for violating drug laws, was suspended by the league four times, and twice given "life" suspensions. Of course, "life" in this case was less than 1 year.[125] Former baseball commissioner Fay Vincent blames Howe's light sentence on the players union.[126] Howe has spoken out in favor of Major League Baseball's new testing policies. As noted earlier, the newest policies are far stricter, but may still contain a number of loopholes.

Woody Paige contends that Bill Romanowski, who had committed a slew of offenses prior to getting caught doping, had never been seriously punished. "This is the fool who spit in an opponent's face in a nationally televised incident, beat up a defensive player on his own team, was accused by his teammates of being a racist . . ."[127] in addition to his 1-year suspension for testing positive for THG and his current investigation in the BALCO scandal. Yet Romanowski is still loved by his team's fans because he takes no prisoners on the football field.

Some argue that athletic organizations could do much more to prevent, catch, and deal with drug use, but see little advantage in doing so. Dick Pound, as president of the World Anti-Doping Agency (WADA), asked the commissioners of all the major sports in the spring of 2003 to consider adopting the World Anti-Doping code. The NHL refused to reply, the PGA said they had no drug problem, and the NFL, NBA, and MLB said they were satisfied with their policies and testing programs.[128] Many organizations fear spectators, with their much-needed financial support, would be turned off if widespread drug use were identified. Christine Brennan argues in *USA Today* that baseball simply doesn't want the public to know if its athletes are cheating.[129]

Some have asserted even the U.S. Olympic Committee tests some athletes too infrequently and provides athletes too many opportunities to avoid testing. At least 15,000 serious, national-level athletes compete in the United States, yet the U.S. Anti-Doping Agency tested only 4,700 athletes between late 2000 and 2002, and most of those only one time.[130] Obviously the best way to truly find out if an athlete is using prohibited drugs is to conduct unannounced tests, yet less than 40 percent of the U.S. Anti-Doping Agency's tests have been unannounced.[131] Athletes will often withdraw from events where testing is likely. For instance, twelve American athletes withdrew from one of the earliest events to test in Caracas, Venezuela, in 1983.[132] Hence the shock when a record twenty-four athletes were ousted from the Athens games and none of them were American. Surely we don't believe our athletes all of a sudden went straight. In fact, the United States has a nasty reputation for allowing athletes to compete despite positive tests. Over 100 athletes were allowed to do so between 1988 and 2000.[133]

Another problem is that the testing agencies often develop incredibly liberal standards, as Dick Pound documents in *Inside the Olympics*. For instance, the legal ratio for testosterone to epitestosterone that could be present in the body was set at 6:1, "despite the fact that there was no empirical evidence of such a level ever being achieved naturally. Knuckles would be virtually dragging on the ground at that level . . . "[134]

Athletes who hold records in their sports often lobby against greater testing, as some would likely lose their accolades and their status in the public eye.[135] Others vehemently maintain they are clean, even arguing for greater testing, as does the women's marathon world record holder Paula Radcliffe.[136] Yet Radcliffe's vocal support for testing does not silence her critics, who maintain she is not clean, just confident her drugs are better than the tests. Barry Bonds is another athlete who has maintained his innocence despite repeated allegations he is doped to the gills. Like Radcliffe, Bonds has not actually tested positive for a banned substance. Many feel this is not an acquittal. "Barry Bonds is a real laugh riot. As he continues his hollow march toward the all-time home run record in a sport that never tested its athletes for steroids until last year, Bonds said that now we can believe he's not on performance-enhancing drugs because he recently took one—I repeat, one— random steroid test."[137] Columnist Woody Paige maintains we should return to the

Puritan practice of branding deviants and place a "C" on Bonds (to represent "the Clear" or "the Cheat" take your pick) and an "RF" on Romanowski for "Roid Freak."[138]

Some athletes maintain that certain ergogenic aids are legal in Europe, so to ban them here only punishes U.S. competitors.[139] Many athletes denounce efforts to ban drugs and to test for their use as paternalistic, and feel that all substances should simply be legal and it should be up to the athlete to decide.[140] Doctors, trainers, coaches, and manufacturers who benefit from the sale of performance enhancing substances are also opposed. "The agreement to carry on business as usual is fueled by the profound ambivalence that exists in society toward athletic performance. On the one hand is a strong demand that sports competition be pure and clean and free of any artificial aids and enhancements. At the same time is an equally strong demand that athletes extend themselves to the most extreme limits that their bodies can endure."[141]

DRUG CULTURE

Ultimately, perhaps it is unrealistic to believe people will truly care about use of performance enhancing substances by athletes. We are a drug culture; any time we are ill, under the weather, or perhaps even when we want to have more sex or when we dislike our hairline, we seek a pill to fix it up ASAP. As Kathryn Jay wrote in the *Washington Post*, "We live in a society that widely accepts physical and chemical enhancements. Every TV-watching football fan in the country has been beaten over the head with ads promising that a simple little pill can rekindle a man's sex life. How big a leap is it to accept that a different little pill can transform a middle-of-the-pack sprinter into a world record holder? Fans who use Viagra and Cialis to improve their 'performance' should not be surprised that athletes use steroids to improve their own."[142]

The problem with doping in sports, and the difficulty eradicating it, clearly resembles greater societal trends in America. We don't often want to know the root of our problems; rather, we want to identify them, drug them, and move on as good as new. Similarly, having identified doping as a problem, we have tried to treat it with shoddy attempts at testing for it, but with little regard for understanding and addressing the reasons for it. In the end, a few athletes get caught and banned, but little else is changed. And other athletes are doping up on new undetectable drugs because they know that is what it takes to succeed.

chapter 3

Eating Disorders and Playing While Hurt

All the fat guys watch me and say to their wives, "See, there's a fat guy doing okay. Bring me another beer."

—Detroit Tigers pitcher, Mickey Lolich

Teams win, and make money, when their athletes are in "peak" condition. Peak condition is *not* defined by the athlete's long-term, or sometimes even short-term, health. Sadly, many athletes are literally failing to *feed themselves*. Others eat but promptly vomit, sustaining precious few calories. Still others huff down mass quantities of laxatives or diuretics. In contrast, other athletes seek to bulk up, eating whatever, whenever, and utilizing a variety of dietary supplements to add desired mass. While eating to get huge is the polar opposite of dieting to stay tiny, both are efforts dictated by the sports machine's emphasis on winning at all costs. In both cases, the cost is the athletes' bodies, their health, and sometimes even their life. Eating disorders on both extremes are far too common by-products of the sports machine.

This is one of the great ironies of higher-level athletics. Public perception is that all athletes are "in shape." In fact, the athletic body is becoming ever more specialized to effectively perform a specific task, which means more specific definitions of the ideal body in every sport. Simply put, waifs can fly higher and spin faster than bulkier competitors in gymnastics and skating, and athletes that are simply "big" are inferior to behemoths in football who can push harder and block better. This is the subject of the first part of the chapter.

Similarly, athletes are expected to endure all the damage to their bodies that comes from playing through illness and injuries, and to do so without complaint. Sometimes playing through pain requires assistance from sources such as a ready supply of Advil or a shot of cortisone. Those who can't play through the pains are regarded as wimps, at best, and certainly never reach hero status. In fact, the sports are a more compelling product when athletes display their superhuman form by playing through pain and injury. As the athlete excels and the announcers drool, the viewers understand that they are witnessing a level of commitment seldom seen in day-to-day life. After all, can we imagine our coworkers steadfastly concentrating on typing reports or answering phones seconds after blowing out an ankle? Of course not, because greatness in most jobs does not require that they do so.

Already celebrated athletes and future hall-of-famers, both Isiah Thomas and Michael Jordan solidified themselves as superhuman by playing at their best in the most adverse situations. Thomas, playing for the Detroit Pistons, scored an NBA record 25 points in one quarter under the spotlight of the 1988 NBA Finals against the L. A. Lakers. The Lakers won the game by a point but Thomas achieved iconic status because partway through his record-setting performance he severely sprained an ankle. Hobbled but determined, he fought on to keep his team in the game. Similarly, Jordan took the court when he should have been home in bed ravaged with the flu. The scene was the 1997 NBA Finals Game 5 against the Utah Jazz. Amid rumors that he would not play, Jordan started the game, scored 38 points, hit a tie-breaking 3-pointer with 25 seconds to play, and solidified his hero status in Chicago. In neither situation was the decision to continue questioned. After all, why question playing while sick and injured when it is easier to celebrate and profit from the feat? Even when continuing to compete is questionable, if it will mean glory for the team and accolades for the individual, many will elect to do so.

We are not arguing that weight-related problems are exclusive to athletes. Clearly many people worldwide, but in particular in the United States, suffer from some type of weight-related problem. According to the American Anorexia/Bulimia Association, more than 5 million Americans struggle with eating disorders.[1] Yet we contend that sports are unique in that these weight-related problems are often not viewed as problems but as normal activity. If it seems you can perform better in your particular sport because you are waiflike, or, in contrast, because you are enormous, few people care if this is detrimental to your long-term health; what matters is that your performance pleases the coaches, team owners, and the fans.

Richard Davies suggested that the 1970s fitness boom, albeit a positive step in many ways, contributed dramatically to an athletic culture that is hyper-vigilant about weight.[2] Jay Coakley argues similarly, and asserts the continued emphasis on female athletes who "look good" is not only destructive to women's self esteem, but most certainly can lead to other body-related problems.[3] The hyperskinny fashion model has shaped the expectations for all women, but is especially problematic for young gymnasts and figure skaters who may already be insecure about their bodies.[4] Obviously, these cultural forces impact athletes in other sports as well. This is perhaps most visible in the case of Anna Kournikova, who, despite never winning a major tennis tournament, earns approximately $15 million a year in endorsements for her long blond hair and sultry gaze. While male athletes stare out from magazine covers with "manly" stares, female athletes are still too often reduced to vixen poses that have nothing to do with their athletic performance. One of *Sports Illustrated*'s best sellers was a 2000 cover featuring Kournikova sprawled on a pillow in a low-cut top, and the perennial best seller is, of course, the swimsuit issue. "This type of media coverage sends an unmistakable directive to today's female athletes: either look good or be ignored."[5] While this has all worked well for Kournikova's pocket book, we wonder what opportunities exist for the outstanding female athletes who are less photogenic or who will not present themselves as "boy toys"? Martina Navratilova is a classic example: despite all her incredible achievements, she received no sponsorship because she was open about her homosexuality.

EATING DISORDERS AMONG MEN

Clearly full-on eating disorders are more common among women in general. Yet much research suggests eating problems among men are getting worse. Leigh Cohn, co-author of *Making Weight*, estimates 2 percent of men suffer from eating disorders.[6] It is difficult, however, to know for sure how many males are suffering from these problems. Males themselves are often unaware, and may define their excessive exercise or minimal caloric intake as normal behavior for guys. Men, too, feel the pressure to have the idealized body. This often means broad, muscular shoulders, a narrow waist, and 6-pack abs. One study from the University of Central Florida found that males felt unhappier with their physiques after viewing TV commercials featuring muscular actors.[7] A study of muscular satisfaction of males in the United States, Austria, and France, found men chose an ideal body size almost 28 pounds greater than their current body size.[8] Even action figures today are huge; GI Joe now, once a muscular but "average" hero, has biceps that would, in scale, be larger than those of Mark McGwire when he was at his "peak" performance.[9] Males who do identify they have a problem are often hesitant to seek help, wondering if their suffering makes them less manly or even gay.[10]

Wrestling

Wrestlers are pressured to compete in weight classifications that require them to shed any excess weight, including that from body fat and water weight. Also, wrestlers may elect to drop entire weight classes in order to make the team. If there's someone better than him (or her) at a particular weight class, a wrestler might try to drop down to the lower weight class in order to fill a slot and earn a varsity letter.[11] They are often expected to shed pounds in short periods of time. To do so, athletes have been known to exercise in rubber suits or layers of clothing, minimize water weight by refusing to drink fluids, and by eating virtually nothing prior to weighing in. Some athletes take drugs to lose weight, typically diuretics and stimulants, which eliminate fluids and reduce appetites, respectively.[12] Wrestlers have also been known to consume scary quantities of laxatives, then losing as many pounds as possible in the toilet before weigh-in.[13] While this is dangerous enough, they often resume "normal" exercise and eating regimens after the weigh-in, putting themselves through an under-and-over eating cycle all season.[14] Many wrestlers will put themselves through this hellish cycle thirty times during a season.[15]

The wrestling world has more recently paid attention to the issue of unhealthy weight loss in their sport, triggered largely by the deaths of several athletes. In late 1997, three college wrestlers died in a 33-day span, all from their attempts to drop pounds. The three were also using creatine, presumably to add muscle without adding fat, which requires excess hydration. Each young man, however, was far from adequately hydrated.[16] Bill Saylor, a freshman at Campbell University in North Carolina, was the first of the three to die. Saylor was attempting to drop weight (from 201 pounds to 195) by riding an exercise bike in a rubber suit. Only 12 days later, Joseph LaRosa, of the University of Wisconsin-LaCrosse, suffered heat stroke. LaRosa was wearing not one but two sweat suits, in addition to a rubber suit, while he rode a stationary bike. His body temperature at the time of death was 108 degrees.[17] Jeff Reese, of the University of Michigan, completed the sad trifecta. Reese died after attempting to shed 17 pounds, which would have been 10 percent of his body weight. Reese was trying to earn the open spot in the 150-pound weight class.[18] Like the others, he had been wearing a plastic suit while riding a stationary bike in a room in Crisler Arena that had been heated to 92 degrees.[19] Reese's father complained that head coach Dale Bahr gave his son only 4 days to complete this task. Bahr denied any responsibility. He retorted that he had given no such edict, and that Reese was just like a student who crams the night before a final exam; he failed to lose the weight at a gradual pace by his own volition.[20] Evidently Bahr felt losing 10 percent of your already healthy body weight is no concern if done over the course of a few weeks.

These tragedies prompted the NCAA to make changes. First, they banned rubber suits, saunas, and diuretics in the preparation for competition.[21] Existing rules already banned laxatives, fluid restriction, self-induced vomiting, and steam rooms.[22] They also banned exercising in a room heated to more than 80 degrees and they moved weigh-in times from 24 hours prior to the match to 2 hours prior. This was intended to make it less likely an athlete would attempt rapid weight loss, as they would have only a few short hours to recover.[23] The NCAA also adjusted the weight classes so they would better reflect the sizes of college wrestlers, thus decreasing the need for having the smallest wrestlers dropping weight to make impossibly light classes. The University of Michigan also made changes, after considering dropping the sport. They banned all plastic, rubber, and nylon exercise suits and required daily weigh-ins as well as participation in a nutrition education program.[24] While these efforts are all applauded, and are certainly more than has been done in other sports with similar weight-related problems, it is difficult to see how these mandates will be enforced except for after-the-fact. Hence wrestlers are likely to go on jogging in rubber suits, while they chow down Ex-Lax, because who will stop them? We expect that the coaches try their best, as none want to have an athlete die. But if a wrestler indulges in a Kit Kat and has to make weight later that day, who is to say what he will or will not do when unsupervised?

Jockeys

Unlike wrestlers, who face limits on their maximum weight, jockeys face trying to meet a minimum weight requirement on a daily basis. The effect is that all of the top jockeys must try to weigh the minimum, or very close to it, or face being unemployed, as owners and trainers put tremendous pressure on them to put as little weight as possible on the horses' backs. So severe is the problem that the jockey's room at Hollywood Park not only has a sauna for sweating off the pounds, but also a designated stall for self-induced vomiting, which is called "flipping" in the vernacular of the trade.[25] While everyone who has seen a horserace understands that jockeys are tiny people, few know the skeletal bodies that are under the racing silks. One physician said 95 percent of the jockeys have dangerously low body-fat percentages and they tend to develop kidney problems from dehydration and pre-cancerous conditions of the esophagus from vomiting.[26] He claimed that the rules of the sport have effectively mandated malnutrition.[27]

Currently, jockeys must weigh-in with their clothes and saddle and try to hit 115 pounds. This requires that they hover around 110 pounds body weight. A movement to increase the minimum weight has met with stiff resistance from owners and trainers who care more about the investment in the horses than the health of the men steering them around the track. They claim that more weight will injure the horses and that it will do nothing for the jockeys except increase competition for the jobs, as more small people would engage in unhealthy eating practices for a shot at the high pay that comes with the jobs.[28]

Meanwhile, jockeys are wasting away, fasting, vomiting, using stair climbers in the sauna, and taking diet pills to stay in their profession.[29] All the while knowing they are taking years off their lives. As two-time Kentucky Derby winner Kent Desormeaux put it, "The reality is that probably 85 percent of riders are dying to ride—literally."[30] As evidence that he is right, it is sad to note that chronic renal failure, a precursor to kidney failure that may result from hours in the saunas, occurs ten times more frequently among jockeys than in the normal population.[31]

EATING DISORDERS AMONG WOMEN

Women's Gymnastics

As perilous as the focus on weight is in the historically male sports, the situation is even worse for females. Gymnasts tend to maintain a stable eating and workout regimen: they eat almost nothing and work out constantly. A petite frame is absolutely essential to success in the current world of women's (often girls') gymnastics. Not only do the elaborate and risky tumbling passes work more easily and look more spectacular with a light body, but physical appearance is also a significant part of the judging.[32] Thus coaches insist on the thinnest athletes. Unlike wrestlers, gymnasts are typically not allowed to ever gain weight. Infamous gymnastics coach Bela Karolyi is a grueling taskmaster when it comes to weight; he limited his 1992 Olympic squad to just 1000 calories per day. Karolyi's henchmen monitored the athletes' food intake as well as their belongings, lest the girls smuggle some contraband carrots. This is not even enough to sustain weight for an average American do-nothing, let alone for an athlete working out at least 8 hours per day.[33]

Karolyi, other coaches, and even some judges, admit saying cruel things to girls they suspect are gaining weight in order to motivate them to stay focused. In the early 1990s Karolyi had pet names for his girls: Erica Stokes was a "pregnant goat," Betty Okino was a "pregnant spider," Kim Zmeskal was a "pumpkin" or "butterball," and Hilary Gravich was a "tank."[34] Karolyi justified his practice of driving young ladies until they break, saying, "These girls are like little scorpions. You put them all in a bottle and one scorpion will come out alive. That scorpion will be champion."[35] Of course Karolyi, while one of the worst, is not alone. Many studies have found gymnasts began unhealthy weight control patterns after their coaches derided them as hefty.[36] A judge at the 1984 Olympics told Mary Lou Retton "You know, if I could, I'd take half a point off because of that fat hanging off your butt."[37] Mary Lou shrugged it off. While some girls can take the constant monitoring and haranguing from coaches, others cannot. Clearly such practices wreak havoc on the self-esteem of these young athletes. Not only do many of these girls battle anorexia and bulimia, many experience amenorrhea (absence of a normal menstrual cycle) and injuries associated with inadequate calcium that may lead to osteoporosis.[38] Amenorrhea, disordered eating, and osteoporosis has been called the Female Athlete Triad and is, according to one source, "extremely dangerous, potentially fatal—and alarmingly common."[39] Studies have found that young women who do not menstruate had the bone densities of women in their fifties and even older, yet most elite gymnasts do not have a period until they retire. Kathy Johnson, a medallist at the 1984 Olympics, started menstruating at age 25.[40]

Christy Heinrich provides an illustration of the trouble with eating among gymnasts. In 1989, 15-year-old Christy weighed 90 pounds and stood a mere 4'11". She embarked on a radical weight loss plan after a judge told her she had to lose weight or she would never make the Olympic team. He was probably right; the average U.S. female gymnast in 1992 weighed 83 pounds. So lose she did. Christy upped her already intense 9 hours per day training schedule, for which she was nicknamed "Extra Tough."[41] At the same time, "food became her enemy."[42] At 18 years, Christy weighed less than 80 pounds. Rather than experience the payoff, Christy was too weak to compete. She ended up retiring from the sport, but could not escape her devastating eating disorder. After starving herself for 5 years, Christy Heinrich died in 1994 of multiple organ failure, weighing less than 50 pounds.[43] She said this about herself: "It feels like there's a beast inside of me, like a monster. It feels evil."[44]

Christy is by no means the only extreme case; the National Institute of Mental Health (NIMH) reports one in ten anorexics die from the condition.[45] Other gymnasts prior to Christy suffered as well; Chelle Stack drank 12-ounce bottles of laxatives two or three times per week,[46] and 1972 Olympian Cathy Rigby went into cardiac arrest twice in her 12-year battle with anorexia and bulimia. Nadia Comaneci has recently come forward to discuss her eating disorder.[47]

Figure Skating

Figure skaters suffer a similar situation, although weight parameters are perhaps not quite so restrictive as in gymnastics. The necessity to be beautiful, on the other hand, is even worse. Figure skating rewards competitors who have beautiful hair and makeup and elaborate costumes. At the same time, however, the females are asked to perform increasingly difficult jumps, requiring strength. Thus female figure skaters are faced with an almost impossible paradox: be slim and feminine, yet powerful. Michelle Kwan won her first world figure skating championship in 1996 when she was 15 years old, then earned a silver medal at the 1998 Winter Olympics when she was 17 years old. But she claims puberty virtually destroyed her career. She first experienced problems on ice when she "got hips," saying, "Even if your body is just a little bit different, it throws you off. Even if you gain 1 pound, it makes you lopsided."[48]

Even male figure skaters have claimed the pressure to be thin is tremendous. A judge at the U.S. Nationals in 1984 told Brian Boitano he needed to lose weight. The impetus for the comment was Boitano's no-no of snacking on some crackers. Boitano, who was 5′11″ and weighed 162 pounds, told his coach he thought about quitting that night. Of course, this was no isolated instance. Judges repeatedly told Boitano he was fat.[49] Boitano did not quit, nor did the comments. A year later Boitano weighed-in at 154 pounds when he ran into a judge after a competition. This time Boitano had the nerve to eat a hamburger, to which the judge said, "You really shouldn't be eating that. You need to lose more weight, another 10 pounds."[50]

Swimming

Reports of weight obsessions are also common among college and elite swimmers. Interviews with eighteen former swimmers for the University of Texas in 1989 found three with bulimia, two who had previously been treated for it, and ten who claimed to use unhealthy means of losing weight (such as fasting and laxatives). Twelve said their coach, Richard Quick, who led the team to five NCAA titles between 1983 and 1988, set weight goals that led the women to have weight obsessions.[51] Most of the women claimed they knew of each other's weight problems because that was virtually all that was discussed in the locker room and dorms. "Food was the thing that was on everybody's mind all the time. It was on my mind from the moment I woke up. The only time I didn't think about it was when I was in the water swimming," said Susan Johnson, a 1988 Olympian and two-time All-American.[52]

Distance Running

Distance runners are also prone to eating disorders. Several studies have found cross country runners have a greater degree of body dissatisfaction, more disordered eating, and more concern over their weight.[53] While the majority of runners don't actually have anorexia or bulimia, many suffer from what has been called "disordered eating" or "anorexia athletica."[54] Coaches encourage this when they tell athletes, as Laura witnessed, that they won't make the travel squad if they don't drop a few pounds. These edicts are often internalized and last a lifetime.

The Move to "Bigger Being Better"

On the opposite end of the spectrum, some sports require large athletes. This type of athlete is said to suffer from reverse anorexia or muscle dysmorphia. They often believe they are too small when, in actuality, they are quite large. It is sometimes the case with bodybuilders who are constantly seeking bigger muscles.[55] Rick Telander called serious bodybuilding, "the male equivalent of anorexia nervosa; the lifters only feel in control of their bodies and themselves when their muscles are engorged with blood and screaming for mercy."[56]

Sumo wrestlers don't seem to struggle with body dysmorphia so much as they just want to be heavy, and the heavier, the better. Athletes in this sport consume enormous amounts of food and supplements in order to reach, or preferably exceed, 400 pounds. And when Americans venture into this traditionally Japanese sport, it is with the intention of excelling. Akebono, born Chad Rowan, was America's sumo star, weighing-in at an eye-popping 510 pounds at his competitive best.

While not so extreme, it seems some football positions are best played by behemoths. Who can forget the poster boy for a bigger and better NFL, William "The Refrigerator" Perry, of the 1984 Super Bowl champion Bears? Following the Fridge's lead, the 1993 Super Bowl featured Nate "The Kitchen" Newton of the Dallas Cowboys, who proudly stated, "Fat's in, steroids are out," and, "All those pretty steroid boys, they're gone. Now it's who's got the most jiggly." The Cowboys' media guide listed Newton at 318, a figure most suggested was complete fiction.[57] He was likely much larger.

The trend of bigger equals better has followed to the lower levels as well. In the college ranks, the average weight of the five starting offensive lineman for the 2004 powerhouse squad at Oklahoma was 304 pounds. Even lowly Western Michigan University (our beloved alma mater), who finished 1–10 in 2004, featured upperclassmen on the offensive line checking in at an average of 290 pounds. But help was on the way for old WMU as they had a sophomore tipping the scales at 330 pounds.

According to ESPN, there were only five players in the NFL weighing over 300 pounds 20 years ago; in 2001, almost 300 NFL players tipped the scales over

300 pounds, and by the 2004 season there were 339 such players.[58] The 2005 NFL Combine featured fifty-seven of sixty offensive lineman over 300 pounds, with the lightest a stealthy 298 pounds. Pittsburgh tackle Rob Petitti was the heaviest at 347 pounds.[59] And, as documented in the last chapter, it is difficult to know how much of this heft is chemically induced, in one way or another. As Kathryn Jay wrote in the *Washington Post*, "Do team officials really think offensive and defensive linemen are just supersizing their meals?"[60]

Former Michigan State star Tony Mandarich is a case study of this chapter and the last one. He is also the single largest human being Peter has ever seen in person. Growing up in East Lansing, Peter bumped into Mandarich (literally) in a video rental store. Peter was so awestruck that he followed the mountain of a man around the store. It remains unforgettable. Rick Telander discussed watching Mandarich prepare to lift weights in *The Hundred Yard Lie*. After rubbing down with Icy Hot, Mandarich downed a 16-ounce bottle of Super tea and a 340-calorie "Maximum caffeine" drink. He chased that with 32 ounces of coffee, which, coupled with his morning's Vivarin (200 milligrams of caffeine) got him adequately hyped. He then did squats until he vomited.

Former University of Kentucky quarterback Jared Lorenzen, referred to as "Pillsbury Throw Boy," "Lord of the Ring Dings," and "Hefty Lefty" was told repeatedly that he should shed weight, as he was likely the heaviest ever college quarterback at just about 300 pounds. In fact, nutritionists for the university set up a plan for Lorenzen, but found he was cheating when a roommate reported Lorenzen would go missing during dinnertime, "the same time various pantry items that were neither green nor leafy also turned up missing."[61] Coaches were convinced a bigger Lorenzen was indeed a better one, though, when he came out 10 pounds thinner but flat and lethargic in 2001. And that's all that mattered; once they realized Lorenzen played better bigger, no one cared that he might be jeopardizing his long-term health. A teammate agreed with leaving Lorenzen alone to weigh-in at whatever, saying, "Jared's just a greasy-food guy."[62] Jared has also upped his chances of a heart attack, but who cares, as long as he makes it through the season. Lorenzen did cut down to a svelte 288 for the NFL Combine and was drafted by the New York Giants.

Clearly these tremendous weights are a substantial burden on the athletes' bodies. Excess weight on a body frame taxes ligaments and joints, leading to more sprains, strains, and tears.[63] In an extreme example, Cincinnati Bengals nose-guard Tim Krumrie snapped his own leg in half from momentum in making an open-field tackle during the 1989 Super Bowl.[64] When football players bulk up but do not lose their speed (perhaps due to weight gain from steroids or other performance enhancers), on-field collisions are all the more violent.[65] "Sheer size, and the speed at which it moves, has made football a game that toys with the tolerance level of the human skeleton, sinews, muscles, and organs."[66] And, while training and equipment seem to have cut down on the number of football deaths, now injuries are common on virtually every play.[67]

The added weight also strains the heart. Ultimately, these athletes are likely reducing their lifespan. A study of 1,800 NFL players from 1921–1959, all of whom played at least 5 years, found their lifespan to be 5 years less than average.[68] Another study found the average life expectancy of an NFL player was fifty-five, and most are 50 percent to 64 percent disabled due to back and leg injuries.[69] The case of lineman Korey Stringer, who died of heatstroke during preseason conditioning drills for the Minnesota Vikings in 2001, is an example of the dangers of playing obese. Stringer not only weighed in at 338, but he had also been using ephedrine.[70] The extra weight Stringer was carrying could not have helped him tolerate a difficult workout in the heat. As Dave Kindred noted in *Sporting News,* obese athletes face great danger, as the fat around their torsos acts as an insulator, refusing to allow body heat to escape. Kindred explains,

It's a product of the Bear Bryant/Vince Lombardi macho culture that demands players prove their 'toughness' by passing physical tests that often mean little other than the players' willingness to bend to a coach's order. Such tests can be a coach's crutch; instead of the hard work of judging talent, character and dedication, a coach too often judges a player by how much pain he is willing to endure.[71]

WHEN EATING BECOMES THE SPORT

The lack of concern about exceedingly large athletes should not be a surprise, given that we are a society consumed with consumption. For some "athletes," eating is not just a means to increase sports performance. For some, eating is the sport. Enter the world of the competitive eater, or "gustatory athletes" as they are called. Competing under the auspices of the International Federation of Competitive Eating (IFOCE), these athletes compete to shovel in a variety of foods as fast as they can in truly bizarre sports spectacles. While we might resist the notion that eating is a sport, it is important to note that competitive eating is getting TV time, billed as a sport, as ESPN brings us live coverage of Nathan's Famous Hot Dog Eating Contest.

According to their Web site, "The IFOCE helps to ensure that the sport remains safe, while also seeking to achieve objectives consistent with the public interest—namely, creating an environment in which fans may enjoy the display of competitive eating skill."[72] Gee, we'll sleep easier knowing that they are working to bring us a safe sport. Never mind that one of their records is for eating salted sticks of butter (Donald Lerman ate seven quarter-pound sticks in 5 minutes).

The characters of competitive eating are worthy of World Wrestling Entertainment. Top performers include the 409-pound "Cookie" Jarvis, and 420-pound Eric "Badlands" Booker. Frankly, we expect these guys to climb into a ring and eat each other. Booker, hoping to capitalize on his eating fame, released a rap album titled *"Hungry and Focused,"* featuring the song *"All Day Buffet."* No joke.[73]

Ironically, it is the lightweights who ascend to the top of the competitive eating ranks. And there is no gender bias. The second best eater in the world is American Sonya Thomas, who weighs only 105 pounds but can put away eighty chicken nuggets in 5 minutes. Thomas, known as "the Black Widow," was victorious at the

December 3, 2005, Tropicana Meatball competition, shoveling in 10.3 pounds in 12 minutes. And the top gurgitator? That would be Japan's Takeru Kobayashi, at a mere 132 pounds. To the chagrin of the American competitive eating community, he is the defending Nathan's Champion with a record fifty-three and a half hot dogs and buns polished off in 12 minutes.[74] But how can the skinny athletes dominate what should be a big man's world? As the theory goes, by having less fat around their midsections, they are better able to expand their stomachs while in the heat of competition. So for the future of competitive eating, put your money on thin athletes with tragically weak abdominal muscles. As a caveat, while the material above is somewhat amusing, we believe it exemplifies the fact that something as harmful as eating straight lard can be considered a legitimate enterprise when it becomes coupled with sports.

PLAYING THROUGH PAIN

When bodily damage to athletes occurs, athletes know what they are supposed to do: play on. And if they do anything to alleviate the pain, it better be something that allows them to keep playing. Sociologists Sabo and Messner refer to this as "taking it," and contend it is an attitude that permeates athletics. In particular, they contend,

> male athletes adopt the visions and values that coaches are offering: to take orders, to take pain, to "take out" opponents, to take the game seriously, to take women, and to take their place on the team. And if the athletes can't "take it," they lose the rewards of athletic camaraderie, prestige, scholarships, pro contracts, and community recognition.[75]

Of course this is a problem in virtually all sports, but is perhaps most dramatic in football. The average NFL player will endure 130,000 full-speed hits in a 7-year period.[76] Former Detroit Lions running back Barry Sanders argued that players become immune to the violence and ignore the damage to their bodies. "I hate to say it, but one of the first things you notice in this league is how steadily people step in and out of the lineup because of injuries. After a while you hardly notice it anymore. You just go on."[77] In the mid-1990s Bears safety Shaun Gayle fractured the seventh vertebra in his neck. Gayle stayed in the game, of course, later chuckling that the injury didn't seem serious.[78] Former Denver Broncos guard Mark Schlereth has had twenty-eight surgeries, including fourteen on his left knee and five on his right.[79]

Coaches and the media encourage this dangerous behavior by praising athletes who do it. Somehow sacrificing one's body for the team or the sport is considered "good character." In September 2004, Tennessee Titans quarterback Steve McNair landed in the hospital after getting lambasted by the Jaguars 312-pound defensive tackle, Marcus Stroud. But because Titans coach Jeff Fisher said medical tests found McNair without any major breaks or tears, he was simply expected to play on.[80] McNair finally succumbed to his injuries and missed most of the season, but it wasn't without trying to play and making the injuries worse. Of course, McNair has a reputation for being an iron man. The previous year ESPN did a piece on his frequent injuries with a computer graphic that put red dots on his areas of injury. It looked like he had chicken pox. This guy simply doesn't have a good joint left. He was, however, praised by fans and the media for his efforts. We are left wondering if it will be worth it if McNair can't walk a dog or give his kids a piggyback ride in his retirement.

In order to deal with pain that inevitably comes from bashing into other players, many football players have taken painkillers, sometimes to the point of addiction. A linebacker in the NFL said in 1996 he deals with pain by taking "bottles of Advil and then you go out and smash some more heads."[81] Carolina Panther, Jason Peter, claims his use of crack and heroin stem from his days as a college player at Nebraska, where he got addicted to painkillers in order to play through various injuries.[82] He started taking two Loriset painkillers per day as a freshman, but was eventually up to eighty pills per day.[83] Green Bay Packers quarterback Brett Favre revealed his dependency on Vicodin in 1996. He voluntarily entered the league's substance abuse program, prompted by a violent seizure from his painkiller abuse.[84] Even football legend Joe Namath, according to his biographer Mark Kriegel, spent his career battling and masking pain. The following constituted Namath's "pain management" regimen prior to the 1969 Super Bowl: five syringes filled with Novocain and prednisone, and a bottle of red pills for the road.[85] Like so many others, Namath apparently used booze to self-medicate as well.[86] Many athletes were using the drug Vioxx, which was just pulled from the market by Merck & Co after studies revealed it could triple the risk of heart attacks and strokes in some patients. Similar problems are associated with Bextra, which is still on the market but may be removed soon, according to pharmacy experts.

Often team doctors and trainers are the ones prescribing painkillers or injecting athletes with Novacaine or cortisone. Moira Novak, head athletics trainer at the University of Minnesota, said they prefer athletes take Vioxx, Celebrex, or Bextra because they are easier on the stomach than traditional painkillers. Never mind the risk of heart attack. A sprinter for the Gophers said he used Vioxx for 15 months, generally without a prescription.[87] The primary task, as doctors and trainers see it, is to keep the athlete on the field or court, not in the training room. On occasion an athlete has successfully contested this treatment. Dick Butkis, Hall of Fame linebacker for the Chicago Bears, was given cortisone and other drugs in the last 2 years of his career in order to deaden the pain in his knees. He sued the team, contending doctors had put the team above his health. Butkis received $600,000 in an out-of-court settlement.[88] Generally, however, athletes want to keep playing so they feel no urge to question what happens in the training room.

Athletes can also score painkillers from friends or acquaintances. Jason Peter claims team physicians were careful about what they prescribed, but that he had no difficulty obtaining drugs from other sources, exchanging autographs and other team paraphernalia for "whatever he wanted."[89]

Football players often ignore or minimize concussions they have suffered on the field. In 2004, three high school football players in Colorado died after saying nothing about a series of blows to their heads. One had confided to his best friend that he had a headache, but demanded he tell no one because he wanted to play that night.[90] Studies have found that, each season, up to 20 percent of all high school football players suffer a concussion. Multiple concussions can lead to long-term brain damage. In athletes with three concussions, 25 percent had persistent abnormalities on neurological tests, while 33 percent and 40 percent with four and five concussions, respectively, have brain abnormalities.[91]

The mismanagement of sports injuries is by no means exclusive to football, or even contact sports. Sociologist Howard Nixon surveyed almost 200 male and female athletes in eighteen varsity sports at one Division I school. Over 75 percent reported significant injuries, and almost all had played while hurt. Over 45 percent had lifetime affects of those injuries.[92] Athletes in endurance sports are prone to overuse injuries and generally should give their body time to rest and heal. Unfortunately, resting is seldom a viable option in the competitive world of high-level athletics. Laura experienced this multiple times as a collegiate cross country and track and field athlete. While she was offered cortisone a few times, more frequently the response to her repeated Achilles tendonitis was to ice it, take Motrin, and maybe run a little easier the next few days. University training rooms always had a ready supply of the most potent Motrin to dole out to whoever came in. Yet when a competitive runner jogs it through practice, there is another athlete ready and waiting to make the travel squad for the upcoming meet. So, can the athlete really rest? Particularly when scholarships must be renewed yearly at the discretion of coaches who tend to have a what-have-you-done-lately mentality.

The overuse injuries among distance runners often begin with the overuse of the standout athletes at the high school level. As high school track and field coaches, we witnessed the destruction of countless promising young female runners. Invariably, it was the coaches pushing to get the most points out of the athletes by running them in too many events per meet. In the end, the athletes would often be sidelined by injury and would leave the sport. The coaches seldom saw the opportunity for the athletes to participate across the lifespan, instead seeing the opportunity to collect a few wins in events against the crosstown rival.

Tim Curry interviewed collegiate wrestlers and found they defined pain and injury as simply a part of their sport. In Curry's study, athletes learned from other athletes that they were to "shake off" injuries, to call special treatment for minor injuries "coddling," to always express desire to play, even if hurt, and to use trainers and physicians as resources to keep them playing. They also learned that painkillers were not "drugs" but necessary components of the sport.[93]

Boxers have long punched through the pain, only to face irreparable damage to their bodies. Despite suffering what many argue was major neurological damage in a 1990 fight with Julio Cezar Chavez, Meldrick Taylor continued to fight into 2002.[94] Taylor had won the 1984 Olympic Gold Medal when only 17 years old and had little else to turn to in life, and he was an outstanding boxer before the Chavez fight. After the fight, medical experts believed Taylor suffered from "dementia pugilistica." Most notably, his speech became seriously slurred. Boxing promoters claimed he simply had a speech impediment. Those who had known the fighter for years claimed this was bunk and that there was no such impediment in his early years in the sport. Regardless, Taylor, like many boxers, kept on swinging and getting hit well after he should have hung up the gloves.[95]

It may surprise many to hear that the beautiful and glamorous sports like gymnastics and figure skating command the same adherence to the sports ethic, and consequently that athletes in these sports suffer great bodily injury. In many ways the problem is worse in these sports, as the participants are young and thus more vulnerable to coaches and others' mandates. As Joan Ryan explains, "A gymnast on the elite level learns to stand still—mouth closed, eyes blank—and weather her coach's storms. A gymnast is seen and not heard."[96] A 1992 NCAA study found collegiate gymnasts suffered more injuries than did athletes in any other sport besides spring football. Fall football ranked tenth on the list.[97]

That these young women suffer in silence is obvious from the number of incidents leading to long-term injury and even death in the sport. Nadia Comaneci cut her hand on the guards the women wear to perform on the uneven bars. She failed to tell anyone until she had blood poisoning in her arm.[98] Betty Okino was a rising star with hopes of making the 1992 Olympic team when, in 1991, she was diagnosed as having a stress fracture in her right elbow and was told by doctors to quit training. She did not, and the arm eventually broke. She refused a cast but did agree to rest it for 2 weeks, at which time she went to the gym to keep working out her legs. Less than a year later Okino suffered another injury; she heard a pop as she sprinted down the runway to vault, and her right leg buckled as she crashed to the ground. She had ripped the tendon away from the bone below her knee. When doctors reattached it with screws, Okino again returned to the gym, only to be told by Karolyi she was a slacker. Rather than telling him to go to hell, Okino worked even harder and won a silver medal in the 1992 World Championships. Her medal came with great cost: Upon return Okino saw a doctor for sharp pains in her back. He found stress fractures in her vertebrae. Still Okino competed, and 2 weeks later pain exploded through her back as she dismounted the bars. She had fractured two vertebrae in her lower back. She was urged to quit, having a 2 percent chance of paralysis, but plugged on. She took anti-inflammatory drugs and eight Advils a day. Okino did get selected to the 1992 Olympic team and helped the team win a bronze medal, but today is unable to write without pain and cannot straighten her arm. Olympian Wendy Bruce, who had fifteen cortisone shots in her feet during her career, claimed, "I didn't think twice about it. I wouldn't have been able to compete otherwise."[99] Other gymnasts agree, explaining that no one came to the gym without a montage of drugs to mask pain.

Further, because a gymnastics career is so short, to lose any time to injury might be the end of a dream for both the athlete and her coach. Both, then, will do anything to help her remain in competition.

THE ROLE OF THE MEDIA

As we described in an earlier chapter, athletes also learn from the media how they are to act. When they play through pain, they are revered by the media and the public. Two recent gymnastics performances highlight the media's love of athletes who sacrifice their bodies. In 1996, 14-year-old Dominique Moceanu competed with a stress fracture in her right leg. She said, "What else can I do? I have to bite my teeth somehow and make it through. This is the Olympics you're talking about here."[100] Kerri Strug competed in the vault in the 1996 games despite a torn ligament in her ankle. Both young women were media darlings, in part because of their so-called courageous efforts. Within hours of completing her historic vault, the sponsorship offers came pouring in for Strug.[101]

By the Athens Olympics in 2004, the storyline had changed little. Competing through injury was still a more glamorous story than competing healthy. Thus, every time American gymnast Courtney Kupets prepared to perform we were treated to a shot of her surgically repaired Achilles tendon. Kupets had torn the tendon only a year prior to the Olympics but still managed to make the team and, in Athens, help the team to a silver medal. She also claimed ninth in the All-Around and a bronze on the Uneven Bars. While we certainly can't decry her participation as inappropriate without more intimate knowledge of the injury, we do suggest that the resulting storyline is unsettling. Younger athletes, and perhaps even adults, watching the coverage are left with two distinct impressions. First, real athletes compete through or soon after suffering horrific injuries. Second, the date of the next big event can define when an athlete should return to competition rather than letting the nature of the injury dictate the convalescence.

THE ROLE OF PARENTS AND COACHES

Joan Ryan asserts that most of the blame for young athletes' weight problems falls on the shoulders of parents and coaches; she calls it a form of "legal, even celebrated, child abuse."[102] Coaches push because they are paid to produce the best athletes, not to turn out happy or well-rounded women with great self-esteem. Part of the problem is the status Americans accord coaches; the mythic tough-but-inspiring coaches have seared their brand of tough love into the American psyche, convincing many that to berate athletes and to drive them to the brink of, if not over, injury is the only possible way to get success.[103] Many coaches are lured to the profession by the power that comes with the position. Sadly, many use this power in beastly ways. Rick Telander tells the story in *The Hundred Yard Lie* of his high school football coach, who refused to let a player leave the field to defecate.[104] Clearly this can only be about control. When coaches try to control their athletes in these highly personal ways, it's no wonder some athletes will do whatever it takes to please them.

Parents likely do not start out doing things detrimental to their sons and daughters, but their ambition for their children often gets perverted. One parent of elite figure skaters in the late 1970s compared it to owning a thoroughbred, saying, "That's your horse. That's your prized possession. That's your showpiece."[105] That a parent considers her child a possession is more than scary. Most parents of elite athletes, like gymnasts under the tutelage of Bela Karolyi or other extreme coaches, are so heavily invested, both emotionally and financially, they "quickly learn to keep their mouths shut when Newman or Karolyi called their daughters bloody imbeciles or fat cows or kicked them out of the gym for crying in pain."[106] Likewise, parents of other young athletes are often not the advocates they should be against coaching excesses.

THE ROLE OF ATHLETIC ORGANIZATIONS

Athletic organizations often deny that weight loss (or gain) and playing injured are problems, or, when they do admit there is a concern, they minimize it. Yet they could indeed reduce the incidence of eating-related problems and of athletes playing through dangerous injuries in a number of ways. In some sports, like gymnastics and figure skating, changes in judging criteria could go a long way toward reducing the number of injuries and lessening the focus on beauty. Dr. Aurelia Nattiv, a leading expert on bone density and menstrual patterns among gymnasts, has argued for downgrading, if not entirely eliminating dismounts, because it is clear they are likely to lead to significant injuries. Yet despite the clear connection between dismounts and injuries, nothing is being done about them.[107] And it is likely nothing will be done about them, as they are spectacular precisely for the risks involved. In fact, the International Gymnastics federation upped the skill level, and hence the points awarded, for required items, making it even more likely girls will attempt riskier moves.[108] Olympic medallist and commentator Bart Connor summed up the attitude: "We have to figure out what our goals are. If we want a team that looks nice in their uniforms, that isn't under all this stress, that isn't playing with pain, that isn't risking injury, then we're not going to win."[109]

Similarly, when figure skating did away with the school figures in 1990, which used to be 60 percent of the skater's total score, they dramatically increased the portion of scoring that comes from the free skate. Now athletes are attempting more triple jumps, which separate the great long program from the merely good. Of course these are more risky, and also easier to perform with a light body, so the cycle continues.[110] Further, the repetition of practicing these jumps wears away the joints and leads to injury.

Boxing is notoriously bad for its lack of oversight. Each state runs its own boxing federation, all with different regulations. Boxers who want to compete, no matter what ails them, can simply shop around for a state that will allow them a match. And some state will because of the dollars involved. When the New Jersey boxing federation refused to license Meldrick Taylor because of his neurological problems (discussed earlier), he simply avoided that state and others requiring neurological tests, landing instead in Alabama, which actually has no boxing commission.[111]

Boxing great Muhammad Ali asked Congress in the fall of 2004 to create a U.S. Boxing Commission, which he asserts would protect athletes from both exploitation and injury.[112]

The U.S. Soccer Federation has taken a neutral stand on the use of headbands that can protect athletes when heading the ball, a major source of injury in that sport. Despite seeing several women on the U.S. team wearing the bands, many players, especially males, are resistant to do so without a specific requirement.[113] It seems that wearing protective equipment runs counter to the "coolness" of the soccer image. Interestingly, research suggests girls in sports are at greater risk for head injuries than men and the highest rates of concussion were in women's soccer.[114]

Similarly, pay structures often support dangerous practices. USA Gymnastics began awarding stipends to athletes based on their national rankings. While financial support is a great idea, tying it to rankings ups the pressure on gymnasts to compete more frequently and to take greater risks with their bodies.[115]

Sports federations could also more closely monitor coaches, but they do not. Virtually anyone can coach youth sports. As Dr. Lyle Micheli, of Harvard Medical School and former president of the American College of Sports Medicine claimed, "Jack the Ripper could walk off the street and coach your child."[116] As Ryan explains, the gymnastics federation can provide training advice to coaches, but it can't make them follow it. It cannot ban a coach unless he or she has been charged with a crime; neither repeated injuries or allegations of verbal abuse require a coach be banned.[117]

And sadly, some coaches don't know or care enough to protect their athletes beyond the existing rules. As track and field coaches we were appalled at how frequently coaches ran athletes in four distance events in meets. While the rules set forth by the National Federation of High School Associations allow athletes to participate in four events, we always believed this was more acceptable for the sprinters who also typically did a field event or two. However, when coaches entered athletes in the half-mile, mile, 2-mile, and 2-mile relay in one meet, we were never surprised to see the poor athlete disappear part way through the season. It is just too hard for a young kid to sustain 4 total miles of racing in meet after meet. We always felt that protection of the athletes should have prompted creation of a rule that limited athletes to four events, but no greater than 3 total miles of running in a meet.

CONCLUSION

In sum, many athletes are doing heinous damage to their bodies when they eat far too little or too much, when they take dangerous substances to rapidly gain or lose weight, and when they play through injuries. But again, this is merely sports in America. We clamber for exciting and intriguing athletic performances, and all else is damned.

The bodies of the athletes must be the perfect size and shape in every way or they will be discarded long before reaching the top echelons of sports. If it takes extreme and dangerous measures to get the body into acceptable form, so be it. And when players break down, they had better demonstrate that they can continue to function effectively or others will quickly replace them. There is always another athlete who has been groomed for this moment and anxiously awaits a call up. In the end, we enjoy the spectacular product and give scant regard to the carnage of broken athletes littered about.

chapter 4

Cheating, Dirty-play, and On-field Violence

I believe the game is designed to reward the men who hit the hardest. If you can't take it, you shouldn't play.

—Jack Lambert

I am the most ruthless, brutal champion ever. There is no one who can match me. I want your heart. I want to eat your children.

—Mike Tyson, who later said he was joking.

In an ends-focused culture, acceptable ways to achieve a given set of ends are often defined quite liberally. Various forms of cheating and dirty practices become increasingly tolerated if they help an organization reach the bottom line in a more efficient manner. Translation to athletes: Be a success. Win at all costs. And as a result of these accomplishments, you can make a lot of money, get on TV, and if the rest of us can bask in the glory of your accomplishment, all will be forgiven. As people begin to perceive that others are cheating to get ahead, whether their perceptions are right or wrong, they too may stretch the boundaries. In a competitive culture there will inevitably be winners and losers. As D. Stanley Eitzen commented, "life is often a zero-sum situation where one wins at the expense of others."[1] Perhaps in no area of life is the zero-sum proposition more apparent than in sports. When our team beats yours, we believe our town, or school, or even our country, is better than yours. In fact, losers are generally viewed as the source of their own failure. That the winners may resort to cheating and violence in order to "defeat" the opposition should come as no surprise. Sport is a microcosm of the society in which we live, thus we can see societal problems play out on the sports fields.

In this chapter we look first at how the sports machine entices athletes, coaches, and teams into cheating or playing dirty in order to win, and how the fans generally accept such behavior, rarely finding it out of the norm. Cheating in sports is not by any means a new phenomenon, as we will demonstrate, which only makes it all the more problematic. We are focusing on the major sports in the United States—baseball, football, basketball, and hockey—as well as the strange world of professional wrestling, but we will also demonstrate that cheating is not exclusive to these games. We are not, however, suggesting that all athletes cheat. There will always be those who maintain integrity despite the system's push to give in. The concern is that the long history of sports cheating, coupled with the high stakes of sports, make it unlikely that cheating and dirty play will decrease soon.

In the second part of the chapter we look at violence in sports. Sports-related violence encompasses many things, depending on how the term "violence" is defined. We have limited our consideration to actions between and among players that take place during the course of a game or event, although we certainly recognize that fan violence is a problem (for example, "Basketbrawl"—the melee at a 2004 NBA game between the Detroit Pistons and the Indiana Pacers—could alone provide material for an entire book). We have elected to focus on the major sports here, adding boxing and wrestling, as they are clearly violent by design. And we will provide some brief examples to show the reader that violence is no stranger to other sports as well.

A CULTURE OF CHEATS

There is no doubt we live in a culture of endemic cheating, as David Callahan documents in *The Culture of Cheating*. According to Callahan, "Our culture has changed a lot the last 25 years and not for the better. We have become a more materialistic, more individualistic society. The individualism of the 1960s teamed up with the materialism of the 1980s to create a cultural environment hospitable to cutthroat behavior. The 'Me Generation' has met the 'Greed is Good Generation.'"[2] It is not just the dregs of society who cheat to get ahead, either. CEOs cheat their employees and tax payers out of billions. Even high profile academics have "borrowed" others' work, as is the case with historian Stephen Ambrose who failed to give credit to the authors from whom he cut and pasted.[3] In a 2002 poll of 12,000 high school students, 74 percent admitted cheating in the past year.[4] Sadly, we have caught our students cheating at times, as we type a choice sentence of "their" work into Google and quickly find a whole paper they printed and handed in.

According to Vahe Gregorian of the *Saint Louis Post-Dispatch*, modern America accepts and even applauds incivility. A November 2004 editorial in the Austin, Texas *American-Statesman* puts it this way: losing control is seen as cool. "Thug life is lauded for 'keeping it real.'"[5] We love it when a celebrity, or better yet, a politician, loses it and shrieks at the paparazzi. We love our *Jerry Springer*, our

Montel, and our *Geraldo*. We love nothing better than hearing and seeing people's dirty laundry get aired and the subsequent nastiness that ensues when it is. While we are saddened when celebrity couples like Jennifer Anniston and Brad Pitt call it quits, a part of us revels in their displeasure. Movies and television help make the "bad" look exciting and daring, while the "good" are boring drudges. For instance, in cop films the "bad" cop typically does not play by the rules—he does whatever it takes to put the derelict behind bars. These *Dirty Harry* characters are viewed as quirky and likeable, while the by-the-books guy is just uptight.[6] The message is clear: The way to get ahead in the dog-eat-dog world is to do whatever it takes, not to let those pesky rules stand in your way. It's even easier when so many do it you can define that behavior as normal. "The culture of cheating has become so self-perpetuating in that people think if everyone is doing it, it's a disadvantage not to," said Callahan.[7]

Sports, too, are rife with numerous forms of cheating and dirty play. None of this is new; as we will document, many sports have dirty roots. In fact, sports have been and continue to be so nasty we struggled in sifting through all the possible examples we could provide. Cheating is deeply rooted in sports history. Pelops, grandson of the god Zeus and founder of the Olympic games, was said to have sabotaged the chariot of King Oenomaus, who demanded that his daughter's suitors defeat him in a chariot race.[8] Corruption was again documented in 388 BC, when boxer Eupolus of Thessaly was caught bribing three opponents to take falls.[9] Nor was it just the common athletes who used sleazy behavior in ancient times; judges in AD 67 accepted bribes from Roman Emperor Nero to award him first place award in a chariot race, despite the fact that he fell out of his vehicle and failed to finish.[10]

What is striking about sports cheating today, however, is the myriad methods used by all parties involved and how much it is accepted as simply part of the vast majority of sports. As sociologist George Sage commented in *Power and Ideology in American Sport*, "The competition is waged not only against opponents but also against the rules—to see how often and how thoroughly they can be stretched and outright violated."[11] The masses now see more cheating and dirty play in sports than ever before, thanks to televised coverage of games and events. We can see the same examples over and over, thanks to reruns and stations like ESPN Classic. But, rather than be appalled by the lack of moral vigor, cheating seems to have become normalized, and is even seen as cute. Further, the enormous amount of money fueling the sports machine encourages cheating of all types. Linda Robertson of the *Miami Herald* explains, "What is different as 2004 comes to a close is that the stakes of sports are higher than ever before. Bigger money and greater exposure entwine in a volatile embrace. The egos of athletes and fans—vying for their TV moment—get inflated in the process."[12] Enormous sums of money provide incentives to cheat at both extremes; those on top will try to stay there, while those in the lesser ranks might cheat to get what the "Bonds,'" "O'Neals,'" or "Rodriguezs'" have. This might strike the reader as odd; even the rookie baseball player, for instance, makes at least $300,000 per year. That's a damn good wage, and far better than the millions who struggle just to best the poverty line. Yet, as many sociologists have noted, people are more likely to look upwards than downwards for comparison.[13] According to Kevin Towers, general manager of the San Diego Padres, "A big, big year means a big, big contract," while a bad year might mean a return to the minor leagues or no job at all.[14] As Ed Graney of the *San Diego Union-Tribune,* said, "So focused on money, many athletes will take the ultimate risk (read: their health and quality of life) to be swimming in the bling, bling."[15]

Violence in sports follows a similar pattern, in that, while it is not new, it is demonstrated with far more frequency and in a wide variety of sports. All involved—players, coaches, owners, and fans too—generally accept it. As Don Atyeo explained in *Blood and Guts,*

The thing about sport is that it legitimizes violence, thereby laundering it acceptably clean. Incidents routinely occur in the name of sport, which, if they were perpetrated under any other banner short of open warfare, would be roundly condemned as crimes against humanity. The mugger in the parking lot is a villain; the mugger on the playing field is a hero. The pain inflicted in sport is somehow not really pain at all; it is *Tom and Jerry* pain, cartoon agony which doesn't really hurt.[16]

The level of acceptance for dirty play of all sorts is high among coaches, owners, fans, and athletes at all levels. Phil Taylor, of CNNSI.com., said, "Cheating is not only accepted in sports, it's embraced . . . We've come to think of deceit as part of the competitive spirit, so that if you're not cheating, you're not trying."[17] According to the Josephson Institute of Ethics in California, 45 percent of male high school basketball players think illegal holding and pushing are fine, as long as you don't get caught. Over half felt that inflicting pain to intimidate opponents was acceptable.[18] Thirty-nine percent of male high school athletes and 22 percent of females had no issue with a coach demanding that a player fake an injury to get an extra time out. And, as with doping, even athletes initially opposed to cheating find themselves caught in a vicious cycle, where they do it because they know or believe their opponent is or their teammates and coaches expect them to. As Nathan Aaseng explained, "like a convoy of speeding trucks, modern athletes who bend the rules find safety in numbers."[19] "That's just the way it is," is the mantra and serves to defend cheating and on-field violence as the status quo.

Baseball Cheating: Jimmy-rigged Balls, Bats, and the Like

Steve Rushin of *Sports Illustrated* probably sums up the breadth of cheating in baseball best:

Cheating is to baseball as Bernoulli's principle is to fixed-wing aircraft: the invisible constant that keeps everything aloft. Hitters erase the back line of the batter's box; catchers "frame" pitches to induce strikes; infielders occupy a different congressional district from second base when turning a double play; sluggers juice up on steroids till their forearm veins resemble bridge cables; and outfielders pretend that a one-hopper was in fact caught on the fly, holding the baseball to the umpire like a prized tomato in a produce aisle.[20]

In fact, we are at a point that an outfielder has little choice but to try to elicit an "out" call when the ball really took a one-hopper. Can you imagine the repercussion if the player admits the ball wasn't caught and the team ultimately loses the game? The fans, teammates, coaches, and local media will gangpile on and any notions of fair play surely will be shouted down.

Historically, baseball has had some of the all-time greatest cheating scandals. Few baseball fans are not familiar with the 1919 Black Sox scandal, when eight Chicago White Sox players allegedly took bribes to throw the World Series against Cincinnati. The *New York Times* wrote in 1920, "Many players believe that the recognized code of sports does not apply to baseball."[21]

Through the evolution of the game, ball players have tinkered with their mitts, bats, and balls in efforts to catch more and hit farther. In the late 1990s, Brian Moehler was suspended for ten games for taping sandpaper to the thumb of his pitching hand. He used the sandpaper to rough up the surface of the ball, altering the way air passes over it and allowing the pitcher to throw outrageous curves. Players say he wasn't the only one doing this type of thing. Pitchers also doctor balls by putting tacks in their gloves or adding baby oil or lubricating jelly to their caps. In 1987, Joe Niekro was caught on the mound with a nail file in his pocket. That he was filing his nails between innings and innocently forgot the file didn't fly with baseball administrators, who issued Niekro a ten-game suspension. In addition to the everpopular corking of the bat's interior, made famous recently by slugger Sammy Sosa, players have been known to add layers of lacquer to their bats to make them as hard as aluminum.[22] Regarding Sosa's claims of innocence, we concur with Rick Telander's appraisal of the incident: "Sosa said he keeps a corked bat to use during batting practices because 'I like to put on a show for the fans. I like to make people happy and show off.' I believe that. I believe gangsters keep shotguns in their trunks to shoot rabbits. I believe the Tooth Fairy is married to the Easter Bunny. I believe—I guarantee I believe—that Sosa is a liar."[23]

Don't forget the young baseball cheaters, either. Danny Almonte led his Bronx, New York, team to the 2001 Little League World Series, even tossing a perfect game in the opener. The team was later stripped of the title when it was revealed that Almonte was not 12 years old, the required age limit, but 14 years old. As many have wondered, "What was the first clue—Almonte's towering teenaged frame or his 5 o'clock shadow?"

Football Cheating: Slippery Uniforms, Doctored Balls, and Shaky Tackles

As with baseball, cheating in football can occur before the game even begins by doctoring up the equipment. Altering pads and helmets is possible (recall the case of the sharpened helmet buckles from Introduction), but more frequently it is the ball that gets tweaked. The NFL began hearing complaints about the issue in the mid-1990s. Prior to the 1997 season, they instituted a fine of $10,000 for any player found to have tampered with a ball. According to McCallum, "Footballs have been steam-bathed, baked in aluminum foil, dunked in water, brushed with wire, bonked with hammers, buffed with strips of artificial turf, jumped on, shot out of Jugs machines, pounded into the walls of racquetball courts, inflated and deflated more often than Oprah Winfrey, armor-alled, shoe-polished, and lemonaded, crushed under weightlifting plates, and, like a female wrestler at a county fair, dunked in evaporated milk."[24] All of these extreme measures were to eek a few more yards out of kickoffs and field goal attempts. Clearly the fines were not enough, so the NFL attempted to address the problem of rigged pigskins in 1999, requiring that only twelve balls per game be delivered to punters and kickers. These would be inscribed with the letter K and sent out replete with antitampering tape. A box is delivered to the officials' room $2\frac{1}{2}$ hours prior to kickoff, and only then can the teams remove the balls from their enclosures.[25]

Phil Taylor of CNNSI reports on an interesting incident involving baking products in the college ranks. "In the most creative use of a food product since my college roommate's mom sent us a loaf of homemade bread that was so heavy we used it as a doorstop, it was discovered last week that four Sacramento State defensive lineman had sprayed their uniforms with Pam, the nonstick cooking oil, in order to make it more difficult for opposing players to hold them."[26] Both the greasing and the holding they were trying to avoid are illegal.[27] Just another example of how cheating is seen as a reasonable way to outfox the other cheats in a perpetuation of the they-did-it-first mentality. Interestingly, the players didn't exactly do it on the sly. They were caught after a University of Montana photographer caught them on film applying the substance on the sideline during a November game. "This wasn't just a Martha Stewart moment (can't you just hear her? 'A bit of nonstick cooking oil applied just below the shoulder pads will really keep those pesky left tackles away'). It was a group of athletes so accustomed to dishonesty passing for gamesmanship that they didn't even bother to hide their little scheme by greasing up in the privacy of the locker room."[28] Taylor argues that the players were reprimanded but not suspended illustrates how commonplace cheating has become.

The 2004 NFL season featured a finger-pointing battle over which team is dirtiest. Denver Broncos coach Mike Shanahan and Pittsburgh Steelers coach Bill Cowher were slinging allegations against each other for their players' use of cut blocking. Shanahan has been accused of encouraging his players to use the technique, which involves one player diving at another's legs, for the 10 years he has been in Denver. In October of 2004, the Bronco's right tackle, 6'5", 338-pound George Foster, delivered a cut block on Cincinnati defensive lineman Tony Williams that broke Williams' ankle and ended his season. Most appalling about the play was that the ball carrier was well down the field and Williams was no threat to make a tackle. Cowher had claimed that Foster's block, while technically within the rules, was not a clean play. Cincinnati coach Marvin Lewis concurred. Shanahan defends his team and his coaching, arguing that all the teams do it.[29] Ironically, a week later Denver safety John Lynch cried dirty play; upset he was hurt on a block 30 yards away from the play in a game against Atlanta. Falcon's coach, Jim Mora, replied, "What goes around comes around."[30] Clearly the concern over cut blocking didn't prompt teams to end the practice, merely to seek revenge.

Basketball Cheating: Taking the Foul

Apparently, 1990s flamboyant star Dennis Rodman was a great rebounder, in part, because he liked to pin his opponent's arm between his own arm and his body, making it impossible for the opposing player to jump.[31] Center Bill Laimbeer was so well known for his dirty play that he easily became one of the most hated men ever to grace the courts. But perhaps not surprisingly, nearly every team in the league coveted his services.

One common cheating technique players like to use is taking a foul for another player. When on offense, good free-throw shooters will sometimes waltz to the free throw line when it was actually a weak-shooting teammate who was fouled. The refs or opposing coaches usually catch this one and the offending player will brush it off with a, "Gee, I thought I was fouled." At the other end of the floor, a player might try to get credited for a foul to keep a better teammate from fouling out of the game. This nifty trick occurs most often when a ball handler drives the lane and several defenders swipe at the ball. As soon as the whistle blows a weaker player will protect the stars by raising his hand and saying, "Yep, I fouled him." In both cases the announcers will drone on about what great strategy it is to try these cheeky tricks.

Hockey Cheating: Stick Bending

Hockey players have long been known to alter their equipment to influence play. Players will illegally curve their stick blades for added puck control and goalies wear illegally wide pads to prevent scoring. According to the *St. Louis Post-Dispatch*, a 1998 NHL documentary features superstar Brett Hull shouting at his equipment manager, "I need my legal stick! I need my legal stick!"[32] The stick-bending tricks do not only happen at the top level either. Peter's older brother learned these tricks as a teenager in youth hockey, carefully heating and bending his stick blade like it was an art form passed down through generations of players. Jon Marthaler of the *Minnesota Daily* contends the problem is really exclusive to the NHL's regular season. During the playoffs, he maintains, penalties for cheating and violence are issued immediately and dramatically, and no player wants to take the chance his actions might jeopardize the team's playoff chances. During the regular season the league usually turns a blind eye.[33]

Soccer Cheating: Going down in a Blaze of Glory

Soccer players are regular cheats, according to some observers. Most notable was Diego Maradona's famous "hand of God" goal in the 1986 World Cup quarterfinal, where tapes revealed Maradona had punched, rather than headed, the ball into the goal. It was Maradona this time who was on the good side of the Lord, as he claimed the "hand of God" scored the goal.[34]

Critics contend the vast majority of major league and international games include some type of dirty play. While not necessarily outright cheating, teams will often use aggression to neutralize the advanced skill of opponents, sometimes escalating the abuse until the refs act to stop it through yellow card warnings and ejections. The women's teams are also accused of pushing the boundaries. Brazil's coach, Rene Simoes, accused the U.S. Women's Olympic team of playing dirty in a game that allowed the United States to advance to the quarterfinals in Athens. According to Simoes, two of his players were hospitalized after the game due to the American's overly physical second-half play, which was a tactical change after the Americans were clearly outclassed before the break. One player had suffered a broken collarbone, while the other was knocked unconscious. Of course U.S. coach April Heinrichs vehemently denied the allegation they had changed tactics, and, big surprise, maintained there was all together too much focus on this issue and not enough on the Americans' win.[35]

Of course, it's difficult to fish out the truth here, as soccer has long featured players feigning injuries, hoping the official will award a penalty kick. Particularly difficult to watch is the way forwards topple to the ground like awkward toddlers when they are bumped inside the penalty box. Make no mistake: This practice is taught to goal scorers at the youngest levels. While playing for a traveling youth team, Peter was taught that when inside the penalty box you either get off a good shot on goal or you "get tripped" and score the penalty kick. The problem is so destructive to the image of sports that officials now are giving yellow cards to players who clearly dive to try to get a beneficial call.

Cheating on the Links?

Even "the gentleman's sport" of golf may not be so pure. Tiger Woods has on numerous occasions bandied about the accusation that players on the PGA Tour are using doctored drivers. His claim is that ridiculous increases in driving distances by some players may be more a result of the materials and composition of their clubs than of lifting weights, increasing flexibility, or time spent at the range. The Tour has elected to implement voluntary testing of drivers at every tournament,[36] offering the use of a machine that tests the rebounding properties of the club's face. Players can then police their own equipment as they police their own play on the course by calling rules infractions on themselves. Some have dismissed Woods' comments as sour grapes made at a time when his play was not at its peak. But others have concurred with Woods that there is indeed a problem. Other rules infractions that occur on the PGA Tour include sharpening the grooves on the irons to give the player more ball control, caddies warming balls in their pockets on cold days (yes, that really is illegal), and caddies signaling club selection to each other early in a tournament so players can help each other make the cut and earn a check for the week. The gentlemen's game, indeed!

The Sweat-free Marathon

Sometimes cheaters do something so obvious it is laughable. When Rosie Ruiz rolled across the Boston Marathon finish line as the first woman, minus any sign of perspiration, some eyebrows probably should have been raised. Ruiz managed this feat by jumping into the marathon for the last half of a mile. Of course, this trick was old hat to Ruiz, who qualified for Boston by her stellar run and ride-the-subway combo in the New York City marathon.[37] She didn't conjure up her tactic out of the blue, either. U.S. marathoner Fred Lorz was denied the gold medal in the 1904 Olympics after it was discovered that he had completed 11 miles tucked safely and sweat-free in an automobile.[38]

Cheating in Fishing and Equestrian

Just when we thought there was one sport left where athletes couldn't cheat, professional fishing succumbed to the dark side in 2002. A Canadian angler tried to con tournament judges at the greater Ontario Salmon Derby by cramming $7\frac{1}{2}$ pounds of lead pipes, small rocks, and sinkers into the guts of a Chinook he claimed he caught. The loaded fish weighed in at an incredible $34\frac{1}{2}$ pounds. The same offender, Gary Morrison, was implicated in an earlier incident involving a salmon. But the sports' authorities say the jig is up. The Bass Anglers Sports Society (BASS), which hosts twenty events a year, requires competitors take polygraph tests when a cheating allegation is issued.[39]

What's the best way to get a horse to run fast? Sure, you can whip it, but an even more effective technique is to shock the heck out of it. It's illegal, of course, but that hasn't stopped jockeys from hiding buzzers, which are like mini cattle prods, in the end of their whips or up their sleeves. Officials suspect that jockey Bill Patin used such a device in leading Valhol to the Arkansas Derby win on April 10, 1999.[40]

VIOLENCE IN SPORTS

Ellis Cashmore explains the difference between the sports violence of old and the new variety. He says physical encounters are less restrained than they used to be when pride was at stake, not millions of dollars. And, while those who object that sports today is hyperviolent point to examples of nasty athletes of yonder years—Ty Cobb and Jake LaMotta, for instance—Cashmore explains, "My point is: they *do* stand out. Nowadays, there are so many sports performers with the same approaches that we do not regard them as extraordinary."[41]

Baseball: Hardly a Pacifist Sport

One might think that baseball, a sport where the skills of catching and throwing a ball and hitting it with a bat, is one of minimal aggressive contact between players. Yet, as Steve Rushin documented in *Sports Illustrated*, baseball is not necessarily the sport of pacifists. Rather, baseball is a sport that has attempted to maximize its minimal onfield violence in the name of profit.[42] Some Major League Baseball players have worked hard to cultivate a nasty reputation, as was the case with the Cincinnati Reds, "Nasty Boys," who won the 1990 World Series. Pitcher Norm Charlton displayed the nasty boy mentality when he hit a Dodger batter and stated, "I threw it at him. He'll be lucky if I don't rip his head off the next time I'm pitching."[43] This attitude continues as the fans are treated every season to games featuring pitchers beaning batters in retaliation for beanings of their teammates.

Perhaps the current king of the beanball is Pedro Martinez. He hit eleven batters in each of his first two seasons with Montreal, and in seven seasons with Boston hit another seventy-seven.[44] Although it is sometimes difficult to tell whether a pitcher was aiming at someone or simply miscalculated the pitch, on July 7, 2003, Martinez hit the first two Yankee players to bat, Alfonso Soriano and Derek Jeter, knocking each out of the action. When we consider that this is a guy who can hit the "O" on a stop sign from over 60 feet, we should be more than suspicious when he plunks batter after batter in rivalry games. His worst act while on the mound came in the 2003 American League Championship Series, when he actually threw behind the head of batter Karim Garcia.[45]

We also see the drive to win take precedence over interests for another player's health when base runners round third and head home to find the catcher waiting with ball in mitt. The base runner is expected to lambaste the catcher in an attempt to dislodge the ball so a run can be scored. And the collisions are often bone crunching. In one of the more egregious poundings at the plate, Pete Rose crushed catcher Ray Fosse in the 1970 Major League Baseball All-Star game. Fosse suffered a separated shoulder and was never the same player again. In response to questions about the play, given the exhibition nature of the game, Rose responded, "I play to win. I just did what I had to do."[46] This type of response, all too common when these situations occur in sports, leaves us flabbergasted. Men who stormed the beaches at Normandy did what they had to do. Pounding a defenseless catcher in an exhibition game is about something else entirely. It is about an ego molded and reinforced by a life in the sports' spotlight.

Bench-clearing brawls are also a relatively common occurrence in baseball that gets ESPN anchors drooling all over themselves. Fortunately, little ever happens during these confabs on the mound. But, occasionally an elderly man gets tossed on his rump. During one bench-clearing brawl between the Yankees and Red Sox, Pedro Martinez tossed elderly Yankee's bench coach Don Zimmer to the ground. Jack McCallum of *Sports Illustrated* said, regarding baseball and basketball, "They can release statistics about fighting being down, and they can whine the media are exaggerating the unruly incidents, and they can suggest that their games used to be rougher and tougher in the old days. But perception nowadays is reality, and right now the perception is that both great American pastimes end in brawl, not ball."[47]

Violence in Wrestling: Battles of Good and Evil

The original form of wrestling was often a fight to the death, according to legend. Theogenes, a wrestling hero from 900 BC, has been credited with a perfect record—1,425 victories—all of them clean kills.[48] The pankration, a hyperviolent hybrid of boxing, wrestling, and judo, featured athletes attempting to gain their opponent's submission by breaking various limbs and utilizing strangle holds.[49]

It may strike the reader as odd that we elected to include professional wrestling in our discussion of sports cheating and dirty play. Certainly professional wrestling is not a true "sport." Rather, it is cheap entertainment that boasts a shockingly large fan base. It is painfully obvious that pro wrestling is little more than a vehicle for men to claim their masculinity, while dressing in garish costumes and makeup. However, there are aspects of pro wrestling that we believe affect young viewers and can shape their understanding of the world of sports. Clearly the performers are extremely athletic and perform feats that make most NFL tackles look tame. For young viewers, this can provide erroneous definitions of the limits of the abuse the human body can, or should, suffer in the name of sports. During our years as high school teachers, we both had students who swore that pro wrestling is real, is a sport, and that well-trained athletes can handle being pile-driven into the mat without suffering injury. It was scary stuff that left us shaking our heads in dismay.

The "soap opera for men" offers an interesting glimpse into the broader cultural phenomenon of the blurring of good and evil. Wrestling has long been configured as a battle between good and evil, or "the faces" versus "the heels." Long ago, according to Patrice Oppliger, author of *Wrestling and Hyper-Masculinity*, the faces were the clear winners and they did so by playing by the rules, while the heels could only win by cheating. Now even the faces are expected to ignore the rules. Referees rarely challenge illegal acts during matches, and announcers praise dirty tricks. Acts of revenge after the ending bell are common. Fans hoot and holler, and the cycle continues.[50]

Professional wrestling both entertains and appalls us with its violence, both pseudo and real. Even the titles of matches stress the violent nature of the sport. *Smackdown*, "*No Mercy*," and *Armageddon* are all televised shows.[51] Fans pay big bucks to see these events, and many believe the more violence they see, the better. Even former President Jimmy Carter's mother, Lillian, was a staunch pro wrestling fan who claimed, "The more brutal it is, the better I like it."[52] Critics have contended that professional wrestling is the most violent programming on television. As Oppliger stated, "Just as violence has gradually increased in cartoons, video games, song lyrics, and sports, so too has wrestling become more elaborately violent."[53] Researchers at Indiana University counted the number of aggressive and lewd acts televised in wrestling over 1 year. In 50 episodes they found 609 instances of wrestlers using garbage cans, chairs, and tables as weapons.[54]

Audiences easily become desensitized to the same old moves, so wrestlers push the boundaries more and more. While a jump from the top rope used to thrill the crowd, now it takes hurtling from the 16-foot high metal cage surrounding the ring. According to Oppliger, "The goal of wrestling is not necessarily to be declared the winner of matches; rather the goal is to shame opponents through physical punishments, humiliation, and verbal abuse."[55]

Pro wrestlers are seemingly superhuman, based on the amount of violence they appear to endure. A wrestler who gets "busted open" is highly regarded, as bleeding is a status symbol. While expressions of pain are not acceptable in other sports, here they are highly dramatized. Yet this serves to devalue the pain, as audiences cannot and are not supposed to be able to tell the difference between a real injury and an exaggerated one. In addition, the public may underestimate the true amount of violence in wrestling, as much of it is presented as comedy. Comic violence is not unique to wrestling; films as old as *The Three Stooges* have made aggression seem amusing. Violence presented as hilarious antics may actually be more harmful to audiences, especially young children, who may interpret this behavior as silly and fun.[56] Thus, should we be surprised when violence shows up in child's play on the playground? Of course not. Clothes lining a buddy while playing touch football might be nothing more than an acceptable application of a cool move seen on wrestling in the mind of a fourth grader.

Boxing: The Most Brutal of All?

Although the Greeks are credited with inventing boxing, it was the Romans who perfected it as a violent enterprise. It's common knowledge the gladiator fights were brutal (between two humans as well as creative combinations of humans versus animals) and often to the death.[57] In fact, boxing under the Romans was so lethal it virtually vanished for a 1000 years.[58] Violent prizefighting reemerged in England, and was enthusiastically accepted in the American colonies. No surprise, it was the least powerful in society, the slaves, who were the first fighters, forced into pugilism to turn even greater profit for their owners.[59] The pattern continues today, where boxing promoters link up with impoverished city youth (Mike Tyson, for instance) and offer them boxing as a way out of the ghetto.

The twentieth century, however, "marked a renaissance in pugilism."[60] While the advent of boxing gloves gave the sport an air of respectability, little real reduction in the amount of violence occurred. Gloves weighed only 4 ounces, less than half the weight used today, and were chock-full of insulation tape, at best. Others loaded their gloves with studs or pins. While they no longer fought until death literally, there were still no time limits for fights, so in order to win an athlete fought until the other was knocked out. Fights routinely lasted several hours, with the longest reaching 7 hours and 19 minutes in 1893. Eyewitnesses said both fighters' faces looked like hamburgers. Jack Dempsey earned his heavyweight title, and the nickname Man Killer, by pounding Jess Willard seven times to the floor. Reports of the slaughter described Willard's face as pulp, and "at the feet of the gargantuan pugilist was a dark spot which was slowly widening on the brown canvas as it was replenished by the drip, drip, drip of blood from the man's wounds."[61]

It was not until 1928 that the link between boxing and brain damage was first suggested. In that year H. S. Martland coined the phrase "punch drunk" to describe five boxers he examined. The condition still is a result of fighting, but is now termed "dementia pugilistica." Vocal boxing critics surfaced in the United States in the 1950s, and outcry against the sport reached a crescendo with the death of Benny "Kid" Paret in March 1962. Emile Griffiths, his opponent, had smashed Paret in the head twenty times, while he lay slumped against the ropes. All Griffiths remembered is that he was instructed to keep punching, no matter what. Paret's death was followed in quick succession by several others in the United States and elsewhere, including that of Davey Moore, memorialized in the Bob Dylan song alluded to in Chapter 1. Since 1900, there have been over 500 deaths in the sport.[62]

Because there is no nationwide boxing regulatory agency, boxers today can move from state to state in an effort to be the one to do the pummeling. It is still the most brutal fighters that command the big bucks and the huge crowds. Heavyweights in particular have always been a big draw, as they are best suited to beat the tar out of one another and to deliver knockout blows. And, when their actions in and out of the ring are particularly extreme, such as Mike Tyson biting Evander Holyfield's ear during a 1997 match, they receive even more press coverage and even bigger payouts. In a textbook case of rationalizing, Tyson explained that his cannibalism was necessary, asserting that Holyfield had been head-butting him and the ref wrongly called the acts unintentional.[63] In fact, as one boxing promoter admitted, "Tyson and the despicable thing he did made boxing hot. I'm not saying this is right and this is good. It's a commentary on the people more than anything."[64] As former light-heavyweight champion Willie Pastrano explains, boxing is still "the last of the gladiator sports, baby."[65]

Boxing has also spawned other sports that are equally violent. *Ultimate Fighting*, which started as a pay-per-view television event matching martial artists of varied disciplines, conjures up images of the ancient pankration. Contestants fight in The Octagon (literally an octagon of chain link fencing) and, "The desired effect is minimally controlled mayhem; the model is an alley fight or a barroom brawl."[66] Beyond the few rules (no eye gouging, throat grasps, biting, long toenails or fingernails, and no headgear with dangerous straps), anything goes. Among the most successful fighters are those trained to take the opponent down to the mat before applying a submission hold, forcing the opponent to "tap out," which ends the match. The viewers quickly learn that the term "submission hold" means, "You better start tapping that mat or I'm gonna break your arm at the elbow . . . punk."

Good Tackle or Football Violence?

American football has always been violent. In fact, Harvard pulled out of all competitions in 1884 because the sport was so brutal, but returned in 1887 after proponents asserted the game "teaches character." At the turn of the century the sport was just as brutal; at the first Rose Bowl in 1901, Stanford had to request an early end to the game because they were out of healthy players. In 1905, eighteen college and high school players were killed and more than 159 were seriously injured. Even Teddy Roosevelt, a staunch supporter of rough sports and "an almost pathological destroyer of wild animals"[67] called for the end of the game. Rather than end the game, an Intercollegiate Rules Committee was created. A major change was to legalize the forward pass, which would, in theory, open up the game. Yet 1909 was even more deadly, with 33 killed and 246 injured. Rules changes continued, as did the violence. In 1931 the game killed forty players, but by that time the game had become extremely popular and its critics were largely silenced.[68]

While deaths in the pro ranks are rare, major injuries and shortened life expectancies from the game's brutality are not. Former player Jean Fugett called the game "legalized violence," saying, "Out in the real world you just can't go around beating on somebody's head the way we do. I can go into a game and just literally try to break somebody's neck."[69] Conrad Dobler, voted the NFL's meanest player in 1978, asserted, "If you ever forget that football is a violent game, they'll catch you gazing at the stars and put your lights out."[70]

Some players thrill in the blood and gore of the game, making it their mission to be as violent as possible. Former Chicago Bear, Mike Singletary, Defensive Player of the Year numerous times, described his tackles with pride. Describing a brutal hit on running back Eric Dickerson, Singletary said, "I don't feel pain from a hit like that. What I feel is joy. Joy for the tackle. Joy for myself. Joy for the other man."[71] How nice that Singletary wished his opponent's enjoyment from being knocked silly. Former Detroit Lions linebacker Jimmy Williams, one of those players with God on his side discussed in Chapter 1, claimed, "I like to hit a man and hear that . . . little moan."[72] Some college players feel the same. Purdue's Jon Golsberry embraced his role as ass-kicking fullback. His "intensity" earned him the title of "Top Kamikaze Special Teams Player" in the Big Ten by *Sporting News*.[73] That an award would be so titled reflects the privileging of the game as a compelling product over the interests of the players and their safety.

Coaches often encourage players to make especially violent tackles, rather than tackles simply to take the player down. *Sports Illustrated* documented three helmet decals athletes can be awarded by coaches for extra hard hits. A lineman at Florida would get a "dead roach" if he knocked a player on his butt, legs, and arms in the air. "Decleaters" are awarded to athletes at Wisconsin who stand up to "dee opponent and knocks him off dee cleats," while a player at Miami can receive a "slobber knocker" for slamming an opponent's saliva out of his mouth.[74] Telander tells of reading a notebook from a course on *The Coaching of Football* taught by Woody Hayes at Ohio State in 1966. The section on tackles read: "We don't like to see a kid making a tackle like he is trying to *hug* the man down. We want to give him cancer of the breast by knocking his titty off. We want to knock his anus up through his *haid* (head)."[75]

Obviously there is no less violence in the NFL. In 1997, for instance, a Kansas City Chiefs player stated on a radio show that coach Marty Schottenheimer offered to pay the fines his team might incur were they to break the jaws of Denver players.[76] Former Atlanta Falcons football coach Jerry Glanville once remarked, "I love it when they knock each other out," about watching his special team's players beat each other in practice.[77] Imagine his elation when his players assaulted the other team on Sundays.

Some of the explanation for football's violence clearly lies in the rules and the enforcement of them. Another part of the problem lies in the equipment used. As Atyeo explains, football players shunned protective equipment for decades, arguing it was an attack on their masculinity, but "when it did become accepted they were unsure whether to use it for protection or treat it as another weapon."[78] According to Telander, "Modern-day helmets allow face-first tackles, burying 'your nose in his numbers' as the coaches say, so that the helmet is now less a protective device than a weapon, a rock-hard spear point . . . "[79]

According to Atyeo, there are two primary reasons there are few critics of football today. First, the game is so important that we see the violence and even enjoy it, but don't recognize it for what it is. Because it has become accepted as a routine part of the game, football violence has escaped the condemnation that other forms of violence receive. Second, the way the audience sees football is somewhat insulated from the reality of the game. Today's giant stadiums have moved fans farther from the action. Protective equipment provides the illusion of safety: "to the bleacher-bound eye the players appear impregnable, impervious to pain and something less than human."[80] Viewing a game on television, a fan may see a particular injury shown repeatedly if it is spectacular, but will not likely grasp the perpetual violence of the game. Especially when contrasted with the rest of the television world, which features gratuitous violence. Football violence, the fan might say, is for a purpose, so is distinct from the violence of a Chuck Norris show.

In perhaps the worst example of the media glorifying the violence of the NFL, *ESPN*'s NFL show presents us with the week's top ten players who got "jacked up." As the highlight reel rolls through the ten hardest hit players, the announcers chant in unison, "You got jacked up!" The featured players are frequently being blind-sided or are caught off guard when they think they are no longer involved in the play. And there is no shred of sympathy in sight as the announcers giggle about how hard players collide.

Hockey Violence: A Sport Made for Fighting?

Hockey for many is nothing without the violence. Fights have been a staple since the NHL began in 1917. Originally fighters were referred to as "policemen," as they were there to protect the stars. In the 1970s they became known as goons, and were beautifully parodied by the Hansen brothers in the film *Slapshot*.[81] Today they are dubbed "Enforcers." While fighting is not technically legal, it is certainly encouraged. Players who fight earn the respect of teammates, opponents, and fans alike, and general managers love those who can both play at a high level and fight.[82] Fighting is not always about sheer brutality but is also an integral part of game strategy. Wayne Gretzky was allowed to dominate in his early years partly because opponents feared they'd have to face Edmonton Oilers' tough guy, Dave Semenko.[83] There is an unwritten rule in the sport that demands players always support a teammate, "like soldiers under fire."[84] When a fight erupts, said one player, "You've got to help him. It's more or less just a policy with hockey players, you just do it. There's no question about it. You just drop your gloves and grab the guy . . ."[85]

Huge brawls seem to electrify a team, at least at the box office. In 1970 the Philadelphia Flyers were struggling to sell tickets; in 1973 they set attendance records in five cities and sold out the Spectrum for the entire season because they were winning with violence.[86] Part of the escalation of violence was due to the competition for athletes between the NHL and the World Hockey Association. The NHL scrambled to get players, settling for less talented but rougher ones.[87] Barring the 2004–2005 season, which was cancelled due to a lockout, the NHL generally plays to 90 percent capacity with the bulk of those fans claiming to like the violence.[88] In the 2003–2004 season there were 780 fights in 1,230 NHL games—about two fights in every three games. That rate had been roughly the same for the last seven seasons but is lower than the rate of one fight per game in the 1980s.[89] The fans also become ardent supporters of The Enforcers. For years Bob Probert was a hugely popular fighter for the Detroit Red Wings and local fans proudly wore shirts reading, "Give Blood . . . Fight Probert!"

Most of these fights end in routine injuries—cuts, scrapes, and bruises. Injuries to the eyes and teeth are the most common. "From an opthalmologist's point of view, hockey is the most dangerous sport outside of boxing," said one doctor.[90] Few players leave the game with more than snaggle teeth remaining. Some of the assaults are more serious, however. In 2000, Boston Bruin Marty McSorley used his stick to attack Vancouver Canucks forward Donald Brashear with 3 seconds left in the game. Prior to McSorley's attack on Brashear there had been twenty-seven suspensions in the league, and the game was held in early October. McSorley claimed he did not intend to hit Brashear. The Bruins also claimed far worse occurs in the league and that McSorley was a victim of selective enforcement. In the first criminal trial for an on-ice attack since 1988, a judge found McSorley's claim ludicrous. Judge Kitchen stated, "McSorley slashed for the head. A child, swinging as at a tee-ball, would not miss. A housekeeper swinging a carpet beater would not miss. An NHL player would never, ever miss." McSorley was found guilty of assault with a weapon and sentenced to 18 months probation. The league suspended him for the remainder of the season.[91]

In 2004, Vancouver Canucks star Todd Bertuzzi viciously attacked Colorado Avalanche player Steve Moore from behind, breaking vertebrae in his neck as he was driven to the ice and pummeled.[92] Bertuzzi would plead guilty to assault causing bodily harm in a provincial court in Canada, agreeing to pay a meager $500 and serve 80 hours of community service. Although it was nice to see a court address an issue of violence in sports, the punishment is paltry given that Moore still suffers from headaches, memory loss, and mood swings and has a minimal chance of ever playing again.

Certainly, some injuries in the sport are due to accidents, but "most injuries are the end results of a game which has adopted violent assault as its *modus operandi*."[93] Thus, when players suffer "routine" injuries, such as broken noses and teeth, nobody cares much. It is only when a stick is used or a player breaks the code of acceptable violence by attacking another from behind that anyone seems upset. Of course, then the media shows the hit over and over for days, pumping up viewership.

BASKETBALL VIOLENCE: BAD BOY MENTALITY

Let us begin this section by acknowledging that professional basketball has attempted to address the problem of on-court violence better than have the other major leagues. While there is still violence in the sport, the NBA is far from the dark days of the late 1970s. Commissioner David Stern recalled, "We were looked upon as a league that was too black, too violent, and too drug-involved during the late seventies."[94] The 1976 season had forty-one fights that lead to at least one player being ejected, and there were countless other incidents that were broken up shy of an ejection. Team owners voted in 1977 to strengthen the league's rules against fighting. Now the commissioner can fine a player up to $10,000 and suspend him indefinitely for fighting, whereas before the maximum fine was $500 and the suspension could last only 5 days.[95]

Yet despite these changes, what has become known as "the punch" of 1977 has lived on in infamy. Kermit Washington of the Los Angeles Lakers hit Houston Rocket Rudy Tomjanovich during the course of an on-court scuffle. Like Hockey's enforcers, Washington's job was to protect team star Kareem Abdul-Jabbar, which meant, "he did the dirty work defensively and on the boards and if any kind of skirmish broke out, it was his job to make sure nothing happened to Abdul-Jabbar."[96] The job of the enforcer had become so important that *Sports Illustrated* featured a cover story about it early in the 1977–1978 season, prior to the fight.

After lying on the court for several minutes, surrounded by a widening pool of his own blood, Tomjanovich was assisted off the floor and into the training area. He demanded the trainers fix what he thought was a broken nose and get him back on the court. No mere broken nose, the top portion of Tomjanovich's skull was an inch out of line with the lower portion and the funny taste in his mouth was not blood but spinal fluid from his brain. His head looked like a watermelon that had been tossed off a roof onto a parking lot.[97]

Some have asserted the violent play of yonder years is coming back with a vengeance. The Detroit Pistons of the late 1980s were the model for the resurgence of bad-boy basketball.[98] Seattle Supersonics player Danny Fortson has been dubbed a dirty player in the latest go round. After eleven games in the 2004–2005 season, Fortson had earned four technical fouls, picked up five fouls in six different games, fouled out of two, and was suspended for a game by the NBA. Fortson believes the problem stems from a game in November 2003, when he was still with the Dallas Mavericks. Fortson was called for a flagrant foul against then-rookie Zarko Cabarkapa, whose wrist was broken. Suns chairman and CEO Jerry Colangelo dubbed Fortson a "thug," while *New York Post* columnist Peter Vecsey claimed Fortson had "attempted murder."[99] Now branded as a cheap-shot artist, the NBA will keep Fortson on a short leash. All the while, however, the physical play in the league will continue to escalate as long as wins result.

At the college level, revered Temple coach John Chaney admitted sending in a goon to rough up a St. Joe's player in February 2005. The goon did his job, and the result was a broken arm for the St. Joe's player and an end to his season. While Chaney suspended himself for a game, Temple upped the suspension when they learned the St. Joe's player had a broken arm. That Chaney is a great coach in the win-loss department is without question, but that he has, "temper issues second in the game only to Bobby Knight" is also true.[100] Yet it's unlikely Chaney is the only coach to send a player in the game with the intention of taking an opposing player out.

The problem is that one-on-one incidents have become free-for-alls, exactly what was supposed to have changed since the 1970s. Steve Rushin explains, tongue-in-cheek, "The Knicks and the Heat annually reinvent the concept of the bench-clearing basketball fight, a practice condemned by the NBA but one that actually speaks to the best nature of man. What's wrong with loyalty, with coming to the aid of a comrade-in-arms? Chivalry isn't dead—it's living in the NBA rule book, under an assumed name: Leaving The Bench during A Fight."[101] Indeed, others lambasted Pat Riley for encouraging thuggery as coach of the Miami Heat. Said Rick Reilly of *Sports Illustrated*, "He had style before he decided the true way to teach the game is by opening another branch of the office of Assault, Mayhem and Thuggery." And Riley did the same with the Knicks, although at the time the players received most of the blame. Reilly recommended the league fine Coach Riley, saying he is, "taking the league down the sewer with this stuff. . . . There is not a player in the NBA who can just go out and start turning guys into steak tartare without his coach's tacit approval."[102]

Most recently we witnessed the brawl between several members of the Detroit Pistons, the Indiana Pacers, and assorted Detroit fans. With 45.9 seconds to go, Pacer Ron Artest fouled Piston Ben Wallace as he went in for a lay-up. Wallace retaliated after the whistle, shoving Artest and grabbing at his neck. Other players tried to separate the two. Artest ended up reclining on the scorer's table waiting to see if Wallace would be ejected, and the event was seemingly over. Far from it, however, as Artest was hit by a cup thrown from the stands and charged into the seats to attack the fan. More chaos ensued between fans and Pacers.[103] Prior to this debacle, Artest was known throughout the league as a hack with a violent temper. In 2003 he attacked a TV monitor after a game, verbally abused Miami coach Pat Riley, and made obscene gestures to the crowd at two different games.[104] He had further diminished his reputation with the fans by requesting 2 months off from playing so he could promote his new rap CD. He claimed that he was too tired to perform on the court because of his commitments off of it. In an era of multimillion dollar contracts, this obviously was a ludicrous request. Following the brawl, Artest was suspended for the entire season in the most severe ever punishment for fighting. Many denounced the punishment as too severe, as it would leave Artest without an income for a year. No matter, he wanted time off to promote his rap CD anyway.

CONCLUSION

To give credit where it is due, efforts have been made in all of these sports to curb cheating and violence. For example, as noted above, Commissioner David Stern came down hard on Artest and some of the others in the brawl. Likewise, the NFL levied a fine of $75,000 on the Broncos' John Lynch for a vicious hit on Colts' tight end Dallas Clark. But, like their drug-testing policies, the punishments doled out by the leagues are often not enough. MLB player Alex Rodriguez was suspended a few games and fined a whopping $2,000 for his part in a bench-clearing brawl.[105] This is a guy who makes more than $2,000 per at bat. Heck, he probably makes $2,000 every time he breathes at the stadium.

Nor are the rules and penalty changes consistently applied. Sometimes it seems the leagues want to make an example out of certain players. Of course, the disparity in treatment of athletes is no shocker; it is simply a reflection of our culture. We "get tough" on those who do wrong unless they have loads of money and fan appeal. Leagues will respond when something lands in their laps, or when public outcry requires a response, but the responses are typically reactive. As Phil Taylor explained in regard to the Sacramento State spray-grease incident, "We still tend to get upset over the obvious rule-breaking, like college athletes taking under-the-table payments or ballplayers puffing themselves up with steroids. But the mundane, run-of-the-mill cheating has come to seem like business as usual."[106] Sports leagues simply do not seem to be trying to thoroughly investigate the source of their own stink, nor do they always want to prevent cheating and violence if it might mean reduced fan interest. As Minnesota Vikings safety Joey Browner stated, "It's not good for business if you care for a second whether blood is bubbling from a guy's mouth."[107] And what's good for the blood-gurgling guy is simply not that important.

In America, we love a good comeback. So, even when an athlete is penalized for cheating or for excessive violence, their sins are quickly forgotten. Baseball historian John Thorn claims, "We cover sports now the way the *National Enquirer* covers Britney Spears. We like to build our heroes up. We like to see them fall. We like to see them contrite so we can build them back up again."[108] Take figure skater Tanya Harding, who orchestrated an assault on competitor Nancy Kerrigan. Her punishment was rather minimal, especially when the publicity and subsequent financial windfall of the attack are factored in. Harding paid $160,000 in fines, but received $600,000 from *Inside Edition* for her story. One year after the attack *People* and *Esquire* named her one of their favorite celebrities, and respondents for one survey named her among the twenty athletes they most admired. Huh? Of course, Harding was one of the least nasty of the crew favored by those surveyed. They also included alleged murderer O. J. Simpson and convicted rapist Mike Tyson. Harding also launched a new career as a celebrity boxer, earning $50,000 in March 2002 from Fox for trouncing Paula Jones (of Clinton sex scandal fame).[109]

We feel it is unlikely that the vast amount of dirty play, cheating, and violence in sports will be eliminated or even reduced any time soon. Richard Lapchick, director of the Institute for Ethics and Diversity at the University of Central Florida, concurs. One reason, as we discussed at the beginning of the chapter, is that we live in a culture that accepts and even expects cheating as a necessity for success. "Americans demand winners in school, business, politics, and sports, coaches are fired if they are not successful; teams are booed if they play for ties. Super Bowl losers are defined as *losers*, not as runners-up."[110] Likewise, we may pay a lot of lip service to reducing violence, usually couched in "for the children" verbal diarrhea, but reality is we are a violent society. Why would sports be any different? Former NBA player Greg Anthony commented on the Pistons-Pacers incident, saying, "I do really think there is a moral renaissance, if you will, or moral revolution in our society, where we're starting to get to the point where we're immune to these things. You know, we have a war in Iraq right now. And what's our biggest story? We're talking about a fistfight at a professional sporting event. And I just think that this is a microcosm of what's going on in society."[111]

Another reason we don't expect these problems will be alleviated soon is due to the complex and changing nature of what is defined as moral and as good sportsmanship. "The words 'fair' and 'unfair,' those words are difficult to define outside sports, but they're even more difficult to define in sports, because you come back to those notions of strategy and gamesmanship," said Marica Sage, former president of the Sports Ethics Institute.[112] League regulations don't exactly clear it up. The NFL rule against unsportsmanlike conduct reads: "Any act contrary to the generally understood principles of sportsmanship."[113] Because sportsmanship is not well defined, some players have simply failed to internalize it as a goal. NBA player Allan Iverson has been quoted saying, "I would rather win than have good sportsmanship."[114]

Yet another important factor constraining a reduction in dirty play and violence is the way that most of the major sports are so integrally tied to notions of masculinity. In commentating on the brawl involving Pistons, Pacers, and fans, former player Greg Anthony tied it to "a skewed sense of what it means to be masculine in our society that leads people to make these kinds of decisions to take matters into their own hands, so they're not seen as soft."[115] Mike Messner maintained that, as traditional forms of masculinity are perceived to be unavailable, males are increasingly looking to sport as a vehicle to express their manhood.[116]

The media also share some of the responsibility for the acceptance of sports cheating and the adulation of aggressive athletes. Patrice Oppliger, in *Wrestling and Hyper-Masculinity*, asserted that while sports promoters claim to want less violence in the events, sports appear to be getting more violent, or are at least marketed as such. This, she claims, is in order to compete with other media for the highly sought after 18–34 years old male crowd. It is well known that violence sells well internationally, as it is essentially a universal language.[117] George Schlatter, a television producer, commented, "we make entertainment out of violence. We salute it. We rerun it."[118] *Sport* magazine featured hero worship of violent pro football players in an article called "Heavy Hitters From Hell."[119] Sports are even promoted as violent when violence is not a part of the actual event, such as the "Ice Wars" in figure skating.

The media presents, and we watch, athletes do heinous things to themselves and others with a mixture of horror and admiration. When Tyson bit Holyfield's ear, people were appalled but also found the event amusing and worthy of much attention. Headlines such as "Ear Today, Gone Tomorrow," and "Undisputed Chomp" were some of the media's finest.[120] Fans are conditioned to believe that sportscasters are experts about sports. When they give great amounts of attention to certain aggressive athletes or to players who stretch the boundaries of legal play, fans often uncritically accept that these players' actions are not so problematic. As George Sage explained, "a powerful cheerleader/boosterism mentality is promoted by all sports organizations. Their message to fans and players is to give uncritical support; if you don't, you're not being loyal or you're not a team player."[121] Even the format of televised sports talk shows, like *Around the Horn* and *Pardon the Interruption (PTI)* are combative. In *Around the Horn* the goal is to always have one commentator become the stooge in the debates over current sports issues, while *PTI* features two commentators yelling at one another, often even when they agree!

It's also difficult to truly address problems in sports when we get too mired in the nitpicky details at the expense of real systemic problems, as is the *modus operandi* of the NCAA. In 2003 they went after Utah basketball coach Rick Majerus for the following violations: purchasing a deli dinner in 1994 for player Keith van Horn after van Horn's father had died; buying a player a bagel when his brother had recently attempted suicide; and twice allowing assistants to buy groceries (totaling $40–50) for players who hadn't received their scholarship money yet. Rick Reilly aptly lambasted the NCAA, "It's not an easy job, picking nits this tiny, but nobody is up to the task like the NCAA. Take the time the organization told Aaron Adair, a third baseman in Oklahoma, that the book he'd written about surviving brain cancer meant his amateur career was over."[122] And in the mean time, boosters across the country heap on secret payments to stars and provide them with jobs that have high pay and no duties.

What the NCAA and the major sports organizations should be doing is some serious self-analysis. What are our problems? Why do we have them? What could we do about them? But they probably won't, as that could lead them to uncomfortable truths. Even more importantly, we as fans should consider what behavior we want to accept in athletics. We could decide not to attend sporting events where athletes play dirty or violently, and we could turn off our televisions when such events are on. But we probably won't. We'll keep going to the games and keep sedating ourselves in front of the boob tube, an implicit nod to the world of sports to carry on, business as usual. A December 2004 Gallup poll confirmed that few fans are losing interest in the major sports despite recent cheating scandals. Thirty-eight percent of respondents identified themselves as pro basketball fans, about the same as the 39 percent who claimed they were NBA fans in May (prior to Basketbrawl).[123] And, as parents, we should work to teach our children a love of sports that are clean and nonviolent. Perhaps that would prompt real change in big-time sports.

chapter 5

Recruiting Scandals and Academic Fraud

We're not attempting to circumcise rules.

—Pittsburgh Steelers coach, Bill Cowher

Son, looks to me like you're spending too much time on one subject.

—Texas A&M Men's Basketball coach Shelby Metcalf, to an athlete receiving four "F's" and one "D."

In January of 2005, Andy Geiger, the athletic director at Ohio State University, announced he would retire in 6 months. Geiger's announcement came a year earlier than planned. While he claimed it was a decision made for personal reasons—he no longer found his job fun—and that it was made under no duress, many have doubts. The Buckeyes were knee-deep in trouble the previous year for a number of recruiting violations and instances of academic fraud that likely have their origins deeply rooted in the athletic culture at OSU, which boasts one of the largest and most successful athletic departments in the country.

Most of the allegations of universitywide athletic wrongdoing at OSU came from star football player Maurice Clarett, who was suspended for taking illegal payments and lying to investigators about it. Clarett first made allegations of wrongdoing after the Buckeyes won the 2002 National Football Championship. He claimed he received cars and cash, as well as passing grades for work he did not do.[1] A few other ex-players chimed in, saying they were paid for bogus summer jobs and that tutors did their coursework for them.[2] Because it is primarily Clarett making the accusations, however, many dismiss them as his own personal vengeance. Perhaps those who doubt Clarett forget how Ohio State famously lined up a cupcake summer schedule to keep star Andy Katzenmoyer eligible a few years prior. The OSU case is by no means the most egregious example of irregularities in an athletic department, but it exemplifies the problem that many big-time schools face: How to get and keep the best athletes to build and sustain a winning program. The answer for many is to simply cheat.

RECRUITING AND ACADEMIC FRAUD

Recruiting violations and academic fraud cover many different types of ethical and often illegal acts committed by athletic departments, coaches, and "friends of the program." Sometimes the problems violate NCAA policy only, while at other times they violate assorted criminal laws as well. In recruiting, the most common offense is offering some type of financial or material inducement to athletes or their families. Academic fraud generally includes sneaking unqualified athletes into universities by circumventing the normal admissions process. Once they are in, school officials may "fix" their grades or arrange for someone to do their coursework for them. Schools have to keep their "investments" eligible at all costs.

Many of the repeat violators have been caught for combinations of all of these offenses. In August 2004, the University of Georgia men's basketball team was rocked by NCAA sanctions for providing recruiting inducements, providing athletes extra benefits, and committing academic fraud. The NCAA found that the Bulldogs paid money to former player Tony Cole when they were recruiting him, failed to report excessive long-distance phone usage by players on road trips, and committed academic fraud when they gave As to Cole and two other players for work they didn't do in a physical education course.[3]

Assistant coach Jim Harrick Jr., who got great student reviews, taught the Principles and Strategies of Basketball course in question. Small wonder, as all thirty-nine students in the fall of 2001 semester received As. Class attendance was optional, as was the final exam.[4] Of course, it didn't matter that the final was optional given that any basketball fan would ace it. Questions tested one's ability to identify how many points are scored for a 3-point basket and being able to identify how many halves are in a game.

The Bulldogs will be on probation for 4 years, will lose three scholarships, have to "vacate" thirty wins from the 2001–2002 and 2002–2003 seasons (under head coach Jim Harrick), and have to pay back revenue earned from their berth in the 2002 NCAA tournament. The University of Georgia is a repeat offender, so if any of their twenty sports teams commit any major violations in the next 4 years they could be required to disband those sports under the NCAA's "death penalty." Harrick has been suspended from coaching and Jim Harrick Jr.'s contract was not renewed. Georgia's football team under former head coach Ray Goff garnered the earlier offenses.[5]

Harrick is no stranger to the NCAA's inquiry. He was fired as head basketball coach at UCLA in 1996 for "recruiting irregularities." Harrick filed a false expense report for a recruiting dinner attended by five of his current athletes and three recruits.[6] UCLA was placed on a 3-year probation after Harrick made excessive phone calls to recruits and provided an AAU coach with excessive tickets to UCLA games and a 1995 NCAA championship ring.[7] Harrick Jr. was involved at UCLA as well; he was implicated in a controversial sale of an SUV to a recruit, Baron Davis, who did attend UCLA (think the kid got a sweet deal on that vehicle?).[8] Frankly, it is amazing that UCLA let Harrick go, given his success on the court during his tenure. Harrick was hired as the Bruin's coach in 1988. The team won a national title in 1995 and three PAC-10 Championships in his tenure. They played in eight straight NCAA tournaments, reaching the Sweet Sixteen in 1990, 1992, and 1995, as well as the Elite Eight twice (1992 and 1995). Thirteen of his former UCLA players went on to play in the NBA.[9]

Following his ouster from UCLA, Harrick moved on to the University of Rhode Island, which was looking for a high-profile coach to put it on the map. He put it on the map all right . . . he was involved in a sexual harassment claim (the school settled the $45,000 suit),[10] in addition to changing grades for players, having student managers write papers for players, and arranging pay, lodging, and cars from boosters.[11] Once again, Junior followed suit. He was accused of falsifying meal and hotel expenses for recruits.[12] But Harrick's legacy at URI is a mixed bag. He championed a fund-raising effort that resulted in a $45 million basketball arena and his team went 25–9 and reached the Elite Eight in his first year, creating a fervor that saw an attendance increase of 31 percent.[13] But when he dashed off to Georgia he left a sad wake of scandal behind him. Thus the quandary for smaller schools wishing to gain national attention for athletic success: an unscrupulous coach can bring wins and revenue but can sully a school's reputation to do it. And by the time the repercussions are felt the coach is off to another high-paying gig.

We have little trouble believing there could have been widespread favoritism for high-profile athletes at Ohio State because the problem is endemic among big-time programs in general. A number of other schools have been or are under investigation for the same troubles as OSU, indicating this is the standard operating procedure on the road to championships. The same day Clarett was suspended for the season for accepting illicit benefits and then lying about it, the NCAA put Fresno State's athletic program on probation for academic fraud and recruiting violations.[14] At Fresno State a team statistician wrote seventeen papers for three players who were enrolled in correspondence courses at the University of Southern Colorado, in a blatant attempt to keep the athletes eligible. The statistician, Steven Mintz, was paid $1,500, with much of the money coming from an agent who wanted to represent the players when they left college for the NBA.[15]

It's not just the repeated accusations of recruiting violations and academic fraud that make us inclined to believe kids like Clarett and scoff at the pronouncements of innocence from athletic department officials. At the core of the problem is the win-at-all-costs mentality of college coaches. Given that most coaches in high-profile sports have to win to keep their jobs, many will find it difficult to take the high road. As Rick Telander explained in *The Hundred Yard Lie*, "College coaches have less security than anyone else on campus. They have no tenure and no union.

Imagine if you can, the chairman of the university math department getting fired after having a 'bad year.' "Just what is a 'bad year' at a university, anyway?"[16] Former University of Florida Basketball coach Norm Sloan, who resigned in 1989 in the wake of recruiting violations, explained how the same techniques are recycled over time: "As a college player, I accepted cash from my coach. As a college coach I gave cash to my players."[17] Ian O'Connor of the *Cincinnati Enquirer* warns parents not to let their sons grow up to play Division I athletics, as coaches, "Often major in self-gratification and minor in youth corruption services."[18] Several have been fired or even prosecuted in recent years for serious violations involving sex, which we will discuss in Chapter 7, but even more have engaged in some type of recruiting or academic scandal. And, while it may seem like many are getting caught, there are probably many more who cheat but never get caught, as those who know about the cheating are often the beneficiaries. And because junior staffers handle most of the orders in big-time programs, it is often difficult to piece together a paper trail implicating a head coach in recruiting or academic fraud.[19]

It is not difficult to see why an athlete might accept cash or other gifts to attend a school or why a coach might offer it, but why would an athletic director cheat? Perhaps it's because "Now, it ain't cheatin' even if you do get caught. Cheatin' is just part of doing business."[20] Or, if he or she is not directly involved in anything nefarious, why not exercise greater oversight of your charges to ensure they are not? It is likely because failing to see and stop cheating can be highly profitable for all involved. School administrators and athletic directors don't inquire because football and basketball are a major source of income. For instance, Ohio State made approximately $38 million in their national title run. They also got a surge in donations.[21]

As we documented with doping and other forms of cheating, recruiting violations and academic fraud are not unique to today's sporting arena. In 1929 the Carnegie Foundation documented multiple cases of grade tampering and illegal payments to athletes. Twenty-five years later, West Point was at the center of the scandal, with a number of athletes expelled for cheating on exams.[22] Wilt Chamberlain admitted being paid $20,000 to play for the University of Kansas in the 1950s.[23]

The 1980s saw the real surge in academic fraud. University of New Haven professor, Allen L. Sack, conducted a study of improper payments in 1989. Thirty-one percent of the 1,182 active and former NFL players who responded admitted accepting improper payments during their college careers, and 53 percent saw absolutely nothing wrong with doing so.[24] After winning the 1981 football national title, Clemson was charged with sixty-nine counts of cheating, mostly in the form of payment to athletes.[25]

In 1987, Southern Methodist University (SMU) in Dallas was barred from football competition for paying student athletes and eventually received "the death penalty," a complete shutdown of the football team indefinitely.[26] Eight freshman from the stellar 1983 recruiting class (out of twenty-two) admitted having been promised monthly salaries of up to $750.[27] The school had been sanctioned for fifty rules violations in 1985, but continued to pay thirteen players.[28] The roots of the scandal ran deep; in 1987 Texas governor William Clements, who was former head of the school's board of trustees, confessed to personally approving cash payments to players in 1985, *after* the NCAA sanctions.[29] Said one athletic director, "Illegal payments to college athletes have been so common that kids come in here knowing the going rate. They come in expecting what the market will bear."[30] Football was reintroduced at SMU 2 years after the death penalty was given, but has never had the same level of success.

From 1973 to 1988, Oklahoma football coach Barry Switzer oversaw, or failed to oversee, some of the all-time worst violations of both NCAA regulations and criminal sanctions ever documented. The Sooners were placed on a 3-year probation for "major violations," including offering cash and cars to recruits and providing players with airline tickets. Former Sooner quarterback Charles Taylor described the culture of Oklahoma football in his book, *Down and Dirty: The Life and Crimes of Oklahoma Football*. He told of older players teaching the freshman about "freaking." Freaking had a double meaning: it referred to looking for women as well as dealing with boosters and alumni who courted the players. "Freaking with boosters and alumni meant they showered you with gifts and money, and sometimes drugs."[31] He said he had dozens of business cards from boosters willing to do whatever he needed if he called. One booster arranged for a girl he was dating to fly to the 1987 Orange Bowl in Miami. Players made a lot of money in Miami too, scalping their complimentary game tickets.[32] Taylor also detailed the academic fraud that was widespread at Oklahoma. One instructor volunteered to allow Taylor to complete only half of the required assignments, because he was so busy with practice. Switzer was well aware of most, if not all, the indiscretions. Switzer provided beer and booze for the team on a regular basis and was frequently drunk himself. According to Taylor, "our role models—Switzer, alumni, and boosters—were not only indulging us with money and gifts, but were showing us a side of their lives that said: this is what successful people do—drink, do drugs, and cheat. I knew right from wrong, but I saw very little right being done."[33]

Recruiting and academic fraud were the least of the Sooners' problems, though. Bud Hall, the dormitory where most of the football team lived, might as well have been an armory so many of the players had weapons in it. It was in Bud Hall that player Jerry Parks shot teammate Zarak Peters in a meaningless squabble. Taylor described fairly regular sexual assaults taking place in the dorm as well. Taylor himself was selling cocaine from the residence hall. When word got out about the felony spree the players were on, Oklahoma Governor Henry Bellmon condemned the players, but claimed the university had no responsibility. He even praised and expressed his confidence in Barry Switzer.[34]

The Sooners were threatened with the death penalty if they didn't clean it up. Switzer has claimed, "I didn't create the monster . . . my job was to feed the monster."[35] His comments are in reference to the importance Oklahomans give to Sooner football, but are indicative of his attitude. He fed the monster whatever it wanted to get the wins—regardless of whether that "diet" was ethical or even legal. And, because Switzer was winning, things did not get addressed until they were completely out of control.

In Switzer's tenure at Oklahoma his team amassed a 157–29–4 record and won three national titles.[36] He went on to coach the Dallas Cowboys, also referred to as the Dallas Criminals. In pondering "unfortunate events" of the last century, ESPN included the Sooners and Cowboys under Switzer in the category titled "police blotter." Switzer himself enjoyed some time in the company of law enforcement; he was fined $3,500 and required to complete 80 hours of community service after pleading guilty to a misdemeanor weapon charge. Switzer was caught trying to board a plane with a Smith and Wesson .38 in his bag.[37]

Buying wins continued through the 1990s. Ed Martin, a retired electrician from Detroit, paid $616,000 to University of Michigan basketball players Chris Webber, Louis Bullock, and Maurice Taylor. Head coach Steve Fisher resigned in the brouhaha. At the University of California at Berkeley, basketball coach Todd Bozeman resigned in 1996 after admitting he paid $30,000 to the parents of star point guard Jelani Gardner, who was not even aware of the payout.[38]

The mid-1990s saw Baylor University basketball running amok to secure top recruits. A federal jury indicted the head basketball coach and three assistants, as well as two junior college coaches and two junior college administrators for federal mail fraud, wire fraud, and conspiracy. Essentially, folks at Baylor used a fax to supply an athlete with a paper to submit for credit at his community college. Baylor coaches then got snagged for telling a player to take a correspondence course from Southeastern College of the Assemblies of God because they had the final exam. Finally, Baylor officials accepted a fraudulent transcript that an administrator at Shelton State Community College helped doctor up for a would-be Baylor player.[39]

Although recruiting violations and academic fraud is old hat to some programs, what has changed is the greater stakes for both players and coaches. Coaches now make enormous salaries, but know they have little job security if they don't win. This is virtually a recipe for cheating, as some will do whatever shady thing they can to ensure the wins. It is pretty common for a school's football or basketball coach to make more than the university president. Steve Spurrier reportedly made $2 million a year as football coach at the University of Florida when you include other benefits and radio and television contracts.[40] He was the highest paid public employee in the state of Florida and he helped usher in the era of multimillion-dollar coaching contracts. Today, there are a number of coaches making this type of money and even coaches at second-tier schools often command total compensation packages of $500,000. In addition to the desire to keep their big-time salaries, the emphasis on being visible leads some to do whatever it takes to get their moment (or more) of fame. "Cheating to recruit the players necessary to win . . . makes the team more attractive as a television commodity."[41] This, in turn, helps generate revenue, feeds the university coffers, justifies coaches' salaries, draws more recruits, and contributes to the need to cheat to win for all schools.

It is impossible to overemphasize the importance of winning in big-time college sports, as Notre Dame's firing of football coach Tyrone Willingham demonstrates. Despite success in every area that should matter in college sports, Notre Dame let him go because it did not appear the team was headed for a national title run. Never mind that Willingham had only served 3 years of a 5-year contract. In announcing the firing, athletics director Kevin White proclaimed, "He personally has displayed impeccable integrity and tremendous character. His players have represented themselves, off the field, in a first-class manner. In addition, our football program under his watch never has been stronger in terms of academic performance."[42] Couple these compliments with the fact that the team beat several top-ranked foes, including Michigan and Tennessee, and had qualified for a bowl game, and you would think Willingham should be in line for a contract extension, not a dismissal. But alas, in the win-at-all-costs era, even Notre Dame foregoes its honorable tradition and makes winning all that matters. And coaches everywhere shudder and know that a recruiting "incentive" here and a paper written for a player there might just be the cost of doing business.

Despite repeated criminal offenses, Sam Mack was recruited to play basketball for four different schools in 5 years in the early 1990s. "Like a hotel guest, he checked in, played ball, and checked out when trouble arose."[43] During those 5 years Mack was investigated for a felony sexual assault, was charged with four felonies and three misdemeanors, shot by police officers during an armed robbery of a Burger King (he was acquitted, largely due to the influence of Iowa State basketball coach Johnny Orr, who testified on his behalf), and convicted of theft and forgery. When he left Iowa State after the Burger King shootout, he transferred to Tyler Junior College, where he dominated on the court. After his stellar season there, the University of Houston was happy to pick Mack up, regardless of his felonious history.[44]

Much of the rhetoric from coaches when they recruit known criminals is that the kid deserves a second chance and the team is going to help the kid be a better person, which is good for society. This line of thinking is more smoke and mirrors than substance. Many coaches recruit kids who can play, almost without concern for the baggage they bring and positioning the school as societal savior is bunk. If the kid can excel on the court or field, he will get more chances than we can count. If he is bench fodder, he'll get canned faster than he can run the 40-yard dash.

Case in point: University of Miami football player Willie Williams, who had more than ten arrests on his record when he was accepted to the school in 2004. The university claimed they were stepping back from Williams and delayed his application after his record came to light and the school suffered embarrassment for even considering him. What they really did was wait out the media frenzy and then usher him in later. To make matters worse, some of Williams' crimes were committed while on a recruiting trip to the University of Florida. He was charged with a felony (malicious damage to fire extinguishers) and misdemeanors of criminal mischief and battery from that trip. As the digging into his past commenced, a charge for stealing stereo equipment was found, as well as nine other arrests on his juvenile record going back to when he was 14 years old.[45]

So why would Miami admit Williams? Simple. He can play. According to their own Web site, Williams was widely regarded as the top prospect at his position in the country. He was a hard hitter, had exceptional speed, and was unblockable as a prep athlete. And so his all-American status trumps his all-Jailhouse record, and his application to the university is given the green light.

Proposition 48

In the college ranks, NCAA changes like Proposition 48 have also played a tremendous role in upping the ante for cheats. The NCAA uses a sliding scale to determine initial eligibility, so now a high school student with a 2.0 grade point average who wishes to be eligible must achieve a 1,010 on the SAT or a 21 on the ACT. Ed Lupomech, who investigates cases of testing fraud for the NCAA, explained, "As the bar gets higher, the number of cases gets higher too."[46] The director of the NCAA initial-eligibility clearinghouse, Calvin Symons, believes test scores of athletes are being challenged at a rate three times that of nonathletes.[47]

In basketball, there is the additional problem of high school students going directly to the NBA, which makes it difficult to sell some "blue chip" players on jumping through the NCAA's hoops, or maybe even sitting out a season prior to being eligible.[48] As we write, the Florida High School Athletic Association and the NCAA are investigating "diploma mill" high schools. In November 2005, a *New York Times* article described a south Florida correspondence academy, University High School, which catered to athletes needing a grade boost to become eligible to play college sports. University School is every student's dream: there are no teachers, no textbooks, and not even any classrooms. The method of instruction was for students to read packets of information and answer corresponding questions. According to the *Times,* fourteen Miami-area athletes had graduated from the school in a matter of weeks.[49] Certainly, a good part of the ownership for the fraud that likely took place at University school lies with the owner, a man who was charged with marijuana possession and is currently wanted on a bench warrant.[50] The founder of the school, who sold it last year to the current owner, once served a 10-month sentence for . . . surprise, running a diploma mill in Arizona.[51] Yet, responsibility also lies with the college teams who recruited these athletes with their obviously questionable transcripts. Florida State University, the University of Central Florida, University of South Florida, and the University of Florida were among eleven universities that signed students from this particular diploma mill.[52]

JUCO Too!

The problems of cheating and academic fraud that pervade big-time college sports also exist at the community college level. Former Barton County Community College basketball coach Ryan Wolf was indicted in December 2004 by a federal grand jury on 36 counts of embezzlement and fraud. Allegedly, Wolf used his position at Barton to provide illegal financial assistance and false academic credentials to at least six athletes. Five of the counts related to actions Wolf took for Ricky Clemons, who went on to notoriety at the University of Missouri for a number of criminal and NCAA violations. Allegedly, Wolf paid for some of Clemons' classes on his credit card. Wolf's wife was also involved, as she is alleged to have "fixed" Clemons' papers. Wolf also arranged for another coach to attest that Clemons' took tests, but then told the person not to bother actually witnessing the test taking. Wolf also allegedly misappropriated $120,000 in funds, including Pell grants, work-study monies, and other federal student loans.[53]

Eligibility

It's not over when the players have signed on to the team; keeping them eligible remains a concern. Here too the pressure on coaches is immense—not necessarily to help the athletes get degrees, but to ensure they help the team on the field or court. We are not suggesting that coaches do not care about their athletes. That is probably far too simplistic and not true of most. But we are arguing that coaches often see student athletes as athletes first, then students, if time permits. Nor are we assuming all athletes are dumb jocks who need assistance to remain eligible. We were both student-athletes who had no trouble in the classroom and who obtained our degrees within the normal timeframe, as did most of our athlete friends. Our concern is that, too often, the athlete in a big-time program who wants to achieve academically is on his or her own to do it. Laura knows several football players at a Division I school who were encouraged to take easy courses rather than courses in their degree programs. Some of these students knew they were getting poor advice and registered for the courses that would be most helpful to them regardless of the mumbo jumbo being offered by academic advisors in the athletic department. But many others were unaware that taking Coaching of Basketball II might not contribute to their degree in history and simply did what they were advised to, only to find themselves scrambling to find summer courses to complete their degree.

Coaches are not hired or evaluated based on their commitment to education. Simply, they are hired based on their ability to win and to generate money.[54] Because they need to continue to justify their place in the educational setting, coaches and athletic administrators keep pushing the farce that what they do has educational value.[55] But, in reality, "they don't need well-rounded, erudite student-athletes who can converse on any subject; they need players who can knock your hat off. They need winners. It is not in their best interests for their players to go to class or even read the papers, except as needed to keep them eligible..."[56] As associate commissioner of the SEC in 1992, John Gerdy sat in on a meeting of the conference athletic directors. He was there to review NCAA proposals to increase academic standards for athletes. Exemplifying the attitude held by many in athletic administration, he witnessed one athletic director say, "Hey, this is an athletic conference. We've got to be careful that we don't get lost in all of this academic stuff." Two other ADs at the meeting concurred.[57]

Because the NCAA rules allow a football player who starts a season eligible to remain so until the next grade check at the end of the semester, players don't have to step into the hallowed halls too frequently if they think they can pass without doing so,[58] or if they think a failing grade will simply disappear. In a 1993 survey, only 5 percent of student-athletes said their coaches encouraged them to do more academically than the minimum needed to stay eligible.[59]

Passing Classes

Because passing classes is difficult for many students, not just athletes, shocking numbers resort to cheating. A 1999 poll found 75 percent of college students admit cheating at least once.[60] One way is to have someone else do the work for you. The University of Missouri was recently forced to deal with the fallout of academic cheating that didn't even occur on its campus. The school agreed to name a newly constructed facility "Paige Sports Arena" in a deal that secured a $25 million donation. Paige Laurie, for whom the building was named, is a granddaughter of a founder of Wal-Mart, and her parents made the incredible donation. Paige Laurie never attended Missouri. She attended, and even graduated from USC. She did not, however, actually do her own work while there. Her roommate during their freshman year, Elena Martinez, says Laurie paid her to do the coursework she was unable to do while she partied with celebrities. Martinez claims she was paid about $20,000 over 3½ years.[61] In response to these allegations, the University of Missouri quickly changed the name of the facility to Mizzou Arena.

Having someone else do your work is the method of choice for many athletes who cheat. In September 2004, Ken McFadden, the all-time leading scorer in Cleveland State University basketball history and a former employee of the school's athletic department, claimed a member of the athletic department staff wrote, and continues to write, papers for players. McFadden claims Chris Sedlock, an associate athletic director, wrote the papers, and that many people knew what was going on, including then athletic director, John Konstantinos. An anonymous tipster had already called the NCAA, who investigated CSU for academic fraud.[62]

Boosters

Sometimes it is not the athletic program itself but "boosters" or "donors" who conjure up and implement these cheating schemes. Sometimes they do so with the knowledge but not assistance of anyone involved in athletics at a given school, while other times they take it completely solo. Some anonymous source from Michigan requested $2,500 from both UNLV coach Jerry Tarkanian and then Michigan coach Bill Frieder in the early 1990s. The sum was to be payment for fixing test scores for star recruits. Both coaches claim they told the caller to get lost.[63] However, given the number of borderline students who possess tremendous athletic ability, it is certain that some coaches are taking advantage of such "services."

In 1995, Glenda Rush was amazed to see her 17-year-old son, Jaron, pull up to their South Kansas City home in a brand new GEO Tracker, which retailed for approximately $17,000. Jaron told his mother "someone" bought it for him. That "someone" turned out to be Tom Grant, a 46-year-old Kansas City millionaire and University of Kansas booster. Grant had taken an interest in Jaron when he was eleven, paying his $10,000 yearly tuition at an exclusive private school, inviting him to dinners at his mansion, and doting on him with grandiose gifts and vacations, including a trip to the Cayman Islands and a chance to meet NBA superstar Michael Jordan. Grant spent up to $300 per week on Jaron. Grant claims he disclosed all his expenditures for Jaron in a letter to the NCAA. Yet Grant obviously knew he might be committing NCAA violations and was potentially jeopardizing Jaron's eligibility, as he discussed the issue with the Rushes in 1997. Jaron did initially sign a letter of intent to attend KU, but because he was under eighteen the letter required his mother's signature. She refused. Although the NCAA does not have to make their findings public so it is not clear exactly what happened, it seems that Grant's gifts to Jaron were considered to have given the Jayhawks an unfair recruiting advantage. Because he was not actually committed, Jaron was still eligible, just not at KU. Jaron Rush ended up playing at UCLA, his second choice.[64]

As we write this book a court is hearing testimony about the illegal deeds of University of Alabama booster Logan Young. Lynn Lang, a former high school coach allegedly sold one of his players, Albert Means, to the Crimson Tide. Must be they were the highest bidder, as Lang testified that seven schools made offers to pay for Means' skills on the football field. Young also helped Means be eligible to play by arranging for a former athlete of his to take the ACT for Means.[65] On February 2, 2005, Young was convicted of conspiracy to commit racketeering by breaking state bribery laws, crossing state lines to commit racketeering, and arranging bank withdrawals to cover up a crime. The charges carry a maximum sentence of 15 years, Young was sentenced in June, 2005 to six months in prison, six months of home confinement, and then two years of supervision for his convictions on Money Laundering and Racketeering Conspiracy. He was free, pending appeal, when his body was found in April, 2006. Investigations into his death are still underway.[66]

Colluding with the Cheats

Students sometimes help athletes cheat without direct influence from anyone in the athletic department. One player who allegedly cheated on the ACT (his score suddenly jumped to 21 after he had racked up five scores in the 12–15 range) said, "I had people coming up to me, telling me they'd help me. Not coaches, but students in general. They just wanted to say they helped Terrance Roberson and feel privileged and stuff."[67] Roberson was forced to sit out the 1995–1996 season, but still claims he did not cheat.

A former tutor for the University of Minnesota claimed to have written some 400 papers for men's basketball players between 1993 and 1998.[68] According to

Murray Sperber, author of *Beer and Circus*, three Minnesota tutors, "encouraged and rewarded by athletic department officials, brazenly composed whole papers and answered take-home exams for many basketball players, sometimes on subjects about which the athletes knew nothing, and in polished prose that some of the academically challenged jocks were incapable of writing."[69] Sperber surveyed 1,906 college students and found amazing numbers who would help an athlete cheat. Students at schools with Division I sports were most supportive; 59 percent said sure, they'd help an athlete cheat. Even if they would not help the athlete cheat, 84 percent said they would not turn him or her in. In explaining their rationale, students said things like, "I'd help. It's not hurting me."[70]

The Chain of Command

In some cases, the stench of cheating rises all the way to the top. St. Bonaventure's trustees forced the resignation of President Robert J. Wickenheiser in 2003. Wickenheiser oversaw the transfer of a junior college athlete who clearly lacked the requisite credentials for eligibility to play NCAA Division I basketball. The athlete, Jamil Terrell, had only a welding certificate from Coastal Georgia Community College, not the associate's degree required by the NCAA for Junior College transfers.[71] But who cares, if he can help the team? Other schools who had passed up on Terrell because of the transfer issue got suspicious, as his coach at Coastal Georgia was very upfront about Terrell's academic qualifications. Evidently Wickenheiser went to great lengths for Terrell, sidestepping the recommendations of the school's compliance officer to get Terrell admitted and later changing his grades to keep him on the floor.[72] Athletic Director Gothard Lane was allowed to complete the school year but the board of trustees did not renew his contract.[73] Coach Jan van Breda Kolff's contract extends through 2006–2007. He could be fired, but the school would be forced to pay his salary, about $220,000 per year, for the remainder of that contract unless the NCAA finds him guilty of rules violations. That investigation, however, may take months or even years. Clearly Wickenheiser and van Breda Kolff figured they would never get caught. While the NCAA's Initial-Eligibility Clearinghouse must check high school seniors for academic eligibility, there is no such screening process for transfers. Universities are expected to police themselves.[74] Nor was this an isolated instance. It was evidently quite common for van Breda Kolff or assistant coach Kort Wickenheiser (the president's kid) to go to the president to assert a player's eligibility.[75]

Those in the academic community who protest this type of cheating generally meet with little success. In 1981, Jan Kemp, a remedial English instructor at the University of Georgia, realized that school officials had changed the failing grades of nine of her students. Wouldn't you know, all nine were on the football team and needed the passing grade to remain eligible and to play in the upcoming Sugar Bowl? Kemp was demoted. Fortunately, she eventually won a $2.5 million settlement.[76] One Minnesota professor who suspected academic fraud was told the university would not investigate. He ended up succumbing, and gave the paper in question and the player a passing grade.[77] Later it was found that the professor's allegations were true, but the university still claimed it was an isolated incident, not a systemic problem.

Linda Bensel-Meyers received hundreds of offensive and threatening e-mails when she went public in 1999 with her suspicions of academic fraud at the University of Tennessee. Bensel-Meyers was an English professor and coordinator of tutors at the university and was highly regarded in her field. According to the University of Tennessee Faculty Senate, she "... consistently upheld the highest ideals of the profession, including excellence in teaching, advancement of knowledge, and academic integrity."[78] However, to the fans of the Volunteers, she was a traitor and a snitch. People simply did not take too kindly to Bensel-Meyers' allegations that players for the 1998 national champion football team were steered toward easy courses, had low grades changed, were allowed to delay declaring their majors, and had tutors write papers for them. The goal of the institution, according to Bensel-Meyers, was obvious: Keep the athletes eligible to play before the 108,000 spectators.[79]

The NCAA declined to investigate and turned over the investigation to the university. Shockingly, no evidence of wrongdoing was found and no changes to academic protocols were made. Well, there was one change . . . they did tighten up faculty access to student records making it more difficult for anyone to keep tabs on how frequently football players had "incompletes" and low grades changed to passing or higher grades. While at Tennessee, Bensel-Meyers received dirty phone calls and noticed her papers had been rifled through. She suspected her phone was tapped and her computer files were tampered with. She knew that if NCAA violations were ever found people would blame her. In the end, she learned a powerful lesson: "Their concern is keeping them eligible. Keeping them eligible is quite different from keeping them educated."[80] Bensel-Meyers left Tennessee for Denver University after having received so much hate mail that she had to ask the FBI for protection.[81]

As a professor, Laura experienced the lack of support for professors who catch players cheating. When she received duplicate take-home tests from two football players at a Division I university, she was encouraged to take minimal sanctions. Rather than flunk them for the entire course, as would likely happen to other students, she was told simply to fail them on this assignment, as their academic advisor would speak to them and make sure they "learned their lesson." In another example at the same school, Laura was asked by a player who received a good grade, a B, to change the grade to an A so he could remain eligible. Laura refused. Either another professor gave in or someone pulled strings and changed the grade, because the athlete was indeed on the field the next season.

Another facet of this problem, according to Sperber, is that local media sources are often loath to out cheating by athletic teams, because "most college towns have only a single daily newspaper, resting snugly in the local athletic department's pocket, and the paper refuses to investigate the U's college sports program or listen to tutors brave or foolhardy enough to come forward."[82]

TURNING THINGS AROUND

Why Doesn't the NCAA Do More?

The problem in enforcing the rules regarding recruiting and academic standards is that the NCAA is both "policeman and promoter of college athletics."[83] According to sports writer Ted Miller, "Rules enforcement is about 76th on a list of priorities for a cartel that will absorb more than half a billion dollars in revenue this year."[84] Some say the NCAA simply cannot contain this problem. William Reed of *Sports Illustrated* issued a scathing indictment of college basketball. His comments are just as applicable to football. "Every fan knows that underneath its shiny veneer of color, fun and excitement, college basketball is a sewer full of rats. Lift the manhole cover on the street of gold, and the odor will knock you down . . . And the NCAA is powerless to stop it. Make a statement by coming down hard on a Kentucky or Maryland, and what happens? Nothing, really. The filth merely oozes from another crack."[85] Miller agrees, asserting that OSU will get off easy, because,

egregious violations cases at Missouri, Georgia, and Mississippi State recently resulted in a stern look and 100 lashes with a Nerf whip. All three basically broke every NCAA rule in the book, not to mention commonsensical standards of integrity, but instead of sanctions that would cripple their programs for years—multiyear postseason bans and double-digit losses of scholarships—their penalties were just north of symbolic.[86]

Reform Attempts

A group of professors who call themselves the Coalition for Intercollegiate Athletics has proposed a plan they think will help reduce academic fraud. This group, founded in 2002, includes faculty from forty-four Division I-A colleges. One part of their plan involves having individual colleges track which courses athletes are taking, as well as their grades in those courses.[87] Another change they propose would involve who speaks to instructors about athletes' grades. Currently, coaches at most schools can go directly to instructors, whom they often intimidate (sometimes not intentionally, and often with great intent). The proposal would have academic advisors approach instructors.[88]

The NCAA has approved the Academic Progress Rate (APR) plan, which establishes minimum graduation rates that all Division I teams in every sport must attain beginning in 2005–2006. Failure to meet the standards will result in scholarship reductions. The rate is based roughly on a 50 percent graduation rate over a 5-year period. Schools received a warning in early 2005 if any of their teams fell below the standard.[89] While this plan sounds like a positive step toward increasing academic accountability, we are unconvinced. Given the threat of losing scholarships for low graduation rates, schools can take one of two approaches. They can recruit better students, encourage them to go to class and study hard, and reduce practice and travel time to afford more time for studies. Or they can recruit great athletes regardless of academic ability, put them in "easier" majors with professors who are friendly to the program, and then provide "tutors" who are willing to "go the extra mile" to keep the athletes eligible. In a climate that makes winning paramount in the drive to generate revenue and secure gifts from boosters, we believe the choice is obvious. And, this is the same NCAA that fought tooth and nail against making public the graduation rates of student-athletes, so we aren't convinced that true reform is on their minds.[90]

Sometimes schools will impose penalties on themselves, in the hope that this will satisfy the NCAA. Often this is nothing more than an effort to prevent the NCAA from finding out about even greater problems. The University of Michigan self-imposed sanctions for the booster-payment-to-athletes scandal of the 1990s. They removed championship banners, forfeited nearly seven seasons of victories, and did not allow the team to play in the 2002–2003 NCAA or NIT tournaments. In this case the NCAA took it farther, placing U of M on 3½ years probation and docking them one scholarship for four seasons, starting in 2004–2005.[91]

In December 2004, St. John's announced it would penalize itself for academic fraud, financial aid fraud, and admissions and ticket violations involving their basketball team. Former player Abe Keita said he received $300 per month from a member of the basketball staff. The school has placed the team on probation for 2 years, will forego a basketball scholarship for each of the next 2 years, did not engage in post-season play during the 2004–2005 season, and will return some of the money earned from the 2002 NCAA and 2003 NIT tournaments. Critics have contended St. John's is only admitting to a fraction of the violations they committed. The NCAA is continuing to investigate.[92] The University of Georgia tried the same thing with great success. In 2003, the university yanked the men's basketball team from the SEC and NCAA tournaments after an internal investigation substantiated charges against head coach Jim Harrick and his son, Jim Harrick Jr.

The Broken Filter

Even when someone is caught and disciplined for some type of academic fraud, that person is generally able to bounce right back with his or her career plans. John Gerdy, author of *Sports: The All-American Addiction*, calls athletics an "incestuous culture" where obedience, conformity, and a good ol' boy attitude work best.[93] Jerry Tarkanian, for example, was given multiple chances, despite the fact that two of the three teams he coached were on probation multiple times.[94] Similarly, Jim Harrick was able to move from UCLA to Rhode Island to Georgia, in spite of the trailing stench of cheating, because he has proven he can deliver wins that generate revenue and exposure.

The NCAA also has to be careful they can actually prove a coach or athletic director's involvement in anything shady. If not, they open themselves up to lawsuits. Suits by Jerry Tarkanian and Rick Neuheisel dragged the organization through the mud. Tarkanian sued the NCAA for unfairly targeting him as basketball coach at UNLV. His case was tied up in court throughout most of the 1990s. As with the claims of innocence coming from OSU, many doubt Tark's claim that, "In 37 years of coaching, I've never had a case of academic fraud." The NCAA did agree to pay him $2.5 million, however.

Neuheisel was cleared in October 2004 of any wrongdoing associated with his gambling on the NCAA basketball tournament while football coach at the University of Washington. The school remains on probation, however, for recruiting violations in basketball and for failing to monitor the football team. The football team under Neuheisel was cited by the NCAA for undercharging recruits and their parents for rides on a 65-foot yacht and other private boats, and for allowing contact between a football booster and recruits.[95] In June 2003, Neuheisel was fired from the University of Washington. He filed a wrongful dismissal suit, which was settled in March 2005—Neuheisel will collect $4.5 million. The NCAA must pay him $2.5 million in cash, while the University of Washington is required to pay $500,000. The university has also agreed not to seek repayment for a $1.5 million loan.[96] Clearly the length of the process, as well as the fact that Neuheisel prevailed, might discourage universities from sanctioning coaches without darn good evidence.

Ultimately, college sports are high-stakes and many are willing to sacrifice integrity to win, or sometimes even just to be better than the previous year. As Ted Miller explains, "Fans would rather win a championship and later get busted for cheating than finish 8–4 or 9–3 every year with an upright program of student-athletes. Media rants about the hypocrisy of college sports no longer raise hackles; they're just part of the background noise, like a 13-year-old dropping F-bombs in public places."[97]

chapter 6

Hazing

Are you in a make-work program to find something to write about?
—Mike, in an e-mail to Hank Nuwer regarding his goal to stop hazing.

Hank Nuwer, who has written extensively on hazing, defines it as follows: "When veteran members of a class or group require newcomers to endure demeaning or dangerous or silly rituals, or to give up status temporarily, with the expectation of gaining group status and acceptance into the group, as a result of their participation."[1] There are two types of hazing: physical hazing is the sort that can do bodily damage, while mental hazing refers to situations where those being victimized are forced to do embarrassing or silly things. The two often overlap, with mental hazing escalating to physical hazing.[2]

People tend to think hazing involves only silly pranks, generally alcohol-induced. Think *Animal House.* Laura recalls being hazed, although she wouldn't have given it that label at the time. The women's cross country team at Western Michigan University had a tradition of requiring rookies to drink excessively and do stupid things on a scavenger hunt around town. The alcohol was pleasantly served from an upperclasswoman's running shoe. While not terribly painful and relatively good-natured, the event was hardly required for team bonding, as defenders of hazing often assert. The team bonded far better on bus trips to meets than we did as drunken fools running around town wearing men's underwear over our jeans.

In reality, many incidents of hazing are far more serious. According to Michelle Finkel, an emergency room physician who often treats college students, hazing victims have been brought in with irreversible intracranial damage, blunt abdominal organ damage, third-degree burns, heat stroke, and suffocation, among other physical ailments. She also compares the emotional consequences she sees in hazing victims to that of survivors of domestic violence.[3] Victims who experience hazing that is sexual in nature may be physically and emotionally damaged in the same ways victims of nonhazing sexual assaults are.[4] Far from fun and games, then, hazing is a power trip that can leave significant physical and emotional scars.

Hazing has a long history in the United States, and an even longer one elsewhere. The practice came to the United States with the Europeans, where members of the aristocracy practiced "fagging" in prep schools. Fagging was defined as "the right exercised by the older boy to make the younger do what he likes, and what the younger one generally dislikes."[5] The claim was that it was human nature for boys to behave horribly at times, much like the modern "boys will be boys" mentality. Early instances of hazing tended not to end well; in 1914, a hazing victim shot and killed his hazer at Saint John's Military College in Maryland, while a University of South Carolina student was savagely beaten twice 2 years later—once as part of an initiation and the second time for reporting it.[6]

WHO DOES IT AND WHY

Hazing happens in many different settings—the military, fraternities, and athletic teams are three institutions that specialize in it, but it occurs elsewhere. An 18-year-old ambulance driver died from a booze binge her male employees forced upon her as initiation into the job.[7] Unfortunately, too often hazing is viewed as an inevitable part of attaining group membership and thus is not scrutinized to the degree it should be. Hank Nuwer explains, "Hazing is an extraordinary activity that, when it occurs often enough, becomes perversely ordinary as those who engage in it grow desensitized to its inhumanity."[8] The common feature among all groups that haze is a structure that stresses conformity and plays up on people's desire to belong. Hazing in athletics does tend to differ from fraternity or military hazing in that it typically involves one night of activities, rather than the ongoing ones typical of the pledge period.[9] So rather than daily acts of mortification, sports-related hazing generally requires only one night of tomfoolery. This may indeed serve to up the stakes, however, as the hazers may go to extremes to get as much bang for their buck as possible. Hazing is typically intended as an initiation, and thus victims are most likely rookies. It is assumed the rookie is a naïve rube, and one in need of the "guidance" of upperclassmen. According to Nuwer, "Traditionally, rookies have been treated as untutored and unimportant members of the team who deserve the ill treatment of wily veterans."[10]

Hazing is about groupthink, the term coined by psychologist Irving Janus to explain why humans can act so differently in groups than they do individually. As individuals, most people are well aware that publicly placing food items in the buttocks of another human is both revolting and morally corrupt. It is not even something they would consider doing. But, when that same person is with a group and is told that doing so is required for group acceptance, many will forego their moral integrity. Thus hazing is not the domain of sociopaths but of so-called "normal" individuals.[11] Even our current president was involved in hazing while at Yale.[12]

Hazing is a way for groups to attain new members they feel will value that membership the most, having had to "suffer" to attain it. In groups like fraternities, military academies, and sports teams, an important part of learning comes from observation of and mentoring by senior members. Being a quick study is obviously advantageous in regard to receiving playing time; it is also useful to show you are willing and able to comply with the demands of hazers. The quicker the rookie learns to follow the party line, the faster the hazing generally stops.[13] Here's an example: a friend involved in the shoe-drinking initiation at WMU quickly demonstrated she was willing to chug more beer than anyone else and was rowdier and defined as "more fun," than any of the rest of us. The pressure was off her to demonstrate her drinking abilities, and she was easily considered the "coolest" new runner. This garnered her invites to parties as well as partners on daily runs.

In the middle ages, university students who hazed considered themselves part of a "culture of honor."[14] It is difficult to see the honor in dousing teammates in pig intestines or in sodomizing a hog-tied player. Hazing is ultimately about identifying the "in" and "out" groups. In identifying those who are most like them, groups can maintain the status quo. In other words, all the problems already discussed in this book are likely to be continued if a group selects and "initiates" only those who they see as most likely to hold the party line. According to Nuwer, "Members willing to gain acceptance through hazing may be logically a little less likely to change the old organization the senior members know and love."[15] Surviving some type of hazing makes recipients feel invulnerable.[16]

Part of the explanation for hazing lies in the lack of formal rituals or rites of passage that mark the transition to adulthood. Young people turn to cliques for their rituals, such as fraternities, clubs, and sports teams.[17] In a culture that promotes conformity, it is difficult for many students to resist the pressure from teammates or friends to follow along. Nowhere is the push for conformity greater than in the average public school. Educators in the 1800s even encouraged hazing as a way of quashing individuality.[18] Some still argue that a little hazing is okay if it can keep everyone in line and help them maintain "school spirit." Universities also place a high value on loyalty. Not only do athletes endure hazing to be loyal to their team, but also to their school.[19] So those who refuse to be hazed may feel a double burden; not only have they let their teammates down, but they are also not even worthy of Big-Time U's good name.

Some have suggested that because sports is one of the last "preserves where primitive codes of masculinity can flourish,"[20] it is not surprising that hazing is more prevalent among male groups. Lionel Tiger, a frequent author on hazing and related topics, maintains that hazing activities often take the form of "male on male courtship," whereby males can establish status with other males.[21] In fact, some victims have even asked that they be hazed, despite a group's efforts to elim-inate the practice, because they are concerned their sexuality will be questioned.[22]

Interestingly, despite its being labeled as a way to demonstrate "toughness" in the sense most typically associated with stereotypical masculinity, hazing frequently involves partial or complete nudity, and many instances have a clear homoerotic tendency.[23] By no means are we asserting that homosexuality or homoeroticism are problems. Rather, what interests us is the contradiction between the so-called masculinity of many hazers and the means they use to demonstrate that quality. Sexual-related hazing incidents have included: forced nudity; smearing of initiate's bodies with food products; using duct or athletic tape to immobilize nude initiates; rubbing the buttocks of an older member on the naked body of an initiate; connecting a string weighted with a heavy object to a recruit's penis (as depicted in the film *Old School*); and immobilizing the victim while a stripper performs in his lap.[24]

As mentioned earlier, individuals who refuse to be hazed are generally seen as the deviant, not the reverse. One reason hazing continues year after year is that those who have had to endure it often seek and even enjoy the opportunity to visit the same torture on someone else. Somehow berating and mistreating other humans, they feel, will restore some of their own lost dignity.[25] This vendetta mentality fits well in sports, which thrives on teams getting psyched to beat their most serious rivals. Psychologists Harold H. Kelley and John W. Thibaut assert that a reciprocal rule guides much of our human behavior—that is, we tend to give back about what we get.[26] Many hazers convince themselves that what they are doing is far less severe than the hazing they endured.[27] Further, research suggests that groups tend to reward members they see as making the group better and stronger. Thus hazers may be perceived as toughening up the weaklings.[28] Rather than question their behavior, onlookers may view them as doing a greater good—readying the team for "warfare."

HIGH SCHOOL HAZING

High school sports teams and other clubs regularly haze initiates. According to researchers at Alfred University, approximately 1.5 million high school students are hazed each year, with about half of the victims being athletes.[29] Of these, almost one quarter were required to engage in substance abuse as part of the hazing. Twenty-two percent were subjected to "dangerous hazing," defined as, "any humiliating or dangerous activity expected of you to join a group, regardless of your willingness to participate."[30] Hazing is thought to be more common in competitive, contact sports, where aggression is rewarded.[31] These sports are still to be dominated by males with some, such as football and ice hockey, rarely having female participants at the high school level. Research has shown, however, that noncontact sports may have just as much hazing. What does vary is the brutality of the hazing. Jamie Bryshun, who researched hazing in Canada, explains, "The more aggressive the sport, the more aggressive the hazing. The more sanctions there are against it, the more athletes won't talk about it, the more it is being driven underground."[32] In a recent survey of high school students involved in at least one group activity,

39 percent of the females reported having been hazed and 17 percent were involved in hazing that was dangerous.[33] These statistics suggest that female hazing is on the rise, although it still occurs less frequently than male hazing. When females haze it tends to be less violent. Of the more than seventy deaths identified as hazing-related, only five have been women.[34]

High school hazing has become increasingly brutal. In 1999, a football player at McAlester (Oklahoma) High School suffered a head injury after he was jumped in the locker room. A school in California canceled their wrestling team's season after allegations that older members "probed the buttocks of younger players with a mop handle they had nicknamed Pedro."[35] In Connecticut, eight high school wrestlers were arrested for a hazing scandal. They "hog-tied" the victim with athletic tape, repeatedly stuffed him in a locker, threw him against the wall on a regular basis, and repeatedly sodomized him with a plastic knife over a 3-month time period. The 15-year-old victim was a special education student who had been counseled to join the wrestling team. Seven of the eight perpetrators were expelled from school. Three were charged as adults. They pleaded guilty to assault and conspiracy charges and were sentenced to 2 years of probation, ordered to perform 300 hours of community service, and made to reimburse the victim's family $7,500 for medical expenses. The five others were charged as juveniles and spent a week in juvenile detention.[36] Even worse, there is evidence the school's basketball and wrestling coaches saw the student hog-tied and did nothing.[37]

In 2000, five basketball players and three track and field athletes were indicted on twenty-two sexual assault and kidnapping charges from the hazing of at least ten athletes. The basketball coach was also indicted on three counts of felony and child abuse for failing to prevent the attacks despite prior knowledge they would occur. The hazing stretched over 2 months, and involved younger athletes being held down by older teammates, who pulled down their pants and stuffed markers, pencils, fingers, and other objects in their rectums. These incidents occurred in the school's pole vault pits, on school buses traveling to competitions, and in school parking lots and locker rooms. The three "ringleaders" received 9 months in jail, 2 to 3 years of probation, and community service. Two other perpetrators received 6 months in jail, and the remaining two served 2 months in jail. The incident prompted Arizona to become the 43rd state with antihazing legislation.[38]

The country was shocked by two recent instances of high school hazing. The first was shocking because it highlighted that hazing occurs across all classes—the case involved affluent females at a powder-puff football game. The second was shocking due to the sheer brutality of the assaults veteran high school football players forced teammates to endure. Albeit in different ways, these two cases both demonstrate societal attitudes toward hazing. In both cases perpetrators faced sanctions, but were also supported by many who claimed the hazing to be innocent tomfoolery or "boys will be boys." And, rather than accept hazing as a part of the culture of sports and work on fixing it, these two incidents demonstrated how the blame goes anywhere—to parents, to coaches, to "deviant individuals," and to school systems—rather than to the culture competition sports creates.

In all, six juniors were injured, thirty-one seniors were expelled, and twenty juniors from Glenbrook North High School were disciplined as a result of the hazing that occurred at the powder-puff football game held on May 4, 2003, in Chipilly Woods near Chicago. The community was taken aback when news of the incident broke because the school was so highly regarded. *Newsweek* had recently selected Glenbrook North as among the top 4 percent of high schools in the country. The incident involved both verbal and physical violence. At least twenty juniors total were targeted. Some of the younger girls were punched and kicked and one had a cooler slammed over her head. The victims were covered with urine, paint, fish guts, and trash, wrapped with pig intestines, and smeared with feces. One girl needed stitches and another had an ankle broken. One was forced to eat excrement, resulting in a bacterial infection. All of this was videotaped and viewed around the world.[39]

The girls, as well as a few boys who were involved, were sanctioned by the school and tried criminally. Twenty-eight of the thirty-one expelled students signed waivers allowing them to graduate (but not attend the graduation ceremony), providing they completed community service and counseling. The waiver also barred them from exploiting the incident with a book or movie deal. The juniors involved were also asked to sign the waivers. In their case, their suspensions would be rescinded if they agreed to undergo counseling, community service, and not to profit from the events. Several refused to sign, as they felt that they had committed no wrong in attending the event. When principal Michael Riggle announced the 10-day suspensions, the maximum punishment allowed, several parents responded as though it was too harsh. Three families sought legal orders to rescind the suspensions, claiming that the missed school would irreparably harm the girls. The suit has since been dismissed.[40]

Sixteen students were charged with misdemeanor battery. Twelve pleaded guilty to the charges and the remaining were found guilty. Most received community service and/or probation and were required to steer clear of the victims and remain drug and alcohol free. None received jail time. Three people, including two parents and one young man already on probation for a different offense, pleaded guilty to providing alcohol for minors. Marcy Spiwak admitted in court that she allowed underage teens to drink in her home prior to the event. Judge Timothy Chambers allowed many of the girls involved to travel for college orientations pending the outcome of their cases.[41]

Sixty football players from Mepham High School were taken to a pre-season training camp for 5 days in western Pennsylvania. While there, three players, ages 15, 16, and 17 years, used broomsticks, pine cones, and golf balls to sodomize three freshman players on at least three occasions and over 3 or 4 days. One report says there were as many as ten attacks on the three victims with at least one so vicious it caused a witness to vomit. One assailant was a senior lineman who had lettered in football his last 3 years. He was one of six seniors selected as a bunk captain for the trip and was a Boy Scout. One of the juniors, Kevin Carney, had been suspended before for disciplinary violations. He was described as being a bully who had previously made sexual threats against a female teacher and was kicked off the baseball team.[42]

The assailants seem to have planned the attack, as they allegedly brought the broomsticks used in the attacks to the camp with them, as well as stereos that some have reported were used to muffle the sound of the attacks. According to several reports, the broomsticks were dipped in Mineral Ice, an ointment that burns when applied to sensitive skin, and then used to sodomize the young players. Younger boys were also allegedly sprayed with shaving cream, had powder and gel put in their eyes and hair, and had the hair ripped off their legs and buttocks with duct tape. A black player on the team was also allegedly subject to racial harassment at the camp.[43]

The boys stayed in five different cabins and no coaches stayed with the boys. The coaches claimed they were unaware of any hazing occurring. Initially the victimized boys said nothing, but eventually they told their parents as they were experiencing continued bleeding from the attacks. One had to endure a surgical procedure.[44]

The school board of Mepham High School voted to cancel the football season before it got underway because so many players were obviously aware of the attacks and had done nothing to intervene or to tell the coaches, a violation of the district's code of conduct. The three accused assailants were suspended from school. Head Coach Kevin McElroy later apologized for the incidents, but still denied that he knew anything about them until after the team returned from camp. There is some suggestion, however, that similar incidents had occurred in the past.[45]

COLLEGIATE HAZING

In the college ranks, hazing is perhaps even more common. Researchers at Alfred University surveyed athletes, coaches, and administrators at 224 college campuses. Sadly, the response rate for some sports, especially football, was quite low. Some athletic directors refused to participate, maintaining hazing is a Greek problem, not an athletic one. One AD wrote, "This is a nonissue! We don't have a problem with hazing. We have never had an incident at this campus . . . sorry, but this is one of the more ridiculous questionnaires I've ever been asked to complete."[46] An interesting finding is that only 12 percent of the respondents checked the box indicating they had been hazed, yet when asked about specific activities that were required to join the team, 79 percent admitted they engaged in what would be called "unacceptable" hazing.[47]

The survey differentiated between questionable hazing, unacceptable hazing, and alcohol-related hazing. Questionable activities included being yelled, cursed or sworn at; being forced to wear embarrassing clothes; being tattooed, pierced, having heads shaved, or being branded; participating in calisthenics not related to the sports; being required to associate with only certain individuals; acting as a personal servant to players off the field; and being forced to deprive oneself of food, sleep, or hygiene. Almost two-thirds admitted involvement in these "questionable" activities. Unacceptable hazing included: making prank calls or harassing others; destroying or stealing property; engaging in or simulating sexual activity; being tied up, taped, or confined in a small space; being paddled, whipped, beaten, or kicked, or required to do those things to others; and being kidnapped or transported somewhere and abandoned. More than 20 percent said they had participated in at least one dangerous or criminal act, while over half had been involved in alcohol-related hazing.[48] The involvement of alcohol begins early, as 42 percent of the respondents claimed to have consumed alcohol on a recruiting visit.[49]

According to this study, female athletes were nearly as likely to participate in hazing as males. Male athletes were considerably more likely to engage in "unacceptable" hazing than females, 27 percent compared to 16 percent.[50] Males involved in swimming, football, hockey, lacrosse, soccer, and water polo were the most likely to be involved in hazing.[51] For 17 percent of the respondents, hazing was no one-time incident but a series of five or more incidents.[52] Hazing was much more likely among Division I athletes, with 41 percent claiming they had been involved, compared to 22 percent of Division II athletes.[53] In Division III, however, 37 percent of respondents indicated they had been involved in hazing.[54]

Many acts of hazing in the college ranks are relatively minor, such as the women's swim team at the University of North Carolina at Wilmington making freshmen wear weird clothes to class and run through an automatic car wash in downtown Wilmington. Respondents to the Alfred University survey were asked to write in examples of team-building or initiation activities in which they had taken part. The list included running in diapers and urinating in lockers. Other examples are simply scary, including being forced to take steroids and ephedrine.[55] Others are more physically dangerous, both to the victim as well as to others. An example is when a soccer player at the University of Buffalo was hospitalized for dehydration from drinking prune juice for an entire day. Other players were forced to drink alcohol, but this freshman refused.[56]

In another example of a ludicrous and appalling incident, soccer players at the University of Washington at Seattle were forced to perform 240 hours of community service after campus police found three players bound together in sexual positions and taped to a luggage cart in 1997. The team was also placed on probation.[57] In the same year, seventeen members of the swimming and diving team were suspended for two meets when upperclassmen required rookies to perform calisthenics and drink alcohol for specified time limits.[58] At least one athlete is known to have died from a hazing incident. In 1990, Nicholas Haben, a lacrosse player at Western Illinois University, died from a hazing incident involving consumption of mass amounts of alcohol.[59]

Another instance where university staff failed to respond appropriately to a hazing incident occurred at the University of North Carolina in 2002. Gregory Danielson, an 18-year-old rookie soccer player with a history of asthma, was admitted to an emergency room for acute alcohol poisoning in September 2002. Rescue workers for the Orange County Emergency Medical Services interviewed witnesses who reported Danielson vomiting repeatedly and observed his uncontrollable tremors and twitching. As he was transported he vomited brown liquid and was very confused. All the rookies were aware that they were to be initiated at the party and many recall being nervous about it. Older players had been chiding the rookies about it for weeks. Upperclassmen called it an "endurance test" and said things like, "You are going to puke, but you have to keep drinking."[60]

A team captain picked Danielson and some of the other players up for the party and took them to a fast food restaurant, evidently to allow them to be able to drink more because the food would absorb the alcohol. Once they got to the party they were given silly clothing and nicknames and were forced to drink, with Greg and another player receiving most of the prodding because they were heavier than the other rookies. They were given a concoction called PJ, which was a mix of 190-proof Everclear and fruit and punch. They were required to engage in an event called the "Cooper Test," where a barrel of beer was to be finished in 12 minutes by the seven freshmen. If they could not, they were told, the test would be repeated. During the second round most of the freshmen began to vomit, but they endured two more rounds. After they were thoroughly intoxicated they were given strange costumes—Danielson's involved a plastic cowboy hat, women's bikini underwear, and a halter top—and made to drink vodka from a bong. A scavenger hunt followed, and when they returned, more vodka. At some point someone hacked at Danielson's hair, leaving it in clumps. Danielson recalls stumbling into a closet, which is where he lost consciousness.[61]

That Danielson was treated poorly by teammates is sad enough, but the treatment he endured by university staff was absolutely heinous. Teammates blamed Danielson when coach Elmar Bolowich punished the team by making them run extra the next practice. Upperclassmen called him names and blamed him for the bad press the team received when the incident was made public. He was ridiculed and called names like "Detox" and "Pump." He said, "The initiation did bring everyone closer together—against me. I felt blacklisted and blackballed. It seemed I was the only one around with the plague, and everyone avoided me."[62] One night he was tackled on the street by two drunken teammates who had graduated. They blamed him for the "shitty season," as the team was suspended from a major tournament and several players were kicked off the team.[63]

The day after the incident, Danielson was called into Coach Bolowich's office. Rather than receive any sympathy, Danielson was interrogated by Bolowich and athletic director John Swofford. At one point Bolowich accused, "I heard you drank a full vodka bottle by yourself."[64] Danielson recalls talking to his parents later that night, who had been told by Bolowich that their son was to blame for the incident and that he had jeopardized the season for the entire team. Other UNC staff members made public announcements blaming the victims. Women's soccer coach Anson Dorrance blamed the incident on a kid gone wild at college, drinking too much in his first experience with freedom. Swofford repeatedly made public statements about the problems of underage drinking but never described the incident as one of hazing. Shortly after the incident, Assistant Coach Alan Dawson told the team their actions had killed his passion for soccer. Danielson internalized this comment, made by someone he had held in the highest regard. He began flunking classes because he either couldn't bring himself to attend or he couldn't concentrate when he did. Television cameras followed him around, exacerbating the problem. He became physically ill from all the stress and had to take sleeping pills. At no time did any university spokesperson label the incident as hazing and officially denounce the practice.[65] Again, it seems that hazing is only considered a problem when it sullies the good name of a university.

The punishment for the team was laughable. No player was ever criminally charged. In addition to the missed tournament and the other missed game, the team was ordered by the athletic office to perform community service as Habitat for Humanity volunteers. Sadly, the team treated the members of the landscape committee they were assigned to work with horribly, whining and making rude comments the entire day.[66]

A Case Study in Hazing: The University of Vermont

At the University of Vermont, men's hockey coach Mike Gilligan directed players to lie to university officials about their hazing practices in 1999. The team's season was cancelled and players faced criminal charges for the sexual assaults they perpetrated.[67] The incident also prompted new antihazing legislation in Vermont.[68] Fourth-string, walk-on goalie Corey LaTulippe sued the university and seven players who hazed him. He and others were forced to do the "elephant walk": parading naked in a line while holding the genitals of a person in front of you.[69] They were told they needed to arrive at a party with their pubic hair shaved and wearing thong underwear. They were made to pass a chunk of chewed bread from mouth to mouth and perform pushups naked, while their penises dipped in glasses of beer. The amount of pushups each was able to do dictated whether he was required to drink his own glass of beer or that of a teammate. Thankfully, the team thought to have a puke bucket nearby. LaTulippe left UVM.[70] His lawsuit was settled out of court when the university agreed to pay him $80,000.[71]

In 2000, the NCAA mandated that member schools implement a life-skills program for athletes that included guidelines about hazing.[72] Most universities have antihazing policies, although how clearly they articulate exactly what constitutes hazing and how frequently they are applied is still in question. Coaches and administrators have been known to minimize claims by athletes that they were victimized. In the case at Vermont, LaTulippe told assistant athletic director Jeff Schulman about the party 2 weeks before it happened, as well as another incident where he was made by teammates to use a fake ID at a local bar, an offense for which he received a fine. Schulman and athletic director Richard Farnham interviewed all the hockey players and were told they had committed no hazing and no hazing events were planned. Shocking they didn't admit it! After LaTulippe made them aware of the incident at the party, Vermont officials again interviewed the players. This time they admitted to some minor violations, but nothing as egregious as the claims by LaTulippe.[73]

One of the hazers, Canadian Jean-Francois Caudron, saw no problem with what they did to LaTulippe and the others, as he had been hazed numerous times in various hockey leagues. He stated, "It happened on every junior team I played for. You knew about this night and you were nervous. You feel the pressure that you have to do it. I didn't want to be an outsider. So I did it. But once it was over, I was so happy. I really felt part of the team."[74] In a deposition, LaTulippe was asked whether he thought about declining the invitation to the party, as most certainly he knew some type of hazing would occur. LaTulippe's response demonstrates the way athletes internalize the role of victim as simply a part of their belonging. He said, "I didn't feel I had a choice to. Because this is what you had to do."[75]

HAZING IN THE PROS

Even pro teams have been known to brutalize new players in their perverted sense of initiation. In 1998, the NFL refused to punish several veteran players for the New Orleans Saints who savagely beat some rookie players.[76] Veteran players required rookies to run through a gauntlet with players hitting them with bags of coins.[77] Defensive tackle Jeff Danish needed thirteen stitches in his left arm, tight end Cam Cleeland had a detached fluid sac in his retina, and wide receiver Andy McCullough had to have an MRI after he became dizzy and had a series of bloody noses.[78] Danish filed suit for $650,000 against the Saints, six players, and an assistant coach, alleging they knew or should have known these incidents happen at their training camp. Danish and the Saints settled for an undisclosed amount in 1999.[79]

Hazing in the NHL typically involves a full body shave, although on some teams it has been replaced with a financial burden. During the 1999–2000 season, three Vancouver Canuck rookies were required to split a $10,000 bill for team dinner.[80] Sometimes the hazing done in the pro ranks just strikes us as flat out stupid. Denver Broncos rookie Andre Sommersell was taped to a goalpost and showered with talcum powder, vaseline, and various other ointments. They also shaved off half his beard and his left eyebrow, and gave him his own dunce cap—a fluorescent orange traffic cone. Sommersell was "Mr. Irrelevant" of 2004, the title given to the last player selected in the draft. Sommersell said, "You've just got to deal with it. All rookies go through it."[81] Such stupidity, however, can easily escalate and establishes an overall culture that is conducive to the degradation of some for the entertainment of others. In a strange turn of events, hazing may actually have helped Cleveland Indians pitcher Kyle Denney. Denney was shot in the right calf when a stray bullet hit the team's bus as it headed to the Kansas City airport in September 2004. Denney was likely protected from major injury by the tall white boots he was wearing. He was forced to wear the USC cheerleaders costume as part of a rookie hazing ritual.[82]

BLAMING THE VICTIM

In cases of athletic hazing, it is not uncommon that the victims receive the blame, especially when there is some kind of penalty to pivotal players or even to the entire team. There was much uproar over whether Mepham High was correct to cancel the football season. Die-hard football fans felt the entire community was made to suffer because a few crazy boys took their hazing too far. Kent State University once cancelled an entire hockey season to punish the team for hazing. Both student athletes as well as members of the general student body roared in protest.[83] Penn State, then ranked number one in ACHA Division I hockey, was forced to find a new opponent lickety-split in December 2003 when Eastern Michigan University's season was cancelled due to a hazing incident. Rookie players were made to wear dresses and had their heads shaved at a November party. It was later disclosed that members of the Women's Crew team attended the party and had stuffed marshmallows and peanut butter in the rookies' buttocks, doused them with chocolate and mustard, and made them bob for coins in a pool of crushed food. Team members claimed participation was voluntary and there were no repercussions for those who would not. It was not the first time the Icers were in trouble—part of the reason for the season's cancellation was that the team had failed to comply with sanctions from a 2001 incident.[84] Many students at EMU expressed greater concern about the loss of the remainder of the season than for those who might have suffered.

Even when people express sympathy for victims of hazing, they often feel nothing should jeopardize the athletes' chances to play and the fans chances to watch. Much like the outcry when it was announced that O. J. Simpson was required by a civil court to give up his Heisman trophy, it is as if people think sports achievements are so sacrosanct nothing can tarnish them. This attitude perpetuates problems like hazing, as it tells athletes that their "sports morals" can be far from societal norms as long as they continue to achieve and to provide us all with entertainment. In sum, blaming the victim protects the system.

THE ROLE OF THOSE IN POWER

Coaches sometimes encourage hazing, either directly or indirectly. In 1997 Michael Tate, wrestling coach at Meeker (Colorado) High School, was fired and had his teaching license revoked for a series of hazing-related incidents. The instigating event was the one described earlier—players stripped, duct taped, and sprayed with medicated ointment the genitals of a 15-year-old physically disabled student. The parents felt that Tate had ample opportunity to intervene but elected not to. It turns out Tate also taped the mouth and hands of a 13-year-old student he dubbed too talkative and left him in the hallway to suffer the other students' ridicule. Tate stated, "The whole class was in on it. It was great fun."[85] Another high school coach who recommended his football team haze newcomers stated, "In our mamby-pamby society, people like me are looked at like Neanderthals, but I believe strongly you don't get something for nothing. If you're going to be the best, you've got to work harder, have more intensity and more determination."[86] Perhaps he is right—hard work and determination certainly are impressive values, but it is not clear exactly how hazing contributes.

HAZING AND THE LAW

Some major league sports organizations ban hazing, while others do not. Even those that do are clearly not overly concerned. One executive for the Canadian Hockey Association couldn't even find the hazing rule in the 165-page book of regulations and bylaws.[87] Currently, hazing is illegal in forty-three states. Most states consider hazing a misdemeanor.[88] In seven states it is a crime to observe hazing and not notify authorities.[89] There is a wide range of penalties, including fines, jail time of up to 1 year, and withholding of diploma or expulsion from school. Some of the state statutes include provisions that allow a hazer to be guilty even when the victim "consented," as they recognize that victims who are physically beaten, mentally abused, or legally intoxicated cannot consent.[90]

Like LaTulippe, some victims will file lawsuits against the schools they attend, holding them responsible for the hazing. A University of Oklahoma female soccer player sued her former coach, two assistants, and the university board of regents for physical and mental abuse stemming from a 1997 hazing incident. As a freshman she was forced to simulate oral sex with a banana while blindfolded and wearing an adult diaper. She did not report the incident for a year out of fear she would lose her scholarship. The victim transferred schools and the coach resigned, but at this point the suit has gone nowhere.[91]

Most lawsuits against schools and universities are for negligence. Clearly such suits are difficult to win. First, the plaintiff must establish that the institution owed them a duty of care, and then they must establish the university breached that duty. Historically, colleges and universities operated under the doctrine *in loco parentis*, meaning they were akin to parents to the students. This shifted in the 1970s, as courts began to recognize college students as adults. A plaintiff can also recover damages under a landowner–invitee relationship. Generally a landowner has responsibility for the safety and protection of invitees on his or her land. This can only hold for foreseeable acts, although there is precedent for hazing incidents being considered foreseeable. A third avenue for recourse is to establish that there is a special relationship between universities and student-athletes.[92]

Another challenge in addressing hazing legally is that many state laws only outlaw hazing in initiation or preinitiation. So any incidents that occur later in the season do not apply.[93]

At the pro level, recovery for damages is even more difficult. Only four states do not limit their antihazing laws to acts involving student groups.[94] One possibility is a workers compensation lawsuit against the team, although issues of foreseeability arise here as well. A victim could also assert the team negligently "hired" a player; that is, a player was signed by a team despite a dubious background. Negligent Supervision is yet another claim that could apply, especially if it is clear that the team was aware a hazing was planned. This is the case with the New Orleans Saints incident described earlier. Evidently players made no effort to be secretive about the intended hazing, even announcing it on a meeting room blackboard.[95]

CONCLUSION

In the end, sports-related hazing persists because a lot of people find no problem with it. *Sports Illustrated* printed an article called "Praising Hazing" in September 1999 in which the authors say they would miss hazing were it to be legislated out of sports, and "sports would miss it too."[96] They feel it helps bring down athletes of privilege, allowing them to be treated like the rest of the team. In 1997, Seattle Supersonics coach George Karl (now with the Denver Nuggets) stated, "The rookies should have to go through a ritual to be in our league."[97]

Athletes will often defend hazing as integral for team building. Some men who have been hazed claim they "enjoyed the challenge."[98] Some of the write-in responses on the Alfred University study of 1999 are indicative of this attitude. Athletes wrote: "Don't prevent it. Hazing does and should happen as a part of team chemistry. It makes you stronger... builds mental toughness" and "If no one is hurt to the point they need medical attention, just leave it alone."[99] Athletes often consider hazing harmless. Yet even in cases where no one is physically harmed mental harm may follow. Even the most innocuous instances of hazing can escalate into more dangerous incidents relatively easily.[100]

A typical defense offered by hazers is that the activities were voluntary. One of the seniors involved in the hockey hazing at the University of Vermont said, "I was a captain, and I never heard any complaining (from the freshman)."[101] While sometimes it is true that no one has physically forced the victim to endure the hazing, such a defense ignores the many other forms of coercion a group may exercise upon an individual. Because hazing is so integrally tied to conceptions of hegemonic masculinity, arguments to eradicate it are sometimes perceived as threatening.[102]

Others defend hazing as a matter of personal choice. David, a 23-year-old, wrote in an e-mail to Hank Nuwer,

America is the land of the free (with) the freedom to join whatever group that you want. If I want to join a group that beats the crap out of me every day, I can. If I want to join a group that requires me to drink 6 gallons of wine in a day to join, I can.[103]

A mother, Sue Ellen, echoed the comments made by the high school football coach cited earlier:

No wonder there are so many wimps in society today. EVERYBODY WANTS TO BE A VICTIM! Unless there is extreme physical harm being done then hazing amongst teams, social groups/clubs, is good and a bonding experience. Once you've "been there, done that" you're proud of yourself and it is a brotherhood-bonding thing.[104]

chapter 7

Racism, Sexism, and Classism

Inhumanity to man is every man's concern.

—Peter Hain

Sports are capable of bringing races together, of forwarding gender equality, and of providing opportunity for people of all social classes. For instance, Eitzen explains how the United States may help bring people of different nations together when we set up tours of athletes to sponsor goodwill. On the home front, a 1993 poll found that three-fourths of high school athletes, both white and African American, felt sports had helped them develop interracial friendships.[1] Yet, too often, sports are divisive. Sports commentator Frank Deford maintains, "It is time to recognize the truth, that sports in the United States has, in fact, never been so divisive. Uniquely today, sports has come to pit race against race, men against women, city against city, class against class and coach against player."[2]

Why, if it can be uniting, are sports so often not? We argue that because sports have become about the almighty dollar and the power to entertain, these things are just not that important. In fact, sports as entertainment thrives on exploitation, in direct contrast to equality. The people who are cashing in—team owners, sports organizations, and the media—may pay lip service to equality, but in reality, true equality could jeopardize their bottom line.

CLASS SEGREGATION

Class segregation occurs not only in housing, public schools, and other major institutions—but it is also evident in people's play. While the wealthy can enjoy tennis, golf, sailing, and skiing, poor people might be able to play basketball at their neighborhood court, often with no net on the rims. George Sage offers the example of polo; it costs at least $70,000 to outfit a player with horses, plus thousands of additional dollars to care for them. He quotes one writer as saying, "That polo's reputation as snobby is a given. After all, Ralph Lauren never considered naming his pricey line *Bowling* or *Softball*."[3] This is not by accident or fluke. It is the result of acute class inequality in society at large, and this inequality was purposely built into sports. Most sports clubs, leagues, and organizations were founded on segregation—by class, by race, by religion, and by gender—not inclusion.[4] Men of wealth originally played baseball in "gentlemen's clubs," and the first football teams were at elite private colleges in the Northeast.[5] Organized sports in America was conceived as yet another means for the wealthy to show off their status—what better way than getting tanned during a leisurely game of tennis or an afternoon on the family yacht? They could further assure themselves of their superiority as they watched the poor bash each other in the boxing ring, aghast at "their" brutality.

THE SHAM OF AMATEURISM

Curiously, many people still believe sports to be a great vehicle for the American dream. This belief is largely due to the notion of the sports amateurs. We love the image of the one who does it for love of the game, not for external reward. But the amateur image was a farce from the beginning. The early Greek Olympic athletes were not true amateurs; they were actually rewarded quite handsomely for their achievements, including winning valued items like oxen, horses, and property.[6] The myth passed on to the United States because it benefits those in control of sports. According to Ronald Smith, author of *Sports and Freedom: The Rise of Big-Time College Sports*, "Amateurism in sport was a nineteenth-century upper-class concept created by the English. It was an elitist attitude to keep the lower classes from mixing with their social superiors on the athletic field. It was an undemocratic, nonegalitarian concept designed to make amateurism appear to be superior to professionalism... It was... a reactionary policy to preserve for the traditional power and social elite control over an important area of upper-class life—sporting activity."[7] The amateur sham still has this function; now we convince ourselves our college athletes play for the sheer love of the game and that they are lucky to have the opportunity, which allows us to continue to exploit their labor for the wealth of coaches and athletic administration. Typically this translates into a form of modern-day slavery, as white, upper-class males remain firmly in control of athletes who are often nonwhite.[8]

OUT OF THE GHETTO? NOT VERY LIKELY

Allegedly sports provides the impoverished kid, typically inner-city minority males, the opportunity to leave the ghetto for good. Certainly this does happen sometimes, but, more often, sports do not offer mobility from poverty to the middle or upper classes. One important reason is that sports opportunities are increasingly being cut in both city and rural schools, making it difficult for that ghetto kid to show his stuff. Maintaining sports often depends on passing along costs to the would-be participants. About 30 percent of Michigan schools plan to increase fees for extracurricular activities.[9] These "pay-to-play" initiatives make participation impossible for many students.[10] In some Michigan schools, even the cheerleaders have to pay-to-play. In order to enroll in the required camps and pay for other expenses, girls and their families have to shell out $1200.[11] In some schools baseball and softball cost almost $1000.[12] Estimates suggest that three-quarters of the schools in Massachusetts charge students to participate in extracurricular activities.[13] As Stephen Jefferson, professor of Sports Management at the University of Massachusetts at Amherst said, "What it comes down to is the haves and have-nots. Sports are already elite; with fees they become really elite."[14]

In urban districts sports are typically just cut, completely eliminating the opportunity to participate. Some authors have argued that this denial of opportunity is an example of systemic violence directed at youth. We then point to those same urban kids as violent, do-nothing thugs, and blame them for societal problems, all the while ignoring that we denied them important opportunities to better themselves. Poll after poll has demonstrated that the vast majority of Americans believe poverty to be the result of an individual's lack of effort, not to the systems and structures we create.[15]

MAKING IT TO THE PROS

The difficulty of "making it" clearly compounds as an athlete rises in the sporting ranks. The odds of a male high school athlete becoming a professional are 1 in 10,000.[16] Odds are slightly better for African American males (1 in 3,500), yet are still slim. Of the 40,000 African American males who play high school basketball, thirty-five will make the NBA and only seven will be starters. As African American sociologist Harry Edwards has said, "Statistically, you have a better chance of getting hit by a meteorite in the next 10 years than getting work as an athlete."[17]

The myth that sports is the way "out of the ghetto" is especially destructive for young black males, many argue. Because this dream is so heavily marketed to them, young black males invest too much of their time and energy into sports and not enough toward academic pursuits. Nathan McCall, author of a book of personal essays called *What's Going On?* maintains, "So many brothers get sucked into what seems like a basketball cult because they're conditioned to see themselves—and even aspire to be seen—as athletic mules rather than as thinking men."[18] Penn State football coach Joe Paterno has put it in even more direct terms, saying, "For at least the last two decades we've told Black kids who bounce balls, run around tracks and catch touchdown passes that these things are ends unto themselves. We've raped them. We can't afford to do it to another generation."[19] Achieving upward mobility is even more difficult in some sports, as to excel now requires expensive equipment, camps, and travel that is financially prohibitive. Again, the architects of the sports culture can keep pointing to those who don't make it to the top as individual failures in the land of golden opportunities. They maintain that these opportunities are available, so it must be the individuals' fault for not seizing them.

NO GUARANTEES OF A LUXURIOUS RETIREMENT

Even if an athlete does make it to the pro ranks, this by no means ensures they will be set for life. Some make it to the pros, but only for a short time and at the minimum salary. For instance, 17 percent of Major League Baseball players in 1996 made the minimum salaries of $247,500 for veterans and $220,000 for rookies. Because most careers are only 5 years long, and it is likely that those receiving the minimum salaries will be the same people who have short careers, it is not likely these players will retire filthy rich.[20] Many experience a few years of riches, only to revert back to their former social class. This problem is especially acute in the black community, among athletes as well as entertainers. According to Henry Thomas, president of Thomas Sports Management, many make it rich, and then get involved in risky investments. Boxer Joe Louis is the quintessential example; he sank his winnings into everything from a fried chicken restaurant to a dude ranch. Louis was also known for living the high life, another way athletes and entertainers go from rags to riches and back again.[21] In the end, the Brown Bomber had to work as a greeter in a Las Vegas casino to keep himself housed and fed.[22] Extended family members and friends can also be a drain—as an athlete gains celebrity status, "friends" and "family" pop up from every direction. For those who come from backgrounds where there was not a lot of money, there might be immense pressure to share the wealth.[23]

Still others experience financial troubles because they entrust shady figures with their money. Tank Black, a slick-talking agent, defrauded almost two dozen NFL and NBA players, including Vince Carter, out of $15 million in a series of scams. Black was fun-loving and jovial, like a father figure to many, which was why he was able to bilk these athletes out of so much. "Professional athletes are prime candidates for financial fraud. Many are unsophisticated in financial matters and suddenly find themselves with a six-or-seven figure salary," said Michael Fuchs, a lawyer for the SEC in their case against Black. The Tampa Bay Buccaneer's Jacquez Green testified to the SEC that he had never even had a checking account prior to his dealings with Black.[24]

Financial exploitation is perhaps most acute in boxing, which has no single commission or league to offer some semblance of control. There are no players unions, no long-term contracts, no drafts, and no pension plans. Because there are no guarantees of long-term income, boxers often stay in or return to the ring long after they should have called it quits, risking serious bodily damage (or exacerbating existing problems). George Foreman and Larry Holmes fought into their 40s, while Jack Johnson and Earnie Shavers fought into their early 50s.[25] Boxers might also risk major injury by engaging in gimmick matches for a big payout. Heavyweight Tony Galeno fought a kangaroo, a bear, and an octopus.[26]

MOBILITY IS LARGELY A MYTH

That athletes' wealth is often short-lived shouldn't surprise us, as approximately 20 percent of each generation in the United States experiences downward mobility.[27] Sociologist Michael Messner has documented how retirement from sports is far easier for the athlete who came from the middle or upper classes than for those from low-income families, as the former tend to have better social connections and material support. Further, he found that middle and upper class athletes were less likely to have identities rooted solely in sports, and thus had an easier time with the role exit process.[28] Sports that are dominated by the affluent—golf and tennis, for instance—offer a wealth of experiences that can enhance career opportunities, while sports catering to the poor typically do not. In fact, trainers often encourage boxers to drop out of school, and most never attend college. It seldom involves interactions outside the small network of the boxing world, so athletes are not likely to make crucial social connections. One study of forty-eight retired professional boxers found not one had saved much money for retirement.[29]

THE "FULL RIDE" MYTH

Many fans point to college athletic scholarships as a route out of poverty. Sure, some poor kids do get full scholarship packages, including room and board and book money, but these are actually pretty rare. While greater in football because of sheer numbers, the chance to get a "full ride" in other sports is almost nonexistent. Why are full athletic scholarships so rare? Why can't schools offer kids more opportunities? Simple: there is only so much wealth to spread and after football takes the lion's share, there isn't a lot left. We personally know a NCAA Division I tennis coach who had to try to divide a single scholarship among the members of his tennis team, and a soccer coach who divided the equivalent of three scholarships among his team by rotating financial assistance.

Fans also contend that athletes, even those on partial scholarship, have a great opportunity for upward social mobility through earning a college degree. The college degree will allegedly bring a better job with higher pay. Yet many college athletes never actually earn a degree. Certainly some forego completing college for the pro ranks, but many simply play until they have exhausted their eligibility or until sidelined by injury. And, sadly, many schools don't care; once the athletes' function is gone, they are no longer an important investment. One athlete noted, "It's a business here. We're here to make money for (the university). When we're not useful for (the coaches) they don't pay as much attention to us."[30] The most recent figures released by the NCAA show a 55 percent graduation rate for Division I athletes receiving some type of scholarship. White athletes have better graduation rates (55%) compared to black athletes (48%).[31] Graduation rates also tend to be higher in lower-profile sports, as Murray Sperber notes, "The further a sport is from the money, the higher the graduation rate."[32] Part of the issue is that athletes miss, on average, 2 days per week of classes. Over the course of a semester, athletes may miss up to 40 percent of class instruction.[33]

KIDS MAKING SOCCER BALLS

Another way sports fuel classism, as well as racism and sexism, is through the exploitation of laborers who make sports-related products. As we stated in the Introduction, sports is a huge business. Fans are clearly willing to dole out huge amounts of their paychecks for sports-related products. Yet instead of being happy with what would be a decent profit, companies that make tennis shoes, balls, and other sports-related products are increasingly turning to sweatshop labor in order to turn even greater profits. Nike has been the most visible culprit, but is far from the only one. In 1996, it was discovered that workers in facilities in Indonesia were making an average of $2.46 per day to make Nike shoes. Most were forced to work mandatory overtime and faced physical and mental abuse on the job.[34] Adidas and Reebok pay their slaves in Asia poorly as well.[35] The bulk of employees in sweatshops are young females, as they are the easiest to exploit.[36] Sadly, none of the athletes who endorse Nike products has spoken out about the exploitation. The most visible promoter of Nike, Michael Jordan, is an example of what John Gerdy calls the "politically neutered athlete."[37] This is clear not only in his failure to renounce Nike's exploitation of laborers, but also in his endorsement of a known racist in a 1996 Senate race in North Carolina. Rather than support a black candidate, Harvey Gantt, Jordan supported ultraconservative Jesse Helms, saying, "Republicans buy Nikes too."[38] Guess that's all that matters.

"IT'S AN HONOR": THE RACISM OF SPORTS SYMBOLS

Racism can be fueled at all levels of sports. Perhaps the most obvious example of racism is in the naming of teams and the selection of team mascots. For example, Nathan Bedford Forrest High School in Jacksonville, Florida, uses the rebel as a mascot. Amazingly, the student body is predominantly African American, who wear the confederate army's colors and play for a school named after the original grand wizard of the Ku Klux Klan.[39] In a different example of the same racist symbol, NASCAR has long struggled with its "redneck" image. Although NASCAR claims it is controlling the problem as much as it can without infringing on the right to free expression, any fan can tune in or attend a track event and see the area littered with confederate flags.[40] That this might limit the number of black fans seems intuitive.

More common is the use of Native American names, mascots, and ceremonial acts. Most people know of the pro teams that use Native American names—the Washington Redskins, the Kansas City Chiefs, the Cleveland Indians, the Golden State Warriors, and the Chicago Blackhawks. Defenders maintain these names were selected as a tribute. The trouble is, while some Native Americans do see it as a tribute, others are very much offended. Defenders of these mascots also assert that these names are no different than are others that represent ethnic groups, like the Notre Dame Fighting Irish. Others take this argument even further, calling concern over the mascots "politically correct" in order to dismiss what is, in reality, a legitimate claim that deserves consideration. These folks often bandy about such arguments as, "Everyone can be offended by something. Shouldn't cowboys be offended, then, because Dallas has chosen them as a mascot? And what about animals? Won't the cardinals be pissed their name has been co-opted?" In actuality, some names are more offensive than others, although again, we reiterate there is no consensus among the hundreds of Native nations on this issue.[41] "Redskins," for example, referred to the blood dripping from the scalps that were taken from dead Indians. Yes, that's right, Caucasians did most of the scalping, not Indians.[42]

Some Native Americans find offense in the behavior of mascots rather than in the names themselves. Clyde Bellecourt, an American Indian Movement (AIM) leader, has said, "The word Indian isn't offensive. Brave isn't offensive, but it's the behavior that accompanies all of this that's offensive. The rubber tomahawks. The chicken-feather headdresses. People wearing war paint and making these ridiculous war whoops with a tomahawk in one hand and a beer in the other."[43] Also problematic is the co-optation of religious symbols for public entertainment. Using dances, chants, and Native-style drumming tells Native Americans that what is important to them is simply fodder for getting the crowds worked up.

In August 2005, the NCAA finally attempted to take action on the use of Native American mascots. The NCAA Executive Committee adopted a new policy prohibiting member colleges and universities from using mascots, nicknames, or imagery at any of the eighty-eight NCAA championships. The committee's action did not prevent schools from having these mascots or nicknames, it just prohibited their use at championship events within the NCAA's control. Teams keeping offensive or degrading mascots, nicknames, or imagery are required to cover them up at championship events in which they know they will be participating, effective February 1, 2006. According to the committee, eighteen colleges and universities are currently using imagery or references that would make them subject to the policy.[44] The prohibition may not impact many Division I-A football teams, as there is technically no national tournament or playoff.[45] Of course, the typical outcry ensued, as teams sought to defend their tradition. The Florida State Seminoles threatened to sue over the ban, arguing they have consent from the Seminole Tribe of Florida to use their mascot, nickname, and imagery. The NCAA backed down and is removing the Seminoles from the list of restricted schools.[46]

Recently, the San Jose Major League Soccer team that relocated to Houston struggled with the racial overtones of their name selection. Upon arrival in Houston, the team was renamed "1836." After just 3 weeks, the name would be changed again. Team owners initially selected the name because 1836 was the year Houston was founded. Also, 1836 was the year Texas gained independence from Mexico, and its use was seen by many Hispanics as a co-optation of an important historical date.[47] The authors applaud the team owners for being receptive to survey findings suggesting Hispanics in the area were offended. It is not clear what the new name will be.

WHEN THE RACISTS SPEW

Leaders in the sports world have been known to let leak their racist viewpoints. Football commentator Jimmy "the Greek" Snyder lost his job after he explained the dominance of black athletes in pro football as being rooted in slavery. Snyder commented, "The black is a better athlete to begin with because he's been bred to be that way because of his thigh size and big size."[48] In 1993, Marge Schott, then owner of the Cincinnati Reds, referred to two players as "million-dollar niggers." Schott also explained she would, "rather have a trained monkey working for me than a nigger."[49] In 1996, former Mississippi state senator Brad Lott let loose a racist tirade at an Ole Miss game. With 45 seconds left in the game against Mississippi State, Lott descended the bleachers and parked himself at a fence 20 yards from the field. For almost a minute he yelled at Mississippi State noseguard Eric Dotson, threatening to kill him and interlacing the word "nigger" multiple times. Lott was ticked off at Dotson, who had alleged that Lott, an Ole Miss booster, had given him free meals and car rides as a recruit in 1994.[50] Although they have since dropped the mascot, the tirade was made with Colonel Rebel as the mascot and awash in a sea of confederate flags. In 1997, pro golfer Fuzzy Zoeller made an ass of himself after Tiger Woods' historic win at the Masters, by commenting to reporters that he hoped they wouldn't serve fried chicken or collard greens at the dinner for tournament winners.[51]

In 2003, conservative hate-monger Rush Limbaugh, who had remarkably been hired by ESPN to commentate on their *NFL Countdown* show, stated that Eagle's quarterback Donovan McNabb was overrated because he is black and the media was propping him up. Cohost Tom Jackson denounced Limbaugh for his comments, calling them divisive and harmful. Jackson told of an NFL player's son asking him if it was okay for blacks to play quarterback.[52] Not only is Rush a fool for his comments, but ESPN bears responsibility for fomenting racism by hiring a man known to hold antiminority views.

Each of these bigmouths faced serious consequences, but that does not change the fact that some racists are in leadership positions in the sports world. It is unlikely these are the only folks who hold bigoted views. There likely are others who have a greater social filter and play their cards closer to their chests. Of course, in each of these cases, other loudmouths spoke out in defense of the racist. For example, Mr. Multiculturalism himself, John Rocker, claimed people were just too damned sensitive when asked what he thought about Rush Limbaugh's comments.[53]

A WHITE MEDIA

A major part of the problem is that the media is predominately white. According to Richard Lapchick, director of the Center for the Study of Sport in Society, there are more than 1,600 daily newspapers in the United States. In areas where there are professional sports franchises, only four of these papers have African American sports editors and nineteen African American columnists.[54] A similar pattern holds true of televised sports reporting. While there are some black commentators today, white males are still the voice of authority. Those minorities who do get the opportunity to comment on sports are generally former stars, which is less often true of white commentators.[55] Consequently, we are not only limited in the type of story we might hear, but also in the critical view and commentary a nonwhite reporter might add.

Obviously whites are not the only ones fueling poor race relations in sports, or elsewhere for that matter. In 2001, Nike put on hold a commercial featuring Kings' guard Jason Williams. In the spot, Williams' complexion shifted from black to white. Nike claimed the goal was to show race doesn't matter, only basketball. The corporation discovered perhaps they had not selected the best spokesperson for the "colorblind" message after Williams let lose a string of racist epithets at an Asian American heckler in a game against the Warriors. Williams called Michael Ching a "slant-eyed mother f . . . " and mimicked the sound of a machine gun while saying, "I'll shoot all you Asian mother f . . . Do you remember the Vietnam War? I'll kill y'all just like that. Just like Pearl Harbor."[56] To cap it off, Williams asked Ching if he was a "fag." As Jon Wertheim wrote in *Sports Illustrated*, perhaps Williams should include some history lessons with his diversity training.[57]

HIGH SCHOOL RACISM

Because so many of our schools are still racially segregated (in fact, they are worse today than when Martin Luther King, Jr. was alive),[58] high school competitions often pit racially homogeneous teams against one another. This can have disastrous results. Both authors worked in high schools that were almost exclusively white, and both witnessed the fear and racism that accompanied a trip to the big city to play against—gasp—"black teams." Sometimes coaches fuel racism on their own teams, as was the problem in Wildwood, Florida. After a rough night on the field, coach Gary Hughes expressed his disgust at one player, Clifton Peeples. Hughes told Peeples, "I'd better not see you out there looking like a street nigger again."[59] The school's superintendent suspended Hughes without pay, but not until the end of the season, of course.

RACIAL STACKING

Even integrated teams are sometimes segregated by position, a practice called stacking. In football whites are more likely to play offense and to be in the "thinking" and "leadership" positions, while blacks overwhelmingly play on defense and in positions requiring speed and strength.[60] Historically, stacking has been a problem in football, baseball, and to a lesser degree, basketball and volleyball for women. It is still a problem, but is alleviating slightly in football. Prior to 1999, only three black quarterbacks had been drafted in the first round of the NFL draft, and none among the top picks.[61] Stellar black quarterbacks like Warren Moon often had to make their name in other leagues or in other positions.[62] According to James

Harris, who was the lone black quarterback in 1974 when he played for the LA Rams, "Blacks get two types of opportunities to play quarterback in the NFL. A chance and a 'nigger' chance."[63]

In the current era of the NFL, there are a number of highly successful black quarterbacks, including Donovan McNabb and Michael Vick, who led their teams to the 2004 NFC Championship game. Sadly, the success of the black quarterbacks seems to be ushering in a new era of stereotyping, suggesting the black quarterback is more mobile and athletic and able to alter the game by scrambling for yardage when a play breaks down. The white quarterback is still cast as a pocket passer who leads a structured offense with both arm and brain, while the black quarterback is painted as an athlete who can gallop down the field with blazing speed.

In spite of the emergence of the black quarterback, players are still largely stacked into positions by skin color. Stacking has several negative consequences. First, athletes will generally spend the bulk of their practice time with peers of the same race. While it is theorized that contact between the races can help increase understanding and reduce racism, the "contact" must be sustained and conducted with both parties on equal footing. When some athletes feel superior to others, a situation created by stacking, the contact between teammates of different races is not likely to change perceptions in a positive way. Second, this type of division fuels racist banter about blacks being bred for physical labor and being intellectually inferior. It reinforces the stereotype of blacks as "brutes."[64] Third, stacking may increase in-group animosity, as members of the same racial or ethnic group are required to compete against one another for playing time. In the end, this restricts the overall playing time of members of a specific racial or ethnic group.[65]

Stacking is also an issue for minority women. According to Donna Lopiano, African American women are still often restricted to basketball, track, and field, and within those sports are typically relegated to the "nonthinking" positions. Black girls and women, for instance, are rarely setters in volleyball.[66] At the college level, it is often assumed that African American women are there to be athletes, not scholars, just as this assumption is made of black men. Laura had a female African American student who was casually conversing with a professor in line to buy coffee when he asked her if she played basketball. When she said no, he responded that she must be in track, because he "knew" for sure she was an athlete. She was not, and was highly offended by his assumption that she could only be there on athletic scholarship, as she attended school largely due to academic scholarships.

SEGREGATION ON CAMPUS

Most African American college athletes play for schools that are predominantly white. At most schools African Americans are 5 to 7 percent of the student population.[67] Not only do these athletes differ from the rest of the student body in skin color but also they are often far bigger than the rest and thus are highly visible on their campuses. They may also have dramatically different life experiences, including their academic preparation.[68] Their professors also tend to be white, as only about 3 percent of the faculty on most campuses is African American.[69] Most colleges house athletes in special dorms, or at least in a few select halls, which further serves to segregate these minority students from the rest of the populace. Although the NCAA banned this as official practice, it still occurs in the selection of dorms. When Laura worked at a Division I school, several black athletes expressed to her that class was pretty much the only time they saw other nonwhites on campus. Interestingly, the white athletes at the same school had a tendency to overestimate the degree to which their campus was integrated.

STILL NOT IN THE POWER POSITIONS

Even in sports in which they have a large presence, minorities are still underrepresented as coaches, athletic directors, general managers, and owners. The 2003 *Racial and Gender Report Card* in Sports indicated women and people of color lost ground in professional and college sports hiring. The 2004 *Report Card* showed some progress for women, but even worse situations for minorities. In 2004, all Division I and Division I-A conference commissioners were white, and only three were women.[70] Some have argued the sports world lags far behind other institutions in the promoting of blacks to leadership positions. Michael Lomax, assistant professor of sports management at the University of Georgia, documented the dramatic increase in African American elected officials following the 1965 Voting Rights Act, including more than 400 mayors and numerous city council and school board positions. This type of increase, he says, simply did not occur in the world of sports.[71] A 2003 study found that 90 percent of the jobs in Michigan college athletics are given to white candidates, and three-quarters to men. Ron Stratten, who is in charge of minority internship programs for the NCAA, called it a problem of "entrenched, covert racism in intercollegiate athletics" and argued the situation is unlikely to change until a conscious effort is made.[72]

The first black head football coach at a major university, Ron Cooper of Eastern Michigan University, was not hired until 1992.[73] Twelve years down the road, there continue to be no more than a handful of black head coaches on college campuses in any given year. In 2005, there were only three black coaches for the 119 Division I-A football teams. Division I-AA has only one black coach.[74] And, as the Ty Willingham situation at Notre Dame demonstrated, they are often given less time to succeed before they are sent packing.

In 2002, thirty of the thirty-two NFL head coaches were white. By the beginning of the 2005 season there were six black head coaches, as former Patriots assistant Romeo Crennel took over as head coach in Cleveland (bringing a handful of Superbowl rings with him). He joined Tony Dungy, Marvin Lewis, Dennis Green, Herman Edwards, and Lovie Smith as minority head coaches. But this leaves another twenty-six teams with white coaches presiding over a labor force that is 67 percent black.[75]

It is not that black coaches do poorly, either. According to the Elias Sports Bureau, the black head coaches in the NFL from 1989 to 1997 had a combined regular season winning percentage of 0.555, while white coaches in the same time period had a winning percentage of 0.486.[76] More recently, in 2004, Dungy led the Colts to a 12–4 record, Edwards' Jets finished 10–6, and Lewis continued to breathe life into a woeful Bengals organization to finish 8–8.

One study, comparing coaching success by race from 1990 to 2002, found that black coaches averaged 9.1 wins per season, compared to 8 wins for white coaches.[77] While an extra win a season may seem trivial, in a league that prides itself on parity, this win has tremendous impact. Specifically, teams that won exactly nine games over this period made the playoffs over 60 percent of the time, while teams with exactly eight wins were playoff bound less than 9 percent of the time. Unfortunately, this study also indicated that black coaches were fired more quickly and careful statistical analysis led the author to conclude that, "African Americans are being held to a higher standard when NFL coaches are hired and when they are fired. These findings are consistent with racial discrimination against African American coaches."[78]

Representation in the coaching ranks is even worse for other minorities. Despite the increasing number of Latina/os in professional sports, in particular, Major League Baseball, as of 2001, Linda Alvadrado was the only Latina to be part owner of a professional sports team, the Colorado Rockies.[79] It wasn't until 2003 when the first Latino, Arte Moreno, acquired a professional team (the Angels).

Minority women have it worse yet. Minority women face the double whammy of gender and race. African American women are less than 2 percent of all college coaches and less than 15 percent of all college administrators.[80] In 2004–2005, 24 of the 325 Division I women's basketball teams (excluding historically black schools) were headed by black women. While 41.6 percent of the players are black, only 8 percent of the coaches are.[81]

The year 2005 looked to be a pivotal year, as Arizona businessman Reggie Fowler attempted to be the first black NFL team owner. Fowler's bid for the Minnesota Vikings looked to be solid until midwinter, when the NFL Finance Committee expressed concern about his ability to come up with the needed capital. Further investigations revealed Fowler had several inaccuracies on his resume. Straightlaced real estate tycoon Zygi Wilf ended up purchasing the team, and little has been heard from Fowler since then.[82]

CHANGE EFFORTS

The NFL has attempted to address the dearth of minority coaches by instituting a policy requiring teams to interview at least one minority candidate for any open head coaching positions. While a good move in theory and in sound bites, in reality the interviews are often a sham. And, as with the debate over Affirmative Action, too often the result is a backlash against minorities. People resist efforts to hire minorities, arguing, "He only got the job because he's black." In 2003, the

Detroit Lions were fined $200,000 for violating the policy when they hired Steve Mariucci as head coach. It seems the Lions tried to comply, contacting five minority candidates to set up interviews, but none were interested because everyone knew the Lions intended to hire Mariucci.[83]

The NFL also has a Minority Coaching Fellowship that is intended to provide minority coaches with experience and connections so they may eventually attain head coaching positions. This is certainly a positive move, but the problem seems more one of assumptions of what a coach should look and act like, not one of overt racism. Hence the fellowship may make little difference if those in the position of hiring seek to fill their jobs with those who resemble the successful coaches they know. As Joe Saraceno explains, "It matters a whole lot who owns the ship. Right now, the NFL has a lot of Thurston Howell IIIs in charge."[84] Tony Dungy, now coach of the Indianapolis Colts, probably summarized the problem the best in 1996: "I don't think anyone is going to say, 'This guy's good but he's black, so I can't hire him.' But the thought process is, 'Is this what I really want? This isn't what I perceive the coach to be.'"[85]

FEAR OF BLACK DOMINANCE

Some say that minorities have reached equality in sports because they seem to dominate the ranks in basketball and football. These comments are often made in a self-congratulatory way, like "gee, we've done all we can to ensure racial equality. We're the good guys. And now they are taking over." This is wrong in two very distinct ways. First, the opportunities that exist in sports for racial minorities are not generally due to the benevolent white man who thought racism should be a thing of the past. Rather, integration in sports is a product of the white man's realization he could make *mucho dinero* if he included a wider talent and fan base. As George Sage comments in *Power and Ideology in American Sport*, "Sport opportunities for African Americans in professional sport grew only as discrimination became incompatible with good capitalist financial policy. It was in those team sports in which spectator appeal was strong and growing, and in which the profit motive was foremost, that African Americans were given a chance . . . "[86] Second, racial minorities may dominate these sports, but are still quite rare in others, like tennis, golf, and skiing. In actuality, blacks have a strong presence in only four (track and field, basketball, football, and baseball) of the forty-four sports played in colleges.[87] The few who do engage in the nonmainstream sports often face a tough road.

Until 1990, the PGA played most of their tournaments at country clubs that would not admit minority members.[88] The same type of discrimination is true in tennis, both for players and coaches. According to Gary Sailes, chair of the USPTA Multicultural Committee, discrimination in tennis is still a major problem, making tennis still near the bottom of the list of blacks' favored sports. He argues this is due, in part, to the lack of job opportunities. Most minority tennis pros work in public facilities because private clubs still won't hire them.[89]

The same holds true for other minority groups. Native Americans' participation in sports has been and continues to be limited, due to poverty and its effects as well as prejudice and a lack of understanding of cultural differences.[90] College coaches often do not recruit highly capable Native Americans based on assumptions they hold. One assumption is that the athletes will never leave the reservation, so to recruit them is a waste of time. Another assumption is that, if the athletes do come and play, they will likely leave the team and return to the reservation. Either way, many coaches are unwilling to take what they perceive to be a gamble. Further, the transition from reservation to college life is terribly difficult, yet most coaches are not able, or perhaps not willing, to help Native American athletes make this transition.[91] Many Native Americans have a nonaggressive attitude on the field or court, due to their cultural ideologies emphasizing interdependence and cooperation. Coaches often respond by trying to "deIndianize the Indians."[92]

There is not even racial equality in sports fandom. Blacks are still a minority of the fan base for the NFL, NBA, and MLB, relative to their representation in the overall population (17%, 7.5%, and 6.8%, respectively, in 1997).[93]

END ZONE CELEBRATIONS

A topic of some controversy in 2005 is whether football players should be allowed to celebrate in the end zone after a touchdown. While on its face this is not an issue of race, it generally becomes one, as black athletes are far more likely to dance after a score. Of course, this just reflects the fact that there are more blacks than whites playing at the wide receiver and running back positions, which produce most touchdowns. There is mixed opinion among blacks as well. Some argue that these expressions of exuberance are simply examples of the athletes' individuality and should definitely be allowed; they excite the crowd and hurt no one. Yet others say these crazy antics serve to reinforce the stereotype of blacks as the dumb "sambo." Hall of Fame running back, Jim Brown, told interviewer Bob Costas,

I don't understand the logic of celebration, because it is not natural emotions that are flowing. But some of it is cute and some of it is buffoonery and some of it is stereotypical things we tried so long, as African-Americans, to get rid of. Walt Disney used to do it with his crows and his dialect and all the dance. And I just hate to see it now because it means that these young men sometimes don't understand that they are imitating history and that history was a negative thing.[94]

Other controversies have emerged from the NCAA and NFL requirement that athletes cannot remove their helmets while on the field. The organizations claim they are preventing athletes from unnecessary showboating, but some athletes claim these directives are racist, as they impact largely running backs and wide receivers, most of whom are black. Similarly, the NFL banned players from wearing bandanas, which is far more common among black athletes. In the NBA, commissioner David Stern introduced a dress code requiring all players coming to or from the stadiums as well as those on the bench (when not in uniform) to wear "business" casual clothes. While Stern and his defenders maintain this policy is to help clean up the somewhat tarnished image of the NBA after the 2004 "Basketbrawl" in Auburn Hills, detractors maintain this is yet another way that black athletes are supposed to conform to white expectations.

THE LIMITATIONS OF TITLE IX

In our patriarchal society, where a woman still earns about 80 percent of what a man does for the same work, it is no wonder that female athletes are still not treated as well as males. Certainly major inroads have been made, with Title IX by far the most important. The law, passed in 1972, stated, "no person in the United States shall, on the basis of sex, be excluded from participation in, be denied the benefit of, or be subjected to discrimination under any education program or activity receiving federal financial assistance."[95] Those institutions found to be violating Title IX can have their federal funding terminated, although this has never happened. Nor has the Office of Civil Rights ever established a time line for when all schools should be in compliance or face a penalty.[96] A major setback occurred in 1984, when the Supreme Court ruled that Title IX did not apply to school athletic programs because the athletes, not the schools, were the true recipients of the federal funds. Eight hundred cases of alleged discrimination were dropped. Congress responded by passing the Civil Rights Restoration Act 4 years later, which again mandated equality in all programs receiving federal money. Yet this effort, too, was limited because it did not provide enough incentive for schools to change. In 1992, 20 years after the initial legislation was passed, the Supreme Court ruled that injured parties could sue schools if they intentionally violated Title IX. This has forced schools to at least consider issues of gender equity.[97]

The law has been interpreted to require consideration of three things in regard to women's sports: (1) proportional female sport participation opportunities to the percent of female students in the general population; (2) demonstrate the school has regularly expanded sports opportunities for females; and (3) demonstrate that the interests and abilities if the underrepresented (always female) gender has been accommodated. If a school can answer they are doing one of the three things listed above, they are said to be in compliance.[98] In order to say they are working toward compliance, many colleges and universities have added women's sports. Sometimes these sports are pooh-poohed as "not real" sports, like when our alma mater (Western Michigan University) added women's synchronized skating, which was cut only a few years later. That these comments are made only demonstrates that the world of sports is still considered a man's world and is viewed through a masculine lens.[99]

GENDERED SPENDING AND FOOTBALL

Yet major inequities remain. Colleges still spend more money on male sports; it is not uncommon, according to Eitzen, for a big-time football program to spend twice as much on its football team as it does on all women's sports.[100] A 2001 study reported in the *Chronicle of Higher Education* found that Division I-A schools that are part of the Bowl Championship Series (BCS) have, on average, annual budgets of $6.4 million. In contrast, only fifteen Division I-A schools spent more on their entire women's program than they did on football.[101] Ultimately, colleges have three options in order to move toward gender equity in their sports budgets: they can spend more on women's sports; they can reduce or eliminate male sports; or they can constrict expenditures on football. Football is the huge drain on athletic budgets, as teams in Division I are allowed to have eighty-five scholarship players, and some have up to 130 total players. Football consumes, on average, 60 percent of the total men's athletic budget, meaning all the other sports must compete for the remaining 40 percent.[102] Defenders of the status quo maintain that football brings in enough money to underwrite all the other sports. This is, in general, completely false. Only about one-third of Division I football programs turn a profit, while another third typically run annual deficits of more than $1 million. An easy move would be to reduce the number of scholarship athletes to sixty, which would likely also reduce the number of coaches needed, cost for equipment and travel, training supplies, and assorted other things. Thus schools could put more money into women's sports and not have to cut sports for men.[103]

THE SEXIST MEDIA

Male sports still receive far more media attention than do female sports. Because they are promoted more, they continue to draw in more money, which is used as justification to continue to promote them more in a nasty cycle of inequality. When women do grace the cover of magazines like *Sports Illustrated,* too often it is done in a way that emphasizes their femininity, not their athletic ability.[104] As we write this, ESPN is conducting its annual "hottest female athlete" contest. Play-by-play announcers and broadcasters providing analysis of sports are still predominantly male, and refer to males and females differently. Female athletes are frequently referred to as "girls" or "young ladies," while men are never called "boys." Commentators far more often call female athletes by their first names. These practices emphasize males as dominant and females as subordinate.[105]

In their analysis of sports media, Messner and colleagues found four primary ways of dealing with women's sports: silence, humorous sexualization, backlash, and selective incorporation of exemplary athletes. Silence was the most obvious. In 1999, only 8.7 percent of the news coverage about sports was devoted to women. *SportsCenter* was the worst, covering women's sports only 2.2 percent of their airtime. Even when they are covered, it is often in sexualized ways, such as the excessive documentation of soccer player Brandi Chastain's removal of her shirt after the U.S. World Cup win, or the nauseating attention to everything regarding Anna Kournikova.[106] After *Sports Illustrated* featured a cover story on Kournikova in June 2000, the Women's Sports Foundation issued this indictment: "Female athletes should be portrayed as athletes in athletic uniforms displaying their sports skills. When have we ever seen major sports periodicals depicting Michael Jordan or other male athletes stuffed into tight-fitting uniforms that display their genitalia as a way of getting more women to buy magazines?"[107]

COVERING WOMEN IN A TRIVIAL WAY

When the researchers used qualitative methods to analyze the coverage, they found serious stories about serious issues in women's sports to be quite rare. Stories about a female pseudosport or some type of gag were far more frequent. Nude bungee jumping received airtime on two stations. Often sports news simply includes female nonathletes for sexual titillation.[108] Two of three networks continually offered glimpses of bikini-clad women in the stands at baseball games during Messner et al.'s analysis, while male commentators offered their pig remarks.[109] As she wrote these words, Laura watched an episode of ESPN's *Pardon the Interruption* recently and saw this point clearly. Cohost Tony Kornheiser repeatedly made comments about the girlfriend of a tennis player, and ESPN flashed to video clips of her many times in the half hour. No other issues about females were covered, most certainly none about actual athletes. Evidently it is part of Kornheiser's shtick to ogle his newest "girlfriend" for the public to see. Messner explains, "The sports news' humorous focus on scantily clad women spectators, cheerleaders, and nude or nearly nude women in pseudosports makes a conventionally conservative statement about women's 'place'—on the sidelines, in support roles, and as objects of sexualized humor—in a cultural realm that is still defined, at least in these television programs, as a man's world."[110]

The problem of sexist coverage is not exclusive to mainstream sports. Media coverage of the extreme sports, like snowboarding, follows the same patterns. One female snowboarder denounced advertisements for snowboarding events and movies featuring snowboarding as "too fleshy." She described an advertisement for women's snowboarding gear that featured a woman with no shirt on and argued that, sadly, such ads are common, with more than half featuring a female snowboarder in some seductive pose. Even worse are the ads where a snowboard is clearly intended to be a phallus, often being "ridden" by a young athlete.[111]

THE "IMAGE" PROBLEM

Women who excel in sports are still too often labeled "manly" and their sexuality is often questioned.[112] Jennifer Knight and Traci Giuliano found that college-aged viewers rate athletes who appear to be clearly heterosexual more favorably than were those whose sexuality appeared more ambiguous.[113] The homophobia of the sports world serves to limit women's participation.[114] Not only do some women avoid sports for this reason, but it also impacts women in their quest to coach. Jan Boxill tells how almost every parent she encountered while recruiting inquired if she was married to her assistant and if there were lesbians on the team.[115]

Knight and Giuliano assert the media often uses a "feminine apologetic," where females in traditionally masculine pursuits are expected to overcompensate for their sports "masculinity" by emphasizing their out-of-sports "femininity."[116] This might involve extra coverage of a female athlete's relationships with men. For instance, in their coverage of the United States' women's soccer team's inaugural World Cup victory, *People* magazine ran a few action shots, but even more pictures of the women with their husbands, boyfriends, and children. This same expectation does not hold true for male athletes, perhaps excepting figure skating. It is assumed that "naturally" male athletes are heterosexual. Some women respond by going out of their way to emphasize their femininity. Thus they market themselves, as has Kournikova, as sexualized objects. High jumper Amy Acuff and other female track and field athletes posed provocatively for a calendar, while swimmer Jenny Thompson posed nude with her hands over her breasts, exhibiting her chiseled body.[117] While this is certainly a great example of feminine agency, at the same time we question the harm this may do to other women in a culture that fails to understand the difference between agency and exploitation.

SHOCK JOCKS AND WOMEN

Commentators fuel the backlash against women's progress in sports. The exchange reprinted in part below highlights some people's view on sports equality. The discussion is between Tom Leykis, a shock jock with his own radio show, and a caller and is in response to the research cited above by Messner et al. and their call for greater coverage of women's sports.

Brad: The only pro events that women have are golf and, basically, basketball. But you know what? There's no woman basketball player like Shaquille O'Neal to even be worth reporting.

Leykis: No

Brad: And there's no Tiger Woods in the women's golf league.

Leykis: And what are we supposed to be covering? Little Susie's run at the parallel bars over at the junior high school? I mean, what exactly are we supposed to be putting on TV?

Brad: Nothing! Nothing with women, because there's nothing worth watching!

Leykis: Right.

Brad: There's really nothing, I mean, I don't sit at home and watch figure skating. I don't watch some gymnastics . . .

Leykis: (interrupting) Figure skating is a pussy-assed sport anyway. Figure skating is not even a sport. If figure skating is a sport then so is ballet . . . [118]

In addition to the stupidity of the sexism of both the caller and the shock jock, they are, quite simply, wrong. While there may be no female version of Shaquille O'Neal (none are as big or miss so damned many free throws), there are countless stellar athletes in the WNBA. In regard to golf, how about Karrie Webb, Annika

Sorrenstam, Paula Creamer, or Michelle Wie? We're confident any of these women could spot the caller five strokes a nine and still clean his clock.

Even the names of female sports teams reflect our gender hierarchy. D. Stanley Eitzen and Mazine Baca Zinn identified gendered practices in the naming of teams, all of which serve to trivialize women's sports. For instance, many schools refer to their female teams as "girl" or "gal" or "lady." Elon College has the Golden Girls, while the University of Tennessee has the Lady Volunteers. Others use feminine suffixes—Blue Devils become "Devilettes" or "Duchesses" instead of Dukes.[119]

WOMEN AS SEXY SPECTACLES

Women are still used as entertainment at sporting events. At colleges, women are sometimes used as a means to entice recruits, yet the reverse never occurs. Laura (thankfully) heard no suggestion of any "Bronco Bucks" who would show female recruits around WMU and Kalamazoo. Perhaps the most visible exploitation of women occurs in the not-really-a-sports world of professional wrestling. One commentator made this classy remark about a heavy lady during a recent match: "I have heard of buns of steel, but those are buns of cinnamon." Authors of *The Economist* explain this was one of the milder remarks made about the woman, who was part of a "Kiss My Ass" match between Badd Ass, Bill Gunn, and The Rock. Badd Ass brought the woman to the ring and claimed that when he defeated the champion he would make The Rock kiss her backside. In true wrestling fashion, when Badd Ass pulled the woman into the ring and tried to force The Rock's face into her derriere, The Rock reversed the move and it was Badd Ass himself with the face full of booty. In their scramble for ratings the WWE has also conducted a mock sacrifice of a young lady.[120]

YET AGAIN, THE SORDID CASE OF CU

The University of Colorado gained national attention for using sex to recruit athletes in 2004. The university was alleged to host sex parties for recruits and to hire strippers, call girls, and escorts to entice potential football players to the school. One assistant admitted to hiring a prostitute, but has claimed it was only for himself. In addition, former kicker Katie Hnida has claimed she was raped, and that Coach Barnett fostered a sexist climate. Clearly Barnett's comments about Hnida demonstrate his personal sexism—he denounced her for being a terrible player, claiming she was only on the team because she is a "girl" (notice the infantilizing word choice there). While CU got called on it, they are not alone. According to Chris Leeder, a former Northwestern lineman, "Selling sex to recruits is not something they invented at Colorado. Every school does it."[121] Strange, selling sex is still illegal in most of the country, but is standard practice in the recruiting wars.

In 2001, Vince McMahon, of World Wrestling Entertainment fame, teamed with Dick Ebersole of NBC sports to launch the XFL, a professional football league that collapsed soon after it debuted. The XFL was clearly attempting to capture the 18–35-year-old market with its supersized sex and violence. Cheerleaders were a primary component of the XFL, as McMahon explained, "The audience is going to get to know the girls on a first-name basis. Then when the quarterback fumbles or the (receiver) drops the ball—and we know who he's dating—I want our reporters right back in her face on the sidelines demanding to know whether the two of them did the wild thing last night."[122]

SPORTS STRUCTURES: BY AND FOR MALES

Male dominance is also perpetuated when enormous sums are put into building and maintaining arenas and stadiums. As Eitzen explains, "These stadiums, costing a quarter to half a billion dollars in tax revenue, are for men. They are for male owners, male athletes, male coaches, male trainers, male media, male-controlled corporations, and mostly male fans."[123] Many private golf clubs still do not allow women to hold memberships.[124] This was the cause of the scuttlebutt at the Masters in 2002, when Martha Burk, president of the National Council of Women's Organizations, tried to push the leadership of Augusta National to extend a membership to a woman. Club chairman William "Hootie" Johnson refused to be "bullied," as he called it, and many players were outspoken in their defense of Augusta as a male only refuge. Superstar Tiger Woods refused to speak out, while Mark O'Meara, 1998 Masters and British Open champion, called on the status quo response that the club was private so they should be able to do what they want. Another player, Scott Verplank, minimized the females' complaint, asking, "Why aren't they doing more for women in Afghanistan?"[125] While O'Meara is technically correct and Verplank is right that there are indeed all types of oppression of women, both domestically and globally, change needs to start somewhere. These objections merely serve to preserve the good ol' boys network in sports.

GENDERED COACHING AND LEADERSHIP

Women are still underrepresented in coaching and other power positions in sports. Following the passage of Title IX, there was actually a decrease in the number and proportion of female head coaches and administrators.[126] It seems that while more sports opportunities were opening for women, males, not females, were filling these new jobs. In 1972, women administrators led over 90 percent of women's programs; in 2000 only 17.4 percent were doing so.[127] Similarly, while women coached over 90 percent of women's teams in 1972, in 2000 only 45.6 percent were doing so.[128] The 2003 *Racial and Gender Report Card* found every professional sport had lost ground in the hiring of women, with Major League Soccer receiving an "F."[129] Jay Coakley asks the important question, "What would men say if women constituted over 50 percent of the coaches and 82 percent of the administrators in men's programs, while men held only 2 percent of the jobs in women's programs? They would be outraged. And they would certainly call for major affirmative action programs in an attempt to achieve fairness."[130]

GENDERED ASSUMPTIONS ARE THE REAL CULPRITS

As we explained regarding the hiring of minority coaches, the real problem lies in the assumptions held by those in power. Joe Dean, athletic director at Louisiana State University, has claimed the athletic department to be equitable. Yet at the same time, he says, "If the football team wins here, I am a very good athletic director."[131] The courts didn't necessarily agree, finding the school as well as Dean himself treated two female soccer players unfairly in a Title IX lawsuit that began in 1994. Allegedly Dean told a woman who wanted to get a soccer team started, "I'd love to help a cute little girl like you."[132]

Too frequently people like Dean (and that includes athletes themselves as well as fans) point to the progress that has been made and assert there is no class problem, no race problem, and no gender problem, in sports. While looking at the half full glass is nice, it also serves to obscure legitimate concerns that, with some attention, could be addressed. Ultimately, sports will not be a true vehicle for any type of equality until we all admit that we still have a problem.

chapter 8

Stadium Finance

When you call up a hot tootsie for a date, you're not going to go to the water treatment plant.

> —Former Minnesota Governor, Arne Carlson, on why the Minneapolis area needed a new ballpark.

In the last two decades, construction of new stadiums and major renovation projects for professional sports teams has exploded. More than 160 new major and minor league ballparks, arenas, and racetracks were built in the United States and Canada in the 1990s alone.[1] Once some works in progress are complete, over half (17 of 30) of the Major League Baseball teams will be playing in facilities built since 1992.[2] The figure is only slightly less for the NFL, as 17 of 32 teams in professional football are playing in post-1992 constructed sites.[3] The minor leagues have also seen a stadium boom. Since 1990, more than 100 new minor league baseball stadiums have been constructed with state of the art amenities, and franchise values have skyrocketed to as much as $20 million.[4]

FINANCING

Taxpayers have flipped the bill for major portions, and, in some cases, all, of these new facilities. Between 1993 and 1996 alone, taxpayers spent $5.6 billion on construction and renovation of major league facilities across the nation.[5] One researcher has calculated that approximately $10 billion of public money is tied up in these stadiums.[6] The public tends to pay a greater percentage of the costs in smaller market areas.[7] Of the stadiums built between 1961 and 2003, many are 100 percent publicly funded, including Tropicana Field in Tampa, Shea Stadium in New York, Qualcomm Stadium in San Diego, Cinergy Field in Cincinnati, Three Rivers Stadium in Pittsburgh, 3Com Park in San Francisco, and the Superdome in New Orleans.[8]

Private stadiums being funded by public money is a relatively new phenomenon. Prior to World War II, most stadiums were privately owned and financed. Public contributions increased after the war, but the bulk of the monies for stadiums still came from private sources. In earlier decades, most team owners recognized they could share facilities with other teams from different sports. Football teams typically played in stadiums owned by baseball teams, as there was little need for a separate facility for the relatively few football games held each year.[9] The tides began to shift as televised coverage made sports more popular than ever. As more expansion teams were added in each of the professional sports, each with sparkling new facilities, existing teams wanted the same. In addition, as free agency and player unionization have lead to rising salaries for players, team owners sought new ways and new sources of money to gain a competitive advantage.[10] Once things began to change, they changed fast. By the early 1990s, 77 percent of stadiums and arenas were publicly owned.[11]

That teams will demand ever better facilities is virtually built into the structure of the NFL. Teams are required to share television, licensing, and marketing revenues, thus no one team can gain an advantage here. Most stadium revenues are not shared, however, so a new stadium is considered one of the only ways a team can attempt to get a competitive advantage.[12] Team owners do not want to pay for the new facilities themselves, but they often tell voters that a new stadium is required for their local heroes to either stay competitive or to improve. Better facilities equal to better play by the team, the logic goes. Hence, the demands to get a bigger, better stadium for cheap have shifted the bills largely to citizens. Today, most teams pay little or no rent for their facility, get most or all of the revenue from parking, ticket sales, concessions, on-site merchandise sales, have stadium naming rights, and may even be given land around the stadium.[13] Some teams even negotiate special perks. For instance, the Ravens' deal with Baltimore allowed them to pay no rent or any of the construction costs, plus they received a $50 million cash relocation fee to move from Cleveland.[14]

There are a variety of ways the public has been asked to pay for public stadiums. Citizens pay either directly through new or expanded taxes or indirectly via the diversion of existing taxes from other sources, such as schools and law enforcement.[15] Direct methods are often referred to as "corporate welfare." Some places, like Cincinnati and Tampa use property and sales taxes; some use lottery revenues; Chicago, Detroit, Nashville, and St. Louis use hotel/motel taxes; rental car surcharges are used in Detroit, Chicago, and Houston; team merchandise and ticket taxes are used in Nashville; parking fees in Seattle; alcohol and cigarette taxes in Cleveland; and restaurant taxes in Detroit.[16]

Most of the corporate welfare does not come in the form of direct cash payments; rather, it comes in tax breaks. Tax breaks first appeared in baseball in the late 1940s, when Cleveland Indians owner Bill Veeck first applied a 1935 IRS ruling that allowed player salaries to be written off as expenses of running a sports business which, like any other spare part, depreciates.[17] This tax loophole was slightly reduced by the 1986 Tax Reform Act, but fear not, teams find a variety of other tax loopholes. For instance, some team owners own their own television stations then sell themselves the broadcast rights at flea market prices.[18] New York Yankees owner George Steinbrenner allegedly paid himself $25 million in the early 1980s for his role in negotiating his team's cable contract.[19] Another way to cook the books is to count profits without accurately deducting relevant items. For instance, the owner of the Philadelphia Eagles was making $7 million more than it appeared, because he was not counting that $7 million salary he was paying himself.[20] Because many owners control the team, the stadium, broadcast outlets, and even surrounding areas, there is ample opportunity to fake losses via shifting revenues between the entities.[21]

Or, if owners do not get a tax break from the get-go, many are able to negotiate deals where they pay absolutely no local property taxes if they agree to stay there.[22] One more cheeky tactic: some teams negotiate ticket guarantees, whereby the team stays in the area in exchange for the city agreeing to make up the shortfall for unsold tickets. In 1996, the San Diego Chargers threatened to relocate when their lease expired. Not only did the city cough up $76 million to renovate Jack Murphy (now Qualcomm) Stadium, adding 10,000 seats, but it also guaranteed that it would pick up the slack if less than 60,000 tickets per game were sold for each of the next 10 years.[23]

PERSUADING THE PUBLIC

So, how does this happen? Why does the public go for it? Sometimes, the answer is that they do not, but their voices are ignored. The stadium building enterprise has become less and less democratic in recent years, and sometimes the voters speak but no one cares. This was the case with residents of Pittsburgh and Phoenix.[24] In Pittsburgh, Mayor Tom Murphy promised voters that, if Plan A (a referendum to increase the regional sales tax to fund two new sports stadiums and expand a convention center) failed, there would be no stadium, no "Plan B." In other words, once the voters spoke, they would not be pestered again. Yet despite the fact that citizens voted against Plan A, almost two-to-one, 4 years later both the Steelers and the Pirates were playing in new stadiums paid for largely through tax dollars.[25] In fact, a Pittsburgh public official made it clear there had always been a Plan B, which did not include any public participation.[26] When the Seattle Mariners threatened to leave in 1995 if it didn't get a new stadium, voters said go ahead and leave. State legislators, however, ignored their constituents and authorized $320 million in a special session, only to raise that to $414 million when the Mariners were still not satisfied.[27]

In other cases, there is no mechanism in place, such as a referendum, to poll citizens' support. Thus team owners and politicians cannot say they ignored the will of the people—they simply never sought it.[28] In other cases, proponents of new facilities paid lip service to wanting to hear from the public, but made doing so incredibly difficult. So-called public hearings are sometimes not-so-public, as Minnesota voters found when meeting dates and times would be switched at the last minute.[29] In addition, advocates for subsidized facilities clearly have more funds at their disposal, and tend to outspend opponents ten to one.[30] They are far more able to share their message with citizens than are local opposition groups. It is also true that the average citizen values the opinions of powerful people more than that of his or her peers, leading many to accept the claims, however outlandish, made by those with the deepest pockets.[31]

Sometimes voters do approve these new projects. By implication, then, the project must be viewed as worthwhile. A look at the claims made by stadium advocates provides a different story. It is often taken for granted that building a new stadium for a team will be beneficial to a number of people in a variety of ways. Team owners, local groups seeking community growth, and the media have all typically argued that stadiums will provide an economic windfall in the area by providing new jobs, revitalizing existing businesses, and helping to create new businesses. New jobs will be created for the construction of the stadium, albeit temporarily, but also for the stadium's daily operations. The new stadium will also, supposedly, spawn new ancillary businesses, like restaurants, gas stations, hotels, and shopping areas.[32] One especially outlandish claim was made by a Sacramento civic leader, who maintained, "The Raiders coming to Sacramento would be an event the magnitude of the Gold Rush."[33]

CONSEQUENCES...

While it is assumed that the team will benefit by being able to compete in the most state of the art facility and that owners will reap some profits from the arrangement, the fact that the community benefits from the economic impact of the stadium is supposedly a given as well. While the former is typically true, the latter rarely is. It is, however, heavily marketed to the people as fact. Estimates are that a new stadium or arena can add $10–40 million to a team's annual earnings, as well as double the value of the franchise. The Orioles sold for 147 percent more in 1993, after Camden Yards was built, than in 1989, when the facility was under construction. In 1993, the year before the opening of Jacobs Field, the Indians were the least-valued team in baseball. By 1996, the team was worth $125 million, a 54 percent gain over 3 years for the team owners.[34] In 1989 the Texas Rangers were acquired for $86 million. In 1998, the team sold for $250 million.[35] Buying and selling teams is a sure-fire way to make money, far more effective than trying to profit from only day-to-day operations.[36] President Bush made over $14 million when he sold the Rangers in 1999, in part due to their new facility.[37]

Sometimes voters support building new facilities at one price, yet are saddled with far bigger bills in the end. When Cleveland voters narrowly approved a new facility for the Indians (51.7% supported the Gateway Initiative, as it was called), they were told it would cost $343 million. The project cost was up to $462 million by 1996, and continued to escalate.[38] Taxpayers in Seattle will be paying off the almost $1 billion for the Mariners and Seahawks for some time.[39] Cost overruns are virtually guaranteed, and teams obviously have the upper hand. Once a stadium is partially built, there is little a community can do but fund it until completion.[40] The *Sports Business Journal* calculated the "real" cost of constructing new facilities, including all additional and hidden costs the owners tend not to include, and found the real costs to far exceed the projected costs. The Fleet Center in Boston cost $115 million more than estimated, for instance.[41]

Even when proposals for new facilities are shot down, perseverance typically pays off. In San Francisco, the fifth time was the charm for the Giants owner.[42] Similarly, when one team in an area gets a new stadium or arena, other local teams put the pressure on too. After the Colorado Rockies moved into Coors Field, Broncos owner Pat Bowlen argued his team needed to have a stadium that was just as attractive in order to stay competitive.[43]

In recent years, fewer stadium proponents are using the economic arguments to try to convince a community to build the new facility. This is due, in part, to a small but growing number of skeptics about the role of sports in a community. Further, residents themselves have come to see that the grandiose claims about new jobs and economic revitalization are not true in most places. A simple drive through downtown Detroit shows an area of vacant buildings and demolition projects, not a booming metropolis. The Silverdome, located in what is known to locals as "Ponticrack," simply did not result in massive economic spillover, as was predicted. The Silverdome now sits largely unused, as the Lions have moved on to the greener pastures of Ford Field. Research by sports economists, sociologists, public administrators, and others has repeatedly shown these claims as false as well.[44] Economist Allen Sanderson argued that dropping money from a helicopter over the Twin Cities would result in eight to ten times the jobs allegedly created (168) by a new stadium.[45]

Arguments that new jobs are created have tended to ignore the fact that other jobs will be lost. Proponents of the economic benefits of new stadiums and arenas typically fail to mention that some local businesses will suffer, if not be closed, due to the new facility. This is especially true when the facility includes all types of consumer spending opportunities within its walls, including a variety of restaurants and shopping that inevitably take away from existing businesses offering those services. The first major facility to do this was Camden Yards in Baltimore, where spectators can arrive early to a game to buy all varieties of food, play video games, and shop for souvenirs, all inside the stadium.[46] The city lost a good portion of the 1,000 manufacturing jobs provided by the twenty-six companies that no longer exist because of Camden Yards.[47] A study of the impact of the new Comiskey Park in Chicago found only three businesses still open on one side of the facility, and residents only slightly farther away state the stadium has pulled shoppers away from businesses there.[48]

A number of studies have found new stadiums and arenas to have a *negative* impact on the local economy. Baade and Dye found a decline in the city's share of regional income after a new facility was built in seven of nine cities they studied.[49] In a larger study including forty-eight cities from 1958 to 1987, Baade found no instances of a positive impact on city growth and three cities where the impact was clearly negative.[50] Even when there is increased spending in a city with a new facility, it may not represent new dollars but rather expenditure substitution— money that was once spent on another entertainment source. Spirou and Bennett use the example of Coors Field in Denver. The stadium might actually decrease traffic downtown. Parking can range from $15 to $20, so many who are considering attending are discouraged from doing so, and thus do not spend money elsewhere in LoDo either.[51] In sum, economist Andrew Zimbalist has stated that having a new stadium or arena, or even a sports team in general, does not increase per capita income or employment rates of the community.[52]

Realistically, this should not be surprising. Although professional sports have grown tremendously and are enormously popular in the United States, the entire professional sports industry accounts for a very small percentage of the economic activity in a city or region. According to Rosentraub, the professional sports industry constitutes only about 0.2 percent of the city or region's employment.[53] One researcher has even said that a professional sports team contributes only as much to the local economy as does the local Publix or Meijers.[54] Former senator Sam Ervin likened the professional sports industry to the pork and beans industry.[55]

Confronting (and Evading) the Consequences

Supporters of public monies funding private stadiums have had to become more creative in the ways they "sell" their proposals to the public. One strategy is simply to ignore the large body of research regarding economic impact, or to assert it is not relevant to the specific city. One team owner told Delaney and Eckstein, "Baseball stadiums are different. There is great economic power generated by drawing 3.5 million people . . . "[56] Other team owners erroneously point to cities like Denver, Baltimore, and Cleveland as examples that the economic impact literature is wrong. Yet, Cleveland is hardly thriving, as evidenced by its poor public school system, which was put under state control during the stadium boom,[57] and the city's poverty rate, which rose to over 40 percent in the mid-1990s.[58] Baltimore's downtown was doing well a decade prior to Camden Yards, largely due to the National Aquarium that is open 280 more days than the stadium. And while Denver's Coors Field is located near to the bustling LoDo region, LoDo too, was doing well prior to the building of the stadium, and other areas located closer to the facility have not seen any impact.[59]

Others acknowledge the economic impact studies, but find fault with them. One supporter in Cleveland asserted that, "It seems pretty obvious to me that if you put up a ballpark and arena and bring 4.5 million people into a concentrated area, you are going to spur some economic development."[60] While it is nice that this man has such confidence in his intuition, it is hard to accept that it is more accurate than years of scientific research. Some supporters of new facilities even conduct their own studies, which they then assert are more accurate and useful. Not surprisingly, these studies support building the new facility. Despite the clear bias, what tends to happen is that these studies get promulgated as fact in the media, and few readers stop to question the source or the methodology used. Sociologist Lee Clarke refers to this type of study as a fantasy document, and explains that people who conduct them and disseminate the results use a façade of objectivity and neutrality to pass them off as legitimate.[61] Regardless of the specific tactic, in every city where the public vote has supported a new facility, the claim that it will cost little or that whatever cost will easily be recuperated by the overall benefits has been featured.[62]

Yet another new strategy is to focus on the intangible benefits a new stadium or arena can provide. Allegedly a new sports facility can bring publicity to a city, provide citizens with a sense of accomplishment, and offer a way for the community to unify. A new stadium, it is said, will impact the way citizens view the community as well as the way outsiders view it. To convince the citizens that a new facility will enhance the city's image, stadium proponents often make comparisons to nearby "inferior cities." Thus, in Cleveland an argument was made that failure to build a new stadium would turn the city into another Akron, and Cincinnati was told they could avoid being the next Dayton if they simply built a new stadium.[63] Proponents in Cincinnati working to approve Paul Brown stadium for the Bengals and the Great American Ballpark for the Reds, costing over $800 million total, promoted the slogan "Keep Cincinnati a Major League City." It was splashed all over T-shirts, bumper stickers, and signs, telling citizens that if they did not support the new facilities, the city was destined for the dumps.[64] A Missouri Senator claimed that St. Louis became a second-class city when football left, but returned to first-class status when it returned.[65]

The campaigning is a bit more repugnant in some cases. When the Miami Heat wanted a new facility, popular coach and part-owner Pat Riley was the spokesperson. While the sales tactic started out nice—showing voters all the benefits of a new stadium to the community at large and specifically for families—it went nasty fast. Without a new stadium, Miami-Dade County would become a haven for criminals, according to the ads.[66] In another sad appeal (which thankfully only appeared in Minnesota twice before it was pulled), proponents attempted to tug at the heartstrings of voters. The words "8-year-old" appeared against a black background. A voiceover then announced, "If the Twins leave Minnesota, an 8-year-old from Willmar undergoing chemotherapy will never get a visit from Marty Cordova." The next screen showed Cordova handing an obviously ill boy a present.[67] Certainly it is true that a visit from a sports idol can lift the spirits of a sick child, but that a new stadium for the Twins was linked in this highly exploitative way to a child's major health problem is abhorrent. Even worse, it turned out the boy had already died when the ad was aired.[68]

New facilities are also said to provide a collective conscience to the community, something rarely found in the McDonaldized world.[69] The threat to move the team to another city remains one of the most frequently used vehicles for manipulating collective conscience. This tool has been used with greater frequency since the 1980s, although there was a surge between 1952 and 1968.[70] Prior to the Oakland Raiders' move to Los Angeles in 1982, no established professional football team had moved in two decades. It had been a dozen years since there was a baseball team move, and even though basketball saw tremendous growth in new franchises, there was not much among established teams.[71] Some say the Colts' move from Baltimore to Indianapolis in 1984 signified the coming of a new era. The Colts' move was purely driven by the profit motive, as they had good ticket sales prior to the move. The move netted the team a bundle, but cost taxpayers in the two communities close to $1 billion.[72] Between 1982 and 1997, seven NFL teams relocated.[73] In 1995, it was estimated that 49 of the 113 professional franchises in the four major leagues were considering a move unless they obtained a better deal on their current lease or a completely new facility.[74] Team owners are rarely direct about the threat to move. Rather, they say things like, "We don't know where we're going to play . . . We'll have to look around," as the Miami Heat did.[75] Maryland State Senator Julian Lapides once put football and baseball teams in the same category as blackmailers, hostage-takers, and terrorists, because of their demands.[76]

Many team owners assert that, while they love the old stadium, they simply cannot compete with all the other teams if they don't have a new one. This competitive advantage argument may have some merit, but is often based on falsified or exaggerated claims. Teams can cook their books to show losses, hoping to sway voters. For instance, the owner of the Baltimore Orioles claimed $6 million in yearly losses, which seemed to contradict the high attendance rates and an already great stadium deal. Because Major League Baseball prohibits teams from opening their books to the public, there is no way to verify these numbers.[77] Major League Baseball is also particularly subject to this type of subterfuge, as it has the "freest" free agency.[78] Teams like the Yankees snag up the best players with the highest salaries, and low-salary teams feel pressured to build a new facility as their only hope to compete. In Minnesota, few truly believed the Twins had lost money, but their creative accounting allowed them to use an escape clause in their lease agreement to leverage voters.[79]

In many of these cases, perhaps some work is required to better the facility, but not as much or at the cost stipulated by the teams. When the Tigers proposed a new facility in 1987, citizens formed the Tiger Stadium Fan Club. The Fan Club's response was that the old stadium certainly needed repairs, but they calculated the costs at $6 million, not the exorbitant $100 million owner Tom Monaghan claimed.[80] Denver spent $12.5 million in 1986 to renovate McNichols Arena for the Nuggets, which was only 11 years old. Only 8 years later the Nuggets demanded a new facility.[81] The Nuggets' neighbor, the Broncos, demanded a new facility, arguing Mile High Stadium was so bad it was likely to be condemned. Independent investigations said that, with some minor repairs and regular maintenance, the facility would last indefinitely.[82] Monaghan's successful wheeling and dealing was in contrast to public sentiment, as two-thirds favored renovations and 64 percent opposed city funds being used for a new stadium.[83] If the early efforts are not successful, some teams have found the perception of a crisis to serve them well. Like used car salesmen, owners tell the community they need to break out their checkbooks now, as the "good" deal might not be there tomorrow. In Detroit, a Wayne County official later admitted that the urgent August 1, 1991, deadline he was given by the Tigers was of his own making—a swindle to make the public think they better act.[84]

NEW STADIUMS AND SOCIAL CLASS

As we discussed in Chapter 1, promoters seize on the religious-like support of sports to make unsupported, and sometimes flat out false, claims to a highly receptive audience. They argue " . . . sports can bring people together across social and economic lines. Those lines are obliterated. You can have a CEO of a major corporation sitting next to a homeless person, and they both are there for a baseball game . . . "[85] *Can* seems to be the operative word—while logistically this is possible, it is hardly likely the homeless person will be invited to share the corporate suite in which the CEO is observing the game. A primary feature of the new stadiums is the greater number of luxury seats that are, by definition, only luxury if they are superior in a variety of ways to the normal spectator seat.[86] One key way they differ is in their price. As one example among many, the New York Islanders rent their luxury seats for $260,000 per season.[87] The 114 teams in the four major leagues made $1 billion in luxury suite revenues in the late 1990s. Over 75 percent of the suite tenants are corporations that have earnings of over $100 million annually.[88] Many maintain luxury boxes are clearly for profit making, as they do nothing to make the game more enjoyable for fans or to alter the quality of the game.

More season tickets also mean fewer affordable tickets for local residents, as corporations snatch up most of them. Estimates are that corporations hold 50–60 percent of the season tickets for the NHL and NBA.[89] And, continuing the cycle of corporate welfare discussed earlier, corporations can deduct the cost of these tickets, allowing teams to charge even more.[90]

Many of these new stadiums are funded through the sale of lottery tickets or on so-called "sin taxes" on items such as cigarettes and alcohol. It can certainly be argued that these taxes are disproportionately collected from the poor. In another example of the poor paying to line the pockets of the wealthy, some stadiums have been funded by casino taxes. The new Tiger stadium was partly funded by a casino tax approved by then-Governor John Engler.[91] When the casino is on reservation land, as many are, this takes revenue from Native Americans, who are some of the poorest people in America. This was the case in Minnesota as well, where politicians denounced the greedy Indians, some of whom were making

$600,000 per year, while ignoring that there are baseball players making hundreds of thousands per game.[92] Said one Indian lobbyist, "There's never been anybody standing in line to share our poverty. Now everybody's in line to take away our money."[93]

Consequently, the poor are increasingly being asked to fund facilities they cannot afford to enjoy. The average cost for a family of four to attend a major league game and to purchase average concessions of sodas, hotdogs, beer, programs, and souvenirs, called the fan cost index (FCI), increased for all major league sports since 1990–1991. The NHL saw an 81percent increase; the NBA had an 84 percent increase; and 90 percent and 92 percent increases for the NFL and MLB, respectively.[94] The actual cost to attend is perhaps even more important than the percent increase. The FCI for attending a Major League Baseball game was the cheapest in 2002–2003, at $148.61, and maxed out for attending an NFL game at $290.41.[95] One union activist in Baltimore commented that the higher prices are also making the crowd far more white.[96] How interesting, at a time when the major sports are increasingly dominated by nonwhite players. Nor are the new facilities often as fan-friendly for the average spectator. For instance, upper deck fans (the cheap seats) sat less than half the distance from the field in the old Tiger stadium as they do in the new ballparks like Camden Yards.[97] Old Comiskey Park was 75 feet high, while New Comiskey park is 146 feet high.[98] This is largely due to the new cantilevered upper levels. Stadiums of old featured steel supports, which blocked the view from some seats. Cantilevering alleviates this problem, but puts more seats farther away.[99] Minor league fans are also wondering whether the money is worth it. One fan said he used to buy $5 tickets to sit behind home plate, and now all he can get is an $8 ticket behind a foul pole.[100]

While the above discussion has focused on the ways that citizens pay directly for new stadiums and arenas, the public also pays in more indirect ways. These are the opportunity costs, or the things that the money spent on the new facility *could* have been used for. Poorer cities often find their social services decimated after a new stadium is constructed. The Cleveland Teachers Union says the city schools lost more than $3.5 million in just the year 1995 due to tax abatements granted to Jacobs Field and Gund Arena.[101] In Texas, it was estimated that schools lost $480 million between 1985 and 1995 due to tax abatements.[102] Washington, DC, recently pledged $600 million for a new baseball stadium for the Nationals, while also laying off 300 public school workers, closing the city's only public hospital, and maintaining an infant mortality rate worse than Haiti.[103] In addition, creating the ballpark will mean destroying low-income housing and several homeless shelters.[104] One Minnesota protester said the money being suggested to support a new stadium could pay the salaries of 840 teachers for 10 years or 600 police officers for the same amount of time.[105] Just as bad as the actual financial impact is the symbolic notion that a "nicer place to take a shower" is more important than the quality of education for future generations.[106] Baltimore Ravens owner Art Modell explained, "The pride and presence of a professional football team is more important than 30 libraries."[107]

CORPORATE INVOLVEMENT

While it is easy to chalk this up to greedy owners, that is far too simple. It is impossible today to separate the individual owners from the larger sports industry. Team owners are only acting in the way they are supposed to—to make a profit.[108] The leagues encourage this, sometimes directly and sometimes indirectly. In Cleveland, baseball Commissioner Fay Vincent visited the city 2 days prior to the vote for a new facility for the Indians, telling residents how harmful a "no" vote would be.[109] National League president Leonard Coleman did the same in 1996 for the Houston Astros, as did American League president Gene Budig for the Red Sox.[110] NFL Commissioner Paul Tagliabue is on board as well, stating, "The team is a significant economic asset to the community and the state. So I think investment on all sides is warranted."[111]

Moreover, it is not just the team owners pushing for bigger, better facilities; major corporations are part of the push too.[112] Corporate ownership of teams is the norm today in three of the four major league sports—NFL regulations prohibit corporate ownership. More than fifty companies own at least a portion of the eighty-nine franchises in Major League Baseball, the National Basketball Association, and the National Hockey League.[113] In 2000, forty-five individuals from the *Forbes* magazine list of the wealthiest 400 individuals in the United States owned a direct interest in at least one team in the four major leagues.[114]

Corporations also want to benefit from the access to new luxury suites, which they can use to woo new clients and employees. In a clear reflection of the patriarchal society, all the corporate executives interviewed by Delaney and Eckstein mentioned these suites as invaluable in recruiting new talent, designated by the pronoun, "he."[115] Clearly, wooing and retaining female clients and employees is not viewed as critical. Corporate executives are especially enamored with the notion that they are part of a growing, vital city, and thus are likely to buy the argument that a new sports stadium or arena is a marker of success.[116] And, many corporate executives are simply sports fans who want to believe a new stadium will be great for the community. Law firms that negotiate the deals also do well financially, and thus have little advantage in denouncing the projects.[117]

MEDIA PROMOTION

The media has become increasingly critical in disseminating the message that a new facility is needed. While sometimes journalists are not in favor of public money supporting private facilities, it is the editors who get to decide what makes the news. In every city studied by Delaney and Eckstein (2003), the main local newspaper favored the use of public money for new stadiums and arenas in their editorial sections. As part of the power elite, it may be that these people all share an ideological lens. In fact, in Minneapolis reporters threatened to walk out because the publisher was taking an activist role in promoting the new construction.[118] Even when the media is not overtly favoring stadium supporters, those with the most money get to purchase the larger share of advertising time on television and radio. Microsoft cofounder Paul Allen, owner of the Seattle Seahawks, spent over $9 million in just 6 weeks of stadium lobbying efforts.[119]

The media tend to make it sound as though the local citizens all support the new stadium or arena, and that those opposed are unfeeling morons who do not care about the betterment of their city. On the contrary, as many researchers have noted, there are opposition groups in virtually every city where a new facility is planned. These people are indeed concerned about their cities, but do not see the "corporate welfare," as they often call it, provided to professional sports teams as civic assistance.[120] In fact, voters often say, when given a chance, that there are numerous places they would rather see their money go. Voters in Minnesota in 1997 identified schools as the number one place they would divide their tax money. A new stadium ranked last among the choices.[121] Too often, however, voters are not given choices. Instead, they *might* have the opportunity to vote in favor of or against a new stadium, as described earlier, but no one is approaching them with a plan to spend their money elsewhere.

Even more insidious is that the media and teams are, with greater frequency, controlled by the same corporation. Disney, News Corporation, and AOL Time-Warner, three of the biggest media corporations in the United States, own the Los Angeles Dodgers, the Atlanta Braves, the Atlanta Hawks, the Anaheim Angels, and the Mighty Ducks of Anaheim.[122] Fox Entertainment owns the Los Angeles Dodgers.[123] The Chicago Cubs and their broadcaster, *WGN*, are both owned by the *Chicago Tribune*.[124] When major media moguls own teams, it is difficult to see them providing unbiased coverage of the pros and cons of new facilities.

STADIUMS AND THE WORLD OF AMATEUR SPORTS

Sadly, the bilking of the public to pay for the perks of a few has spread to collegiate sports and even to the high school ranks. At the college level, students frequently find themselves paying greater student fees for new stadiums and arenas. For instance, students at the University of Minnesota were asked to pay $50 per semester toward the estimated $235 million total for a new on-campus stadium.[125] Not all students see the benefits, and many would rather see their money spent on other things, like more parking. Many students are simply unaware of where the money from the various student fees they pay is directed. As has been well documented, teams assert that they need bigger, better facilities in order to attract the best athletes and coaches, and to put the school "on the map." Thus, schools have engaged in what has been called an "arms race" for new or upgraded facilities.[126] Major examples include the $350 million spent at Ohio State, $100 million at California, and $93.5 million at Penn State.[127] In addition, as we explained in the Introduction, NCAA requirements drive the arms race, as teams wishing to play at higher levels (Division I instead of Division II, for instance) must add seating capacity, etc.[128] In 2001, at least 43 of the 117 teams in Division I-A football were upgrading facilities.[129] And, like the major leagues, the trend in new college facilities is to add luxury suites and club seats. In the year 2000, Kansas State spent $13.5 million for an upgrade that included 2000 more club seats and thirty-one luxury suites. The club seats sold for $700 each and required a 5-year minimum commitment, while the suites were leased for 5 years at $32,000 per season.[130]

At the high school level, a new stadium in Denton, Texas, cost $18.3 million and features 12,000 seats, two VIP suites that can each accommodate twenty-two people, and a $900,000 scoreboard with a video screen to show replays.[131] It was built in 2004 and financed by voter-approved bonds. And, frighteningly, it is not an isolated example. Sixteen miles south is a new $19.5 million football stadium in Fort Worth (replete with 950 club seats and a two-tier press box), and 23 miles south is a 4-year-old stadium built for $15.3 million. It is so nice it is loaned to Major League Soccer's Dallas Burn as a home field. The football team at the same school also has an 80-yard-long indoor practice field occasionally borrowed by the Dallas Cowboys.[132] By the end of 2006, twenty-five new high school stadiums, costing some $180 million, will have opened in the Dallas-Fort Worth area.[133] Before this is chalked up to just a Texas, "football-is-king" phenomenon, outlandish facilities have been built for high school teams in Indiana, Oklahoma, California, and Arizona. McGraw Hill Construction estimates that $440 million was spent on high school facilities, largely in Texas, California, and Arizona, in 2004.[134] This stadium arms race comes at a time when schools are suffering, in particular in Texas. In 2004, a judge ruled in favor of the more than 300 schools who claimed the state's funding system did not provide enough to adequately educate children.[135] Yet voters approved these projects. Is it that people in these states do not care about education? Or care more about sports than they do the classroom experience of their children? Perhaps, but that is overly simplistic.

CONCLUSION

The debate about public monies supporting private facilities reflects a broader concern in the United States, which is how to best keep cities vibrant and to help those in decline. Many have focused their strategy on making cities areas for tourism, essentially seeing cities as zones for entertainment and little else. Professional sports, and especially new stadiums, are seen as a way to energize a city and to retain businesses and residents. It seems to be assumed that cities have nothing to offer but fun and games, and that the bulk of revitalization efforts should be addressed to tourists, not residents. This assumption ignores those who *do* reside in the city, often by default because they cannot afford to live elsewhere. These people tend to see the entertainment focus as an incredible affront, expressing that monies spent on stadiums and entertainment facilities are a tremendous misuse of funds. One activist in Minnesota explained that, while recent legislation was intended to stop fraud of the traditional welfare system, perhaps more attention should be paid to those who were receiving corporate welfare.[136] As Cagan and deMause explain, "Seeing once-proud downtowns reduced to clamoring for tourist dollars is oddly reminiscent of third world countries continually redefining themselves and their priorities, or being redefined, by their relationship to the almighty U.S. dollar."[137]

Some cities have become desperate for tourist dollars and have resorted to a variety of gimmicks to achieve that end. They jump on the bandwagon, following the latest fad—be it festival market places or pedestrian shopping malls—as we described in the Introduction.[138] This is the McDonaldized, "themed" America, so such a response is predictable.[139] Yet, in reality, copycatting another city is not always effective. As Delaney and Eckstein point out, "Only the most die-hard football fan will visit Cleveland in early January just to see a football game in the new lakefront stadium."[140] Of course, the other alternative is to better cities by supporting their existing enterprises. This might include putting money into schools and local industries, as well as providing new housing for residents. The choice to use tourism as the growth strategy typically precludes a city from the social support strategy, which may be more effective.[141] It is most definitely the more humanistic approach. The day before the vote on the new football stadium in Cleveland, the public schools announced it needed to cut $52 million in 2 years and was laying off up to 160 teachers and cutting interscholastic sports.[142]

In opposition to the United States, the philosophy in Europe is to save whatever of old facilities they can. Renovations are preferable to destruction, whereas in the United States historic landmarks may fall in the name of progress.[143] Of course, we might want it to *look* like the place is old, hence the new baseball stadiums described in the Introduction that are pseudo-old. The same fakery and subterfuge holds for food available in the new stadiums. Rather than a unique experience purveyed by various local vendors on the streets surrounding the stadium, the new McDonaldized facilities feature the predictable pseudo-ethnic chain restaurant food. Teriyaki chicken purveyed by Applebees hardly qualifies as ethnic food. These stadiums are, as is Disneyland, locations for consumption.[144] Some people don't buy it—they see these new facilities as having no heart.

Two key court cases may significantly impact team owners' collection of corporate welfare. In *Kelo v. New London*, the Supreme Court will decide when the government may use eminent domain to acquire private property for projects that will benefit private businesses. In 1954, the court deemed that a "blighted" neighborhood could be torn down for development efforts. Governments have obviously expanded on this decision to obtain land that is not blighted but would be useful to private businesses, such as land needed for parking lots near a stadium. Between 1998 and 2002, more than 10,000 cases of transfers or threatened transfers of private land to another private party have been documented. In one of the most famous cases, the Texas Rangers, then owned by President George W. Bush, swayed voters to approve construction of a new stadium for $191 million. They then used eminent domain to get local property from the residents, claiming it was applicable because the stadium would be for public use.[145] In *Hamilton County v. Cincinnati Bengals,*

Inc., a federal court in Cincinnati might force NFL teams to open their books, which could put the kibosh on the "you have to pay because we cannot afford to build it" claims.[146] The claim is that the Bengals bilked the citizens when they built a new stadium for $600 million based on claims the team needed the facility to perform better. A key piece of evidence in the case is that, despite moving to the new facility in 2000, the Bengals continue to struggle. Their record in the 5 years prior to the move was 29–51, and the last 5 years have been even worse, at 28–52. The Hamilton County Commissioner's office is arguing they were told the team needed the facility to win a Superbowl, and because they are nowhere near to doing so, the Bengals have violated antitrust laws. How so? Because the NFL limits the number of teams, the Bengals use their monopoly power to threaten voters with a move.[147]

chapter 9

Conclusions and Recommendations

I've been thinking a lot about "sportsmanship." It's hard to define—especially in football, which starts with premeditated mayhem.
—Texas linebacker, Pat Culpepper, 1963

What is the future of the sports business? We'd love to say that signs point to the demise of win-at-all-costs sports, but this is simply not the case. Sadly, younger and younger people are being drawn in. High school and even youth sports are being increasingly corrupted and, consequently, virtually all the problems we have discussed in this book can be seen at those levels as well. This is the topic of the first part of this chapter. On the good news front, however, we see a lot that *can* be done at the individual, institutional, and societal levels to make sports less problematic, which is the focus of the second part of the chapter.

THE YOUTH SPORTS CRAZE

Ever younger kids are being signed to lucrative endorsement contracts in the zeal to beat the competition to the next Michael Jordan. In 2003 Reebok started a national marketing campaign featuring 3-year-old sharpshooter, Mark Walker Jr.[1] Eight of the first nineteen NBA draft picks in 2004 came straight from high schools.[2] Parents fuel this early sports craze when they sign their kids up for every camp and elite team, and when they shell out big bucks for sports equipment and travel. In addition to the costly camps and equipment we have noted elsewhere in this text, some parents are paying for personal training for their budding sport superstars. In Washington, parents pay professional soccer players up to $150 an hour for personally instructing their children.[3]

Kids are starting organized sports at younger ages and are specializing in one sport sooner—travel hockey begins as early as 7 years, and baseball often starts at 8 years—young food for the machine.[4] Rashad Gadson, an 11-year-old, plays an estimated 60 hours of basketball per week—40 hours in a structured tutoring session and the rest in games and practices with his AAU team.[5] Kids are being told that if they ever want to be an athletic success, especially in soccer and hockey, they better take part in elite travel squads. Even more important, this type of success is marketed to parents of these would-be superstars, telling them their "special Johnny" has what it takes to make it big, if they only make the necessary time and monetary investment.[6] These teams often practice multiple times per week, and traveling for games often eats up entire weekends. This is in spite of research that demonstrates this type of specialization is not developmentally appropriate for children this young. The American Academy of Pediatrics recommends sports specialization only *after* a child has reached puberty.[7] In some areas youth programs have become feeders for big-time high school and even college athletic programs. Such is the case with Pop Warner football in South Florida, as documented in the book, *We Own This Game*.[8] The goal of youth sports should be to promote mass participation, something that they are failing miserably at right now.[9]

THE SPORTS ETHIC'S INFLUENCE ON COACHES AND PARENTS

Winning has taken on greater importance, even for coaches at the lowest levels. Jeff Laravie, coach of the third-grade "select" team from Centerville, Ohio, explained, "We don't want to lose a ballgame because we played kids equally. It's sort of like a business: I'm trying to put the best product on the floor."[10] Coaches are sometimes using confrontational, nasty tactics in order to score these wins. A recent study by the Minnesota Amateur Sports Commission found that 45.3 percent of youth involved in sports had been called names, yelled at, or insulted by a coach; 21 percent were pressured to play with an injury; 8.2 percent were pressured to intentionally harm others; and 17.5 percent had been hit, kicked, or slapped.[11] Ejections of coaches at the high school level have reached an all-time high. Reports from 2,200 chapters of the National Alliance for Youth Sports in May 2001 showed that about 15 percent of youth games involve some type of verbal or physical abuse from parents or coaches, up from 5 percent in 1996.[12] Too often it seems coaches are using the worthless mantra: "Do as I say, not as I do," to guide impressionable young people.[13] If these pressures were true in any other context, there would likely be quite an outcry. But because they occur in sports, we accept them and even justify them as necessary to "build character."

Coaches and administrators explain that their work with young athletes is like the relationship between students and teachers, and that the lessons learned on the field or court are every bit as important as those learned in the classroom. This allows them to justify whatever they do to kids, saying it is "educational" and necessary to make them a success. But, as John Gerdy points out, there are practically no educational standards for coaches, so why on earth do we believe them? How can we be sure they have any clue what would be "educational" for our kids? More frequently than ever, community members end up coaching high school teams, many of whom, despite their (usually) good intentions, have no idea about what would be an appropriate educational mission.[14] And, while there usually is some degree requirement for athletic administrators, the focus of these programs tends to be on the business end of sports, not on educational issues. Thus it is not surprising that these adults craft youth and high school sport according to their own personal values and agenda, not necessarily the wishes of young people.

Parents are getting just as bad as the coaches. A father in Sturgeon Bay, Wisconsin punched an umpire for failing to make a call on an 11-year-old pitcher. In Oklahoma a 36-year-old T-ball coach was convicted of assault for choking a 15-year-old umpire. Fred Engh, founder of the National Alliance for Youth Sports, recalls hearing a father tell his son, "You little bastard, you could never get anything right," and another beefy character telling his son, "I'm gonna get you tonight because you let me down, buddy."[15] One attorney in New Jersey has even capitalized on this trend by specializing in representing youth league umpires and officials who are assaulted by coaches or parents. The National Association of Sports Officials even provides assault insurance to umpires and referees at all levels of play—it covers legal fees, medical expenses, and revenue lost from missed games.[16] Sports psychologist Shane Murphy argues that the parents who act this way are not simply aberration, as apologists often claim. He maintains youth sports often bring out the worst in parents.[17]

A big part of the problem is that coaches, parents, and community members too often define sports success as making it to the pros. Anything less than this is considered failure. Even this definition of success is limited—the truly successful athlete is one who makes it in "big-time" sports, defined as those that are televised. Sports that require individual commitment, like cycling, swimming, and cross country, are not nearly as worthy, as they will not likely lead to a lucrative pro career and the visibility on TV. ESPN has furthered the idea that certain sports are more worthy through their coverage of high school basketball games featuring players likely to declare for the NBA draft.

This mentality has severely distorted high school sports such that, too often, only those with the most "potential" are even given the opportunity to play. At all levels of sports, from the pee-wees to the big-leagues, the majority is left on the sidelines to cheer while the most gifted get to show their stuff.[18] We gloat with pride when our daughters and sons "score" in sports, but tend to display only half-hearted cheer at their academic, musical, or artistic achievements, let alone applaud them for simply being good people. As John Gerdy explains, "What is wrong with youth sports is the adults. Youth sports programs are no longer about meeting the educational, developmental, and recreational needs of children but rather satisfying ego needs of adults."[19] Again, adults have co-opted kids' sports and imposed their love of competition and winning. Sport psychologist Shane Murphy explains that youth sport has come to look more and more like the corporate world, seeking the same traits as are sought in dedicated workers who toe the party line.[20]

THE YOUTH RESPONSE

Kids often believe that winning is what matters, too. Some respond by doing whatever they feel it takes to win—be it doping, starving themselves, cheating on the field and in the classroom, and hazing (or being hazed) in order to fit in. Yet others respond by dropping out of sports completely. A survey at the National PTA Convention in Charlotte, NC found 44 percent of parents claimed their child dropped out of a sport because it made him or her unhappy.[21] The number one reason why 10-year-olds play sports is to have fun, according to a 1991 study by the Institute for the Study of Youth Sports. "For the excitement of competition" ranked tenth.[22] When asked what might lure them back, the top three responses were: "If practices were more fun," "If I could play more," and "If coaches understood players better." It seems increasing numbers of kids are no longer participating in high school sports either, and when they're asked why, the vast majority say they hate how competitive it is. These kids want sports to be fun above anything else, in stark contrast to their coach's mission to make winning the most important feature. In a country with an enormous obesity problem, it is sad that only about 20 percent of high school students are involved in a sport.[23] Even worse is the fact that this is so incredibly changeable—if kids think there is too much stress on winning, *the adults* who create this atmosphere must stress the fun of the game if they hope to increase participation.

RECOGNIZING THE PROBLEM

So, is there anything that can be done about the state of sports? Indeed there is. Step one is to simply recognizing the problems that exist. For too long the notion that sports is good and character building has been preached as gospel. "We have become addicted to sport; it is our society's opiate," said John Gerdy.[24] Like an addiction to drugs or alcohol, our societal addiction to sports limits us in many ways. Some people invest more heavily in the lives of sports stars than they do their own intimate acquaintances, or even themselves. "Rather than interacting with a friend or family member, our eyes and attention turn instead to the tube, where we slowly slip into a collective *ESPN* stupor."[25] Rather than get involved ourselves, we sit virtually comatose on the couch, getting chubbier by the moment. "When I feel athletic, I go to a sports bar" is the mentality of many.[26] "Despite claims of the positive effect on the health of our populace, organized sports in America have become more about watching elite athletes perform rather than being active one's self; as likely to be associated with lying on the couch with a 6-pack of beer than with working up a sweat through vigorous exercise."[27] And, like any program for addicts, the first step to recovery is to admit that there is a problem.

Sadly, most don't mind this addiction—they don't even recognize it as such—and thus we cannot proceed to alter it. People believe, "Sport is pure, it is wholesome, it embodies the 'American way,' showcasing champions and providing us with winners to worship and emulate."[28] That sports is rife with major problems doesn't even enter the consciousness of many. Steeped in the sports-is-good philosophy, we tend to interpret all discussion of sports through this lens. So even when we can no longer ignore a problem—the allegations of widespread steroid use in Major League Baseball, for instance—we explain it away as the error of a few miscreants, not as an issue in need of systemic attention. And when we do admit there is a problem greater in scope, we too often shrug our heads and say, "That's just the way it is." Changing the way we look at sports might be difficult, but is not impossible.

As D. Stanley Eitzen explains, we *can* make changes in sports by making necessary changes in social arrangements; we are not passive recipients but active participants in the social order. Sports both produce and reflect cultural values.[29] The "we" here means all of us—as individuals, as parents, as athletes, as coaches, as representatives of the media, as team owners, and as members of athletic organizations—we have the power to make sports better for all involved.

Personal choices can also help change sports. Individuals may serve to challenge or preserve the status quo—we simply need to decide which we want.[30] There are many examples throughout history of athletes who have exercised their individual agency to challenge the dominant order—those who boycotted Olympic team participation because of persistent racism in the United States, for instance. Non-athletes, too, can challenge the hegemonic sports machine through their personal choices. Below we outline twenty changes we believe could occur at the individual, institutional, and societal levels to better sports in the United States. These suggestions represent a synthesis of our positions and those established by other authors who are equally troubled by the state of big-time sports. The following section provides eight recommendations that every individual can and should consider.

First, we can all elect to get off the couch and participate in a sports activity. We're not recommending that people go cold turkey and watch absolutely no sports, or never again attend a sporting event. We advocate (as does John Gerdy)[31] balance and perspective. Rather than an all-day football-viewing festival, perhaps a fan could watch one game and then go for a run. Not only can this make us healthier and fit, but it also sends a powerful message to others—namely, our children, the sports industry, and the sports media. Kids can see their parents, siblings, and their community as role models for athleticism. If we spend more time involved in sports and less as spectators, we are in essence giving a "no" vote to the excesses of big-time sports. This is not enough, however. It is essential that we *tell* those heading up the sports industry precisely *what* bothers us and precisely what we would like to see done about it. If we don't, those in charge of the sports business will simply work harder to compensate for the loss of spectators, and will do so in the same old way—jack up prices and make sports even more elite.

As Kathryn Jay of the *Washington Post* remarked,

Real change (in sports) depends on fans—and their wallets. In true democratic fashion, we get the sports world we deserve, one that mirrors the contradictions of American society. If the latest leaks from the steroid case get us to stop buying season tickets, ignore the Saturday afternoon contest between Big U and Even Bigger U, take down personal Web sites devoted to our favorite teams, or turn off "*SportsCenter*" highlights, only then will the sports industry finally get serious about dangerous drugs.[32]

Her logic applies to virtually all the problems in sports today—our message to those at the helm of the sports business is to clean up your act. And they will, if we make it clear enough that we will not watch games until they do.

Second, it is critical we are aware of where and on what we spend our money. Too often consumers are clueless about who is truly the beneficiary of their purchases. Consumers could elect *not* to purchase sports-related products made under unfair labor conditions, again telling the industry precisely why. Students at several universities have successfully lobbied their student stores to purchase school-named gear only from labor-friendly companies. We can also consider the impact of wearing shirts or shoes that endorse an athlete or team with questionable values. Public pressure has made many high school and colleges change their mascots. If we don't like the hiring practices of a team, or the way the coach treats his players, or the way the players treat each other, or anything else, why on earth should we continue to wear their gear and offer them our bodies as advertisement?

Third, we should all simply be informed. We can learn about both the positives and negatives of sports from sources outside of the mainstream media, especially books that offer a critical commentary. Further, we can learn about the graduation rates at our universities, as these are publicized each year. We can demand more information from our high schools, colleges, and local sports franchises—public monies support these things, and thus the public has a right to know how their money is being spent.

Fourth, we can and should demand better from the media. The media needs to be told in no uncertain terms what we want from them—less sexist portrayals, more diversity in sports coverage, more minority and female staff members, less focus on violence, and a more critical eye to both the successes and problems in sports. They want to make money via ratings and distribution. Show them we will turn off the tube or stop reading if they don't change and we will see a different media.

Fifth, as parents, we can give youth sports back to the kids. It's not actually about *us*, and we can and should let it be about *them*. Studies have shown kids, when left to their own devices, can quite nicely organize and manage their own games.[33] In fact, when children play without the imposition of adult structures and rules, they tend to handicap games to ensure even matches and fun for all.[34] And, when adults co-opt kids' games, they reduce if not eliminate the chances for kids to develop important leadership skills that they can develop through self-management of sports.[35] Other cultures do this far better. Edward C. Devereaux describes watching Japanese kindergarteners playing in a park. For the entire 45 minutes, the children organized their activities without a single adult's involvement.[36] Researchers have described similar self-managed games in Israel.[37]

Sixth, as parents, we can tell coaches whose behavior we abhor that we disapprove, and remove our children from their influence. Years ago Peter's mother did this, something to this day he thanks her for. Peter was playing on a travel soccer team and the coach was verbally harassing him and other players. At the end of the season, she told the coach clearly why her son would never play for him again. And, importantly, she explained to Peter that he deserved a better experience out of sports than what he was getting, and helped him find some other channel for his athletic interests. While Peter wasn't preparing for an Olympic soccer career, the same concept should hold true for parents of the truly gifted athlete. Even though many of the parents described in Joan Ryan's *Little Girls in Pretty Boxes* let Bela Karolyi and his comrades run roughshod over their children and even themselves, others did not. Some parents shopped around until they found a coach for their daughter who they felt nurtured her appropriately, even at the elite level.[38] According to psychologist Steve Danish, the goal of a youth coach should be to help children become personally competent. This includes the ability to make life plans, to be self-reliant, and to seek help when needed.[39] These seem to be the antithesis of the overcontrolling Karolyi model of coaching.

Seventh, parents can become informed about who exactly is coaching their children and what qualifications they have. Rather than take for granted that our school districts or youth programs will hire the most qualified people, often a dubious assumption, we can find out their credentials. Perhaps the worst-case scenario is presented when coaches become physically or sexually abusive. Too often athletes accept a coach's authority as complete and fail to tell other adults about questionable contact. And adults too often give these coaches their unquestioned support as well. Better yet, we can try to get involved with the hiring process so as to ensure someone who values the fun and health benefits of sports is in place. We can push for greater training of all coaches, like that offered by the National Alliance for Youth Sport, which has certified 2.1 million coaches.[40]

Finally, as parents, we can refuse to support the worst excesses in sports by coughing up our hard-earned cash for camps, personal training, expensive equipment, and fees for travel squads. In fact, we should consider the developmental appropriateness of allowing young children to participate in elitist travel teams. If the American Academy of Pediatrics recommends we allow only fun, noncompetitive sports activities for kids until they reach puberty, why on earth would we ignore them?

In addition to these individual-level changes, institutional changes should also occur. We make the following six recommendations for collegiate sports.

First, we recommend completely eliminating athletic scholarships and enforcing the NCAA Division III model throughout college sports. Along with this, professional sports (namely the NBA and NFL) can create their own farm systems that pay the athletes. As Rick Telander wrote in *The Hundred Yard Lie*, "Education and big-time sport have nothing to do with one another. They are not mutually exclusive, but they are not necessarily related."[41] Were we to eliminate athletic scholarships, certain sports programs at some schools would certainly suffer. But, as John Gerdy notes, it is unlikely that most Division I "big-time" programs will die from having no scholarships. Fans of these teams simply love their teams, however we "alter the packaging."[42] New fans may even develop, as research has shown a lot of people want more from their college teams than they are currently getting.[43] Many Division III schools still have excellent athletic programs, as do the Ivy and Patriot Leagues. And these teams tend to feature student-athletes who are actually qualified and capable students.

Many athletes would still qualify for scholarships if they were offered by-need.[44] The Drake group, an organization seeking to reform the problems associated with big-time college sports, recommends replacing athletic scholarships with need-based financial aid. Not only might this reduce some of the problems we have highlighted, but also the monetary savings could be transferred to where they should be anyway—education. More academic and need-based scholarships could be offered, thus countering the argument that eliminating athletic grants-in-aid would significantly reduce the number of people who are able to pursue a college education. Murray Sperber noted in 1998 that Duke gave $4 million in scholarships to 550 athletes, and only $400,000 in academic aid to 5,900 other students. Similarly, the University of North Carolina provided $3.2 million to their 690 athletes, and $636,000 to the remaining 15,000 students.[45] Eliminating scholarships for athletes might also reduce tension between athletes and other students, as non-athletes would feel less resentful of the perks athletes receive.[46]

In conjunction with the elimination of scholarships, we could develop farm or minor leagues separate from the colleges. Those who wish to seriously pursue a career in the pro ranks could go directly there from high school, omitting the step of playing in college. This tends to work well in baseball, which has an expansive minor league system. Colleges would still be able to field teams, but they would consist of students who simply wanted to play the specific sport and who felt competent to balance the practice load with their studies. Students participating in college sports would be subject to the same academic standards as their nonathlete counterparts. Not only would this help rid higher education of the hypocrisy and scandal associated with the current arrangements, but athletes seeking a professional career would also benefit by being able to immerse themselves in this pursuit without the distraction of trying to stay eligible to play. Rick Telander describes asking Barry Sanders when he was at Oklahoma State whether he wanted to be in college. Sanders responded, "No, but I have to be."[47] If the elimination of athletic scholarships and the creation of professional farm systems lead to a downsizing in big-time college sports, so be it. The schools will be able to divert money to academics. Also, it is likely that intramural and wellness programs would be expanded, to the benefit of the entire student body.[48]

Second, we would like to see a dramatically altered NCAA structure and a serious reduction in the power of the NCAA. This power can be given back to leagues and individual schools—and even better yet, the students. Jeremy Bloom, the former University of Colorado football player whom the NCAA refused to allow to continue playing because he accepted endorsement money in his capacity as a world class skier, calls the organization, "the judge, the jury and the executioner" for student-athletes.[49] As we documented in earlier chapters, the NCAA does a great job of nitpicking, but a less-than-stellar one of effecting real change. Sadly, too often school presidents, who have the ability to push the NCAA toward major reform, instead advocate or settle for incremental or cosmetic change.[50]

Athletes should be provided a greater role in managing their sports. Athletics in college *should* be about building autonomous and self-disciplined individuals. The best way to do this is to allow athletes to develop these skills in controlling their own sports as much as possible. D. Stanley Eitzen suggests allowing athletes to determine team rules, team discipline, starting lineups, strategy, and the calling of plays.[51]

Third, we recommend reconfiguring the role of college coaches. D. Stanley Eitzen suggests that college coaches be part of the academic community, meaning they get both the perks (job security of tenured faculty) as well as the limitations (significantly reduced salary). He also recommends that their outside income be limited.[52] Above all, college coaches should be committed to education and developing healthy, good humans.

Fourth, we can redefine the ways we measure success. Of course winning will remain important at this level, but coaches should be evaluated on far more than their wins and losses record. Eitzen recommends coaches be evaluated on their teaching skills, on their treatment of athletes, and on their graduation rates.[53] Ty Willingham would not have lost his coaching job at Notre Dame had this been the case.

To redefine success would need to include better screening of coaches and administrators' backgrounds. John Gerdy explains how, prior to the evolution of recruiting to today's spectacle, the most important criteria in hiring assistant coaches were teaching ability and head-coaching experience at the high school level. Now assistant coaches are hired for their ability to market programs to recruits.[54] A simple check into Jim Harrick, Jr.'s credentials would have revealed he was not qualified to teach at the University of Georgia, thus perhaps averting some of the scandal that now blights the school's athletic programs. That is, of course, if the people doing the checking truly care about the coach's background and not about rubber-stamping whomever the head coach wants.

Following this, if a coach repeatedly demonstrated abusive behavior toward athletes, school presidents absolutely must take action. In a classic example, Bobby Knight was allowed to berate players, demonstrate overt sexism, and even physically assault players while at Indiana. In an interview with Connie Chung, Knight was asked how he handled the pressure of coaching a big-time program. He responded with his infamous comparison to rape, saying, "If rape is inevitable, relax and enjoy it."[55] When university president Thomas Ehrlich issued a wishy-washy statement claiming Knight did not represent the university, Knight threw a tantrum and threatened to leave. Rather than defend his statement, or better yet, tell Knight to take a hike, Ehrlich apologized and begged Knight to stay.[56] This is the kind of "unconditional love" for a coach that degrades the entire athletic enterprise.

Fifth, colleges should work toward greater diversity in hiring coaches and athletic administration. The ratio of black coaches to black athletes is atrocious, as is the decline since Title IX of the proportion of teams coached by women. Diverse hiring committees would be more likely to hire minority applicants. These could include other coaches, athletes, nonathletes, faculty, and even community members.

Sixth, information about the athletic department's finances and practices should be published and accessible to students, parents, and faculty. As we have noted, the idea that big-time college programs generate huge revenue is largely a myth. When they do profit the money tends to stay in the athletic department, paying for more expansion of facilities and the often enormous salaries. Parents and students (the tuition payers) have the right to know, for instance, that in 1999, over 50 percent of Division I-A football programs ran a deficit.[57]

Ironically, students help fund athletics through student fees, but are typically not made aware of the athletic department's finances. Not only do students have no voice in the way these funds are distributed, but the lack of public knowledge about athletic department finances also prevents departments from being accountable.[58] Shannon Daily, a student at the College of William and Mary in Virginia, had no idea she paid almost $1,000 per year in a "general fee" that supports the school's athletic teams. Student fees account for more than 50 percent of the intercollegiate sports' operating budget at the fifteen 4-year, public colleges in Virginia, but most students, like Daily, are unaware of this because the fees do not specify where the money goes. In 2002–2003, James Madison, Longwood, Mary Washington, and Norfolk State all generated more than 90 percent of their sports operating budget from student fees.[59] In order to help achieve gender parity and work toward providing greater sporting opportunity, Eitzen recommends student fees be directed solely to women's sports and minor men's sports.[60]

We also have several recommendations for professional sports.

Teams should be owned by local governments, rather than wealthy individuals or corporations. Since localities already subsidize teams now, generally through stadium funding (as we documented in the Introduction and Chapter 8), it's only democratic that they be allowed to have some stake in the team's finances. The Green Bay Packers are owned by some 1,900 local residents. Interestingly, Green Bay is well known for its dedicated fans—a coincidence? Not likely. No ticket costs more than $28, although tickets are hard to come by because there is a 20,000-name waiting list for season tickets. Charities even run the stadium's concessions.[61] Of course, people have long-admired the Packers' model, which is seen as a great threat to the sports machine. Consequently, each league has passed a specific rule outlawing community ownership!

Teams should exercise moral turpitude clauses and refuse to draft convicted criminals. The Colorado Rockies released pitcher Denny Neagle after his second arrest in 14 months—his first for drunk driving and his second for soliciting a prostitute. Sadly, many have argued the Rockies only released Neagle because he wasn't that good.[62] In the event that a player commits an act of overt violence against another, as in the case of hockey's Marty McSorly, we support taking them to the criminal courts. As Jeff Benedict explains, employees in most professions are bound to uphold the law or face sanctions, and professional sports should be no different. He also recommends a loss of playing time for transgressions of the players' code of conduct, rather than fines.[63] One NFL player explained why lost playing time would be a more effective sanction: "I don't think fines have all that much impact on very many players, even the lower-paid players. The real impact on players comes when it affects their playing time. You work so hard to get on the field and you become proud of what you do."[64]

In regard to drafting players, Benedict argues no team should draft a player with more than one felony, and college players with one felony should be on a probationary list on draft day. If they were later convicted of a crime they would lose their eligibility to play. Because teams already investigate players in the scouting process and this is all a matter of public record, developing this type of draft plan would not be difficult.[65]

At the societal level, there are also things we can change that will not only better sports, but also better our society. The following are the ones that strike us as most important.

First, we need to reconsider the importance of offering athletic opportunity to everyone. When schools are faced with tight budgets, cuts might need to be made. But physical education and sports opportunities should not always be first on the chopping block. These can be reconfigured to cost a district less—perhaps teams can play only local opponents, alleviating some travel costs. Physical education should also be more about play and developing a love of lifelong fitness, not furthering the problems in sports by stressing team sports as the only possibility.

Second, we recommend a greater investment in providing athletic outlets at the community level. One option might be to open up school gyms for nighttime adult activities. While some communities already do this, some do not, and many do it quite sparingly. We also like the idea of community Olympic-style festivals, offering opportunities for participants of all ages and in a diverse array of sports. Corporate fitness challenges also help get local businesses involved and send a message that fitness is important. As more data comes out about the monetary costs of our nation's obesity problems, more and more grants will become available to communities to help fund these activities.

Third, we should all evaluate the role of competition in our lives. We need to ask ourselves whether our hypercompetitive approach to everything is serving us well, or serving us up a raw deal. As educator Alfie Kohn explains in *No Contest*, "Not only do we get carried away with competitive activities, but we turn almost every-thing else *into* a contest."[66] This may be difficult in a capitalist culture, but other societies that utilize a capitalist model do stress cooperation and egalitarianism more than the United States. Even if we cannot completely eliminate structural competition, as Kohn calls it, we can at least work to reduce our personal competitiveness.[67] Kathryn Jay of the *Washington Post* identified the American ideal that winning matters the most as the fundamental challenge to even modest reform in sport. We may pay lip service to cooperation and equality, but we truly value the person who gets ahead, whatever that means.[68] The problems of competition, then, are not exclusive to sport. As Alfie Kohn explains,

Sports not only reflect the prevailing mores of our society but perpetuate them. They function as socializing agents, teaching us the values of hierarchical power arrangements and encouraging us to accept the status quo . . . Sports do not simply build character, in other words; it builds exactly the kind of character that is most useful for the social system.[69]

We need to ask important questions like—Does competition spur quality in human relationships? Does it fuel individuality or conformity, even groupthink? Alfie Kohn argues that competition not only strains existing relationships, but also prevents others from developing.[70] It is difficult to appreciate someone as a human being when our sole goal is to beat him or her as badly as possible in competition. Competition does not help people appreciate diversity—it builds a sense of superiority and contempt for "the losers."[71] We can tell our kids that athletics does not *have* to be the "us versus them" endeavor it so often is. It can be about competing with ones' self to get better, about feeling good, and about cooperating. Rick Telander explains that the notion of competition as an adversarial battle is not necessarily a foregone conclusion. The word compete actually comes from the Latin root words *com* and *petere*, meaning "to seek together."[72] This is the premise behind the "new games" movement, which seeks to replace competitive games requiring specific sports skills with egalitarian games stressing fun and participation.[73] As John Gerdy explains, "Many take their connection to a team so seriously that when their team wins, it is an indication that the values and what they and their team 'stand for' are validated. We won, so therefore we are right and good."[74] But this is not innate to sports, or to humans, and is consequently an attitude we can and need to change.

Lastly, all Americans should engage in an in-depth analysis of our own assumptions about race, gender, and class. Support for Native American mascots and team names, or for trivializing names for women's teams, may not strike us as overtly problematic, but they perpetuate an attitude that these groups are inferior to the dominant Caucasian male. Too often people constrain change opportunities by deflecting attention, perhaps by suggesting matters like team names are not important in the realm of oppression. Yet as D. Stanley Eitzen concludes, "Symbols are extremely important in the messages they convey," and, "We can work to remove *all* (emphasis added) manifestations of racism and sexism on college campuses."[75]

As it stands, sports today is a monster with distorted values. In many cases, it does anything but build character. Because we love it, we want to replace this type of sports with a more just and humane configuration of sports. While certainly not the be all and end all, we feel these recommendations would go a long way toward making sports less like a machine and more the fun lifetime activity it should be.

Notes

INTRODUCTION

1. Pitts, B., and Stotlar, D. (2002), *Fundamentals of Sport Marketing,* 2nd ed. Morgantown, WV: Fitness Information Technology, Inc.

2. Ibid.

3. Coakley, J. (1998), *Sport in Society: Issues and Controversies*, 6th ed. Boston, MA: Irwin-McGraw-Hill, p. 326.

4. Pitts and Stotlar (2002), op. cit.

5. Ibid.

6. Howard, D., and Crompton, J. (2004), *Financing Sport*, 2nd ed. Morgantown, WV: Fitness Information Technology, Inc.

7. Ibid.

8. Ibid.

9. Ibid.

10. Ibid.

11. Ibid.

12. Eitzen, D. S. (2003), *Fair and Foul? Beyond the Myths and Paradoxes of Sport*, 2nd ed. Lanham, MD: Rowman & Littlefield.

13. Sperber, M. (1998), *Onward to Victory: The Crises That Shaped College Sports*, New York: Henry Holt and Company.

14. Eitzen (2003), op. cit.

15. Ibid.

16. Toma, J. D. (2003), *Football U: Spectator Sports in the Life of the American University*, Ann Arbor, MI: The University of Michigan Press.

17. Ibid.

18. Eitzen (2003), op. cit.

19. Ibid.

20. Law, A., Harvey, J., and Kemp, S. (2002), "The Global Sport Mass Media Oligopoly," *International Review for the Sociology of Sport*, pp. 279–302.

21. Coakley (1998), op. cit.

22. Eitzen (2003), op. cit.

23. Ibid.

24. Ibid.

25. Eitzen, D.S. (1999), *Fair and Foul? Beyond the Myths and Paradoxes of Sport*, 1st ed. Lanham, MD: Rowman & Littlefield.

26. Ibid, p. 16.

27. Eitzen (2003), op. cit.

28. Ibid.

29. Coakley (1998), op. cit.

30. Underwood, J. (1984), *Spoiled Sport*, Boston, MA: Little, Brown, and Co., p. 43.

31. http://www.espn.com.

32. Eitzen (2003), op. cit.

33. Ibid.

34. http://swz.salary.com/salarywizard///swzl_compresult_national_AVC170,00014.html.

35. Eitzen (2003), op. cit.

36. Gerdy, J. (2002), *Sports: The All-American Addiction*, Jackson, MS: University of Mississippi Press, p. xv.

37. Zirin, D. (2005), *What's My Name, Fool?* Chicago, IL: Haymarket Press.

38. Ibid., p. 125.

39. Eitzen (2003), op. cit.

40. Gerdy (2002), op. cit., p. 27.

41. Ibid, p. 108.

42. Ritzer, G. (2001), "The McDonaldization of Society." In Adler, P., and Adler, P. (Eds.), *Sociological Odyssey* (pp. 371–379), Belmont, CA: Wadsworth.

43. Ibid., p. 373.

44. Ritzer and Stillman (2001), op. cit.

45. Ibid.

46. Ibid., p. 106.

47. Ritzer (2001), op. cit., p. 376.

48. Eitzen (2003), op. cit., p. 107.

49. Ritzer (2001), op. cit., p. 373.

50. Coakley (1998), op. cit.

51. Ibid., p. 335.

52. Toma (2003), op. cit.

53. Sperber, M. (2000), *Beer and Circus: How Big-Time College Sports is Crippling Undergraduate Education*, New York: Owl.

54. Eitzen (2003), op. cit.

55. Miller (1997), op. cit.

56. Perrin, D. (2000), *American Fan*, New York: Avon, p. 181.

57. Ritzer (2001), op. cit., p. 374.

58. Ibid., p. 375.

59. Coakley (1998), op. cit., p. 326.

60. Putnam, D. (1999), *Controversies of the Sports World*, Westport, CT: Greenwood Press.

61. Eitzen (2003), op. cit., p. 45.

62. Ritzer (2001), op. cit., p. 376.

63. McGraw, D. (1996, June 3), "Playing the Stadium Game," *U.S. News & World Reports*, p. 46.

64. Miller (1997), op. cit.

65. Ritzer (2001), op. cit., p. 377.

66. Eitzen (2003), op. cit., p. 80.

67. Ibid., p. 124.

68. Ibid.

69. Ibid., p. 124.

70. Littwin, M., cited in Eitzen, D. (September 2000), "Slaves of Big-Time College Sports," *USA Today*, p. 29.

71. Ibid.

72. Ibid., p. 118.

73. Eitzen (2003), op. cit.

74. Ritzer and Stillman (2001), op. cit.

75. Miller (1997), op. cit., p. 121.

76. Ibid.

77. Ibid., p. 122.

78. Gerdy (2002), op. cit., p. 25.

79. Ritzer (2001), op. cit., p. 376.

80. Ritzer and Stillman (2001), op. cit.

81. Ibid.

82. Ibid.

83. Ibid.

84. Ibid.

85. Ibid., p. 102.

86. Ibid.

87. Rodak, J. (2004, December 8), "NFL Unveils Its Plans for Experience Fun Parks," *Florida Times-Union*, p. A-1.

88. Miller (1997), op. cit.

89. Eitzen (2003), op. cit. p. 12.

90. Hyman, M. (2003, April 15), "When Sports Wave the Flag-For Dollars," *Business Week Online*, p. N.

91. Zirin, D. (2005), *What's My Name, Fool?* Chicago, IL: Haymarket Books.

92. Putnam (1999), op. cit.

93. Perrin, D. (2000), *American Fan*, New York: Avon, p. 33.

94. Ritzer and Stillman (2001), op. cit.

95. Ibid.

96. Ibid.

97. Ibid.

98. Coakley (1998), op. cit., p. 297.

99. Cited in Welch, W. (1996, May 31), "Federal Taxpayers Shut out of Stadium Payoff," *USA Today*, p. A1.

100. Perrin (2000), op. cit., p. 9.

101. Eitzen (1993), op. cit.

102. Eitzen (2003), op. cit., p. 44.

103. King, C., and Springwood, C. (2001), *Beyond the Cheers: Race as Spectacle in College Sport*, Albany, NY: State University of New York Press, p. 18.

CHAPTER 1

1. Coakley, J. (1998), *Sport in Society: Issues and Controversies*, 6th ed. Boston, MA: Irwin-McGraw-Hill.

2. Ibid.

3. Ibid.

4. In Wiggins, D. (Ed.). (2004), *African Americans in Sports*, Armonck, NY: Sharpe, p. 397.

5. Coakley (1998), op. cit.

6. Ibid.

7. Ibid.

8. Lawler, J. (2002), *Punch! Why Women Participate in Violent Sports*, Terra Haute, ID: Wish Publishing.

9. Coakley (1998), op. cit.

10. In Underwood, J. (1984), *Spoiled Sport*, Boston, MA: Little, Brown, and Co.

11. Novack, M. (2001), "Sport as Religion." In Adler, P., and Adler, P. *Sociological Odyssey* (pp. 320–324), Belmont, CA: Wadsworth.

12. Perrin, D. (2000), *American Fan*, New York: Avon, p. 41.

13. Coakley (1998), op. cit., p. 486.

14. Ibid.

15. Ibid., p. 179.

16. Ibid., p. 475.

17. Ibid., p. 495.

18. Ibid., p. 144.

19. Messner, M., and Sabo, D. (1994), *Sex, Violence, and Power in Sports, Rethinking Masculinity*, Freedom, CA: Crossing, p. 84.

20. Lumpkin, A., Stoll, S., and Beller, J. (Eds.). (1994), *Sport Ethics: Applications for Fair Play*, St. Louis, MO: Marby.

21. McKay, J., Messner, M., and Sabo, D. (Eds.). (2000), *Masculinities, Gender Relations, and Sport*, Thousand Oaks, CA: Sage, p. 156

22. Leizman, J. (1999), *Let's Kill 'Em*, Lanham, MD: University Press of America.

23. Eitzen, D. S. (2003), *Fair and Foul? Beyond the Myths and Paradoxes of Sport*, 2nd ed. Lanham, MD: Rowman & Littlefield, p. 46.

24. Underwood (1984), op. cit., p. 85.

25. Eitzen (2003), op. cit.

26. Ibid.

27. Lucas, S. (2000), "Nike's Commercial Solution," *International Review of the Sociology of Sport*, 35(2), pp. 59, 149–164.

28. Putnam, D. (1999), *Controversies in the Sports World*, Westport, CT: Greenwood, p. 79.

29. In Lapchick, R. (Ed.). (1996), *Sport in Society: Equal Opportunity or Business as Usual?* Thoasand Oaks, CA: Sage, p. 187.

30. Ibid., p. 114.

31. Ibid.

32. In McKay et al. (2000), op. cit.

33. Coakley (1998), op. cit., p. 179.

34. Lesko, M. (Ed.). (1999), *Masculinities at School*, Thousand Oaks, CA: Sage, p. 199.

35. Coakley (1998), op. cit., p. 199.

36. In Lapchick (1996), op. cit.

37. Underwood (1984), op. cit., p. 84.

38. Ibid., p. 97.

39. Leizman (1999), op. cit.

40. Copley, M. (2004, October 11), "Heckling Can Go from Good-Natured to Nasty," *Epley News Service.*

41. Reed, D. (2004, September 22), "Pitcher Faces Assault Charges," *The Mirror*, pp. 14, 16.

42. Ibid., p. 16.

43. Eitzen (2003), op. cit., p. 48.

44. Messner and Sabo (1994), op. cit., p. 41.

45. Thomas (2004), op. cit.

46. Ibid.

47. Putnam (1999), op. cit., p. 73.

48. Perrin (2000), op. cit., p. 79.

49. Ibid., p. 79.

50. McKay et al. (2000), op. cit., p. 127.

51. Putnam (1999), op. cit.

52. Underwood (1984), op. cit.

53. Lawler (2002), op. cit., p. 5.

54. Ibid.

55. Lumpkin et al. (1994), op. cit.

56. "Celebs." (1998, December 25–27), *USA Weekend* (online version).

57. Putnam (1999), op. cit., p. 169.

58. King and Springwood (2001), op. cit., p. 9.

59. In Sabo, D., and Jansen, S. (1994), "Seen but Not Heard: Black Men in Sports Media." In Messner, M., and Sabo, D. (Eds.), *Sex, Violence, and Power in Sports* (pp. 150–160), Freedom, CA: The Crossing Press.

60. Coakley (1998), op. cit., p. 155.

61. Brockway, Sandoz, J., and Winans, J. (Eds.). (1999), *Whatever it Takes: Women on Women's Sports*, New York: Farrar, Straus, & Giroux, p. 91.

62. Eitzen (2003), op. cit.

63. Ibid., p. 11.

64. Lumpkin et al. (1994), op. cit.

65. Ibid., p. 56.

66. Eitzen (2003), op. cit.

67. Putnam (1999), op. cit.

68. Eitzen (2003), op. cit.

69. Messner and Sabo, (1994), op. cit., p. 104.

70. Eitzen (2003), op. cit.

71. Ibid., p. 84.

72. "Anti-Gay Remarks by Athletes," at http://www.outsports.com.

73. Putnam (1999), op. cit.

74. Yaeger D., and Wolff, A. (1997, July 7), "Special Report: Cheating," *Sports Illustrated* (online version), p. 6.

75. Simon, R. (2004), *Fair Play: The Ethics of Sport*, Boulder, CO: Westview.

76. Eitzen (2003), op. cit.

77. Benedict, J. (1997), *Public Heroes, Private Felons*, Boston, MA: Northeastern University Press, p. 111.

78. Ibid., p. 127.

79. Ibid., p. 129.

80. Suggs, W. (1999, July 23), "Minnesota Coaches Did Not Interfere with Probes of Athletes' Conduct, Report Says," *Chronicle of Higher Education, 45*(46).

81. Underwood (1984), op. cit.

82. Benedict (1997), op. cit., p. 218.

83. Ibid., p. 28.

84. Ibid., p. 28.

85. Benedict, J. (2004), *Out of Bounds*, New York: HarperCollins.

86. Smith, G. (2002, April 8), "Lying in Wait," *Sports Illustrated*, p. 2.

87. Underwood (1984), op. cit.

88. Perrin (2000), op. cit., p. 21.

89. Underwood (1984), op. cit., p. 22.

90. Adler, P., and Adler, P. (1991), *Backboards and Blackboards: College Athletes and Role Engulfment*, New York: Columbia University Press, p. 52.

91. Eitzen (2003), op. cit.

92. Perrin (2000), op. cit.

93. Putnam (1999), op. cit., p. 49.

94. Perrin (2000), op. cit., p. 17.

95. Underwood (1984), op. cit., p. 156.

96. Ibid.

97. Ryan, J. (2000), *Little Girls in Pretty Boxes*, New York: Warner.

98. Lumpkin et al. (1994), op. cit.

99. Lesko (1999), op. cit.

100. Lapchick (1996), op. cit., p. 104.

101. Leizman (1999), op. cit.

102. Lesko (1999), op. cit.

103. Kohn, A. (1986), *No Contest*, Boston, MA: Houghton Mifflin.

104. In Leizman (1999), op. cit.

105. Kohn (1986), op. cit.

106. Eitzen (2003), op. cit., p. 42.

107. Lapchick (1996), op. cit.

108. Zirin, D. (2005), *What's My Name, Fool?* Chicago, IL: Haymarket Press.

109. Ibid.

110. King and Springwood (2001), op. cit.

111. Dunbar in McKay et al. (2000), op. cit.

112. Coakley (1998), op. cit., p. 501.

CHAPTER 2

1. Bodley, H. (2005, August 2), "Palmeiro Suspended for Steroids Policy Violation," *USA Today*.

2. Pedersen, W., and Wichstrom, L. (2001), "Adolescents, Doping Agents, and Drug Use: A Community Study," *Journal of Drug Issues, 31*(2), pp. 517–541.

3. Coakley, J. (1998), *Sport in Society: Issues and Controversies*, 6th ed. Boston, MA: Irwin-McGraw-Hill, p. 68.

4. Goldman, B. (1984), *Death in the Locker Room: Steroids and Sports*, Southbend, ID: Icarus, p. 31.

5. Simon, R. (2004), *Fair Play: The Ethics of Sport*, Boulder, CO: Westview.

6. Goldman (1984), op. cit., p. 33.

7. Gloster, R. (2004, July 14), "Regina Jacobs Suspended for 4 Years for Steroid Abuse," *USA Today*.

8. Saraceno, J. (2004, December 3), "Calling Out Barry Bonds," *USA Today*.

9. Haft, C. (2005, September 29), "Senator's Comment Prompts Managers Defense of Bonds," *San Jose Mercury News* (online version), http://www.mercurynews.com.

10. Eitzen, D. S. (2003), *Fair and Foul? Beyond the Myths and Paradoxes of Sport*, 2nd ed. Lanham, MD: Rowman & Littlefield.

11. Davies, R. (1994), *America's Obsession: Sports in American Society since 1945*, Belmont, CA: Wadsworth.

12. Goldman (1984), op. cit., p. 52.

13. Ibid., p. 69.

14. Walters, B. (2004, December 3), "Balco Chief on Sports Doping Scandal," retrieved from http://ABCNews.go.com/2020.

15. Goldman (1984), op. cit., p. 70.

16. Ibid., p. 71.

17. Ibid.

18. Ibid.

19. Ibid.

20. Walters (2004), op. cit.

21. Paige, W. (2004, December 5), "Bonds Deserves a 'C' for Historic 73," *Rocky Mountain News*, p. 1, 19B.

22. Goldman (1984), op. cit., p. 75.

23. Ibid.

24. Simon (2004), op. cit., p. 75.

25. Goldman (1984), op. cit., p. 16.

26. Bodley, H., and Antonen, M. (2005, February 13), "Canseco: Steroids Made Baseball Career Possible," *USA Today*.

27. Manning, A. (2002, July 9), "Kids, Steroids Don't Mix," *USA Today*, pp. 1–2C.

28. Ibid., p. 2.

29. Ibid., p. 2.

30. Ibid., p. 2.

31. Putnam, D. (1999), *Controversies in the Sports World*, Westport, CT: Greenwood.

32. Lenehan, P. (2003), *Anabolic Steroids and Other Performance-Enhancing Drugs*, London: Taylor & Francis.

33. Ibid.

34. Putnam (1999), op. cit.

35. Ibid.

36. Ibid.

37. Ibid.

38. Clayton, L. (1996), *Steroids*, New York: Rosen Publishing Group.

39. Goldman (1984), op. cit., p. 73.

40. Campos, M., Yonamine, M., and Moreau, R. (2003), "Marijuana as Doping in Sports," *Sports Medicine, 33* (6), pp. 395–399.

41. Clayton (1996), op. cit.

42. Putnam (1999), op. cit.

43. Clayton (1996), op. cit.

44. Ibid.

45. The Associated Press (2004, November 11), "Young Dealt Lifetime Ban for Another Positive Test," *Rocky Mountain News*, p. 14C.

46. Clayton (1996), op. cit.

47. Ibid.

48. Blitzer, W. (2004, December 3), "Steroid Controversy," CNN broadcast.

49. Purdy, M. (2005, November 16), "Baseball's New Drug Policy Fails to Close Loopholes," *San Jose Mercury News* (online version), http://www.mercurynews.com.

50. Hummel, R. (2005, August 2), "Palmeiro Suspended under MLB Steroids Policy," *St. Louis Post-Dispatch.*

51. Ibid.

52. Anshel, M., and Russell, K. (1997), "Examining Athletes' Attitudes toward Using Anabolic Steroids and Their Knowledge of the Possible Effects,"*Journal of Drug Education, 27*(2), pp. 121–145.

53. Davies (1994), op. cit.

54. Ibid.

55. Ibid.

56. Manning (2002), op. cit.

57. Klis, M. (2004, December 5), "For the Record, Bonds Debate Brewing," *The Denver Post*, p. 19B.

58. Blitzer (2004), op. cit.

59. *News Wire Reports* (2004, December 3), "Reported Testimony by Giambi Looms Large," *Rocky Mountain News.*

60. Walters (2004), op. cit.

61. Lumpkin, A., Stoll, S., and Beller, J. (Eds.) (1994), *Sport Ethics: Applications for Fair Play*, St. Louis, MO: Marby.

62. Bjerklie, D., and Park, A. (2004, August 16), "How Doctors Help the Dopers," *Time,* pp. 58–63.

63. Lenehan (2003), op. cit.

64. Bjerklie and Park (2004), op. cit.

65. Scanlon, B. (2004), "Using Others' Blood to Dope Not Common," *Rocky Mountain News*, p. 9B.

66. Verhulst, J. (2004, December 5), "The Blood Sport of Pro Cycling," *St. Petersbug Times*, 1P.

67. Macur, J. (2004, November 15), "Hamilton Faces Uphill Climb in Bid to Save Medal and Tour Hopes," *The International Herald Tribune*, p. 13.

68. Macur, J. (2004, November 14), "Gold that Has Lost Its Luster," *The New York Times,* p. 1.

69. Austen, I. (2004, September 24), "Gold is Hamilton's, Even though Test Proves Doping." *The New York Times,* D1.

70. Goldman (1984), op. cit.

71. Ibid.

72. Ibid., p. 77.

73. Goldman (1984), op. cit.

74. Anshel and Russel (1997), op. cit.

75. Lenehan (2003), op. cit.

76. Ibid.

77. Ibid.

78. Verducci, T. (1996, May 27), "A New High," *Sports Illustrated, 84* (32–34), p. 32.

79. Ibid., p. 10.

80. Davies (1994), op. cit.

81. Ibid.

82. Campos et al. (2003), op. cit.

83. Ibid.

84. Eitzen (2003), op. cit.

85. *News Wire Reports* (2004, September 22), "Capel Warned after Positive Test," *Rocky Mountain News*, p. 8C.

86. Putnam (1999), op. cit.

87. Goldman (1984), op. cit.

88. Putnam (1999), op. cit.

89. Chester N., Reilly, T., and Mottram, D. (2003), "Over-the-Counter Drug Use amongst Athletes and Non-Athletes," *Journal of Sports Medicine and Physical Fitness, 43*(1), pp. 111–118.

90. Lumpkin et al. (1994), op. cit.

91. Eitzen (2003), op. cit.

92. Lumpkin et al. (1994), op. cit.

93. Bjerkle and Park (2003), op. cit.

94. "Creatine Side Effects and Rumors," (2005, September 15), available at http://www.creatinemonohydrate.net/creatine_die_effects.html.

95. Ibid.

96. Lenehan (2003), op. cit.

97. Bjerkle and Park (2004), op. cit.

98. Zinser, L. (2005, January 14), "Designer Steroid that Avoids Detection is Found," *The New York Times,* p. D-1.

99. Simon (2004), op. cit.

100. Lenehan (2003), op. cit.

101. Walters (2004), op. cit.

102. Goldman (1984), op. cit., p. 78.

103. Putnam (1999), op. cit.

104. Anshel and Russel (1997), op. cit.

105. Manning (2002), op. cit.

106. Lenehan (2003), op. cit.

107. Ibid.

108. Goldman (1984), op. cit.

109. Putnam (1999), op. cit.

110. Goldman (1984), op. cit.

111. Ibid., p. 50.

112. Eitzen (2003), op. cit., p. 66.

113. Putnam (1999), op. cit.

114. In Lenehan (2003), op. cit.

115. Ibid.

116. Dolan in Putnam (1999), op. cit., p. 21.

117. Layden, T. (2004, February 13), "Hanging from the BALCO-ny," http://SportsIllustrated.com.

118. Blitzer (2003), op. cit.

119. Layden (2004), op. cit.

120. Ibid.

121. Ibid., p. 61.

122. Jay, K. (2004, December 12), "Athletes We Deserve: We Built that Pedestal, and We Can tear It Down," *Washington Post*, p. B01.

123. Evans, L. (2005, February 27), "Drug-testing is a Travesty," *Rocky Mountain News*, p. 15F.

124. Goldman (1984), op. cit., p. 78.

125. Davies (1994), op. cit.

126. Blitzer (2003), op. cit.

127. Paige (2004), op. cit.

128. Pound, R. (2004), *Inside the Olympics*, Etobicoke, Ontario: Wiley.

129. Brennan, C. (2004, September 30), "One Clean Test from Bonds Pales in Comparison," *USA Today*.

130. Reid, S., Heisel, W., and Savedra, T. (2003, May 11), "U.S. Olympic Athletes Reportedly Tested Less Frequently than Other Competitors," *The Orange County Register.* (online version), http://www.ocregister.com/features/olympics.

131. Ibid.

132. Goldman (1984), op. cit.

133. Reid et al. (2003), op. cit.

134. Pound (2004), op. cit., p. 59.

135. Putnam (1999), op. cit.

136. Fordyce, T. (2001, August 1), "Radcliffe Backs Drug Tests," *BBC Sports* (online version).

137. Brennan (2004), op. cit.

138. Paige (2004), op. cit.

139. Lumpkin et al. (1994), op. cit.

140. Simon (2004), op. cit.

141. Putnam (1999), op. cit., p. 125.

142. Jay (2004), op. cit., p. B01.

CHAPTER 3

1. Stanley, D. (1999), *Understanding Sports and Eating Disorders*, New York: Rosen.

2. Davies, R. (1994), *America's Obsession: Sports in American Society since 1945*, Belmont, CA: Wadsworth.

3. Coakley, J. (1998), *Sport in Society: Issues and Controversies,* 6th ed. Boston, MA: Irwin-McGraw-Hill.

4. Ryan, J. (2000), *Little Girls in Pretty Boxes*, New York: Warner, p. 9.

5. Araton, H. (2002, November 1), "Babe in Toyland," *Tennis, 38*(9).

6. Andersen, A., Cohn, L., and Holbrook, T. (2000), *Making Weight: Healing Men's Conflict With Food, Weight, and Shape*, Carlsbad, CA: Gurze Books.

7. *Women's Health Law Weekly* (2004, June 20), "Eating Disorders; Unhealthy Eating Behaviors on Rise in Men," p. 12.

8. Raudenbush, B., and Meyer, B. (2003, June 1), "Muscular Dissatisfaction and Supplement Use among Male Intercollegiate Athletes," *Journal of Sport and Exercise Psychology*, *25*(2).

9. Katz, J. (1999), *Tough Guise* (videorecording), producers: Susan Ericsson and Sanjay Talreja, director: Sat Jhully, Northampton, MA: Media Education Foundation.

10. *Women's Health Law Weekly* (2002), op. cit.

11. Eitzen, D. S. (2003), *Fair and Foul? Beyond the Myths and Paradoxes of Sport*, 2nd ed. Lanham, MD: Rowman & Littlefield.

12. Lumpkin, A., Stoll, S., and Beller, J. (Eds.) (1994), *Sport Ethics: Applications for Fair Play*, St. Louis, MO: Marby.

13. Eitzen (2003), op. cit.

14. Lumpkin et al. (1994), op. cit.

15. Putnam, D. (1999), *Controversies in the Sports World*, Westport, CT: Greenwood.

16. Eitzen (2003), op. cit.

17. Putnam (1999), op. cit.

18. Ibid.

19. Eitzen (2003), op. cit.

20. Putnam (1999), op. cit.

21. Eitzen (2003), op. cit.

22. Putnam (1999), op. cit.

23. Eitzen (2003), op. cit.

24. Putnam (1999), op. cit.

25. Norwood, R. (2004, July 21), "Fed Up With the Hunger," *Los Angeles Times*, p. 1.

26. Ibid.

27. Ibid., p. 1.

28. Harris, B. (2004, April 27), "Sellers, Lukas Disagree on Minimum Weight Limits for Jockeys," *The Associated Press*.

29. Norwood (2004), op. cit.

30. Ibid., p. 1.

31. Ibid.

32. Eitzen (2003), op. cit.

33. Ibid.

34. Ryan, J. (2000), *Little Girls in Pretty Boxes*, New York: Warner.

35. Ibid., p. 22.

36. Ibid.

37. Ryan (2000), op. cit., p. 59.

38. Lumpkin et al. (1994), op. cit.

39. Stanley (1999), op. cit., p. 44.

40. Ryan (2000), op. cit.

41. Putnam (1999), op. cit.

42. Eitzen (2003), op. cit., p. 67.

43. Ibid.

44. Putnam (1999), op. cit., p. 39.

45. Stanley (1999), op. cit.

46. Ryan (2000), op. cit.

47. Stanley (1999), op. cit.

48. Putnam (1999), op. cit., p. 41.

49. Brennan, C. (1999), *Edge of Glory: The Inside Story of the Quest for Figure Skating Olympic Gold Medals*, New York: Penguin.

50. Ibid., p. 152.

51. Sanford, S., and Halliburton, S. (1996), "Spotting, Treating Troubled Athletes Can Be Difficult." In Lapchick, R. (Ed.) *Sport in Society: Equal Opportunity or Business as Usual?* (pp. 168–173), Thousand Oaks, CA: Sage.

52. Ibid., p. 169.

53. Raudenbush and Meyer (2003), op. cit.

54. Smolak, L., Murnan, S., and Ruble, A. (2000), "Female Athletes and Eating Problems," *International Journal of Eating Disorders, 27*, pp. 371–380. .

55. Stanley (1999), op. cit.

56. Telander, R. (1989), *The Hundred Yard Lie,* Urbana, IL: University of Illinois Press, p. 153.

57. Kindred, D. (2005, January 16), "Commentary: He's Thin Compared to the NFL's Biggest Players," *The Los Angeles Times*, p. D5.

58. Dahlberg, T. (2005, February 1), "Fat Flies in NFL, Where One in Four Super Bowl Players Are over 300 Pounds," available from http://www.sports.espn.go.com.

59. Ibid.

60. Jay, K. (2004, December 12), "Athletes We Deserve: We Built that Pedestal, and We Can Tear It Down," *The Washington Post*.

61. King, K., Kennedy, K., and Deitsch, R. (2002, October 21), "Living Large," *Sports Illustrated, 97*(16), p. 28.

62. Ibid.

63. Eitzen (2003), op. cit.

64. Telander (1989), op. cit.

65. Eitzen (2003), op. cit.

66. Telander (1989), op. cit., p. 149.

67. Ibid.

68. Ibid.

69. Ibid.

70. Eitzen (2003), op. cit.

71. Kindred, D. (2001, August 13), "Bodies So Powerful, So Vulnerable," *The Sporting News, 225*(33), p. 64.

72. At http://www.ifoce.com.

73. Ibid.

74. Ibid.

75. Messner, M., and Sabo, D. (1994), *Sex, Violence, and Power in Sports,"* Rethinking *Masculinity*, Freedom, CA: Crossing, p. 87.

76. Eitzen (2003), op. cit.

77. Ibid., p. 61.

78. Telander (1989), op. cit.

79. Eitzen (2003), op. cit.

80. Telander, R. (2004, September 29), "Pro-Football Can Become Self-Destructive," *Chicago Sun-Times*, p. 166.

81. Coakley (1998), op. cit., p. 153.

82. Menzer, J. (2004, September 30), "Ex-Panther Tells of Drug-Abuse," *Winston-Salem Journal*, p. C1.

83. Ibid.

84. Putnam (1999), op. cit.

85. Montagne, R. (2004, September 17), "Biographer Mark Kriegel Talks about Joe Namath's History of Dependence on Painkillers," *National Public Radio.*

86. Ibid.

87. Miller, D., and Goessling, B. (2004, November 29), "U. Minnesota Athletes Still Using Bextra," *Minnesota Daily.*

88. Eitzen (2003), op. cit.

89. Menzer (2004), op. cit.

90. Briggs, B. (2004, September 26), "Deadly Game of Silence," *The Denver Post*, pp. 1BB, 16BB.

91. Brody, J. (2004, October 26), "In Sports, Play Smart and Watch Your Head," *The New York Times*, p. F9.

92. Eitzen (2003), op. cit.

93. Curry, T. In Eitzen (2003), op. cit.

94. Fish, M., Kim, A., and Kennedy, K. (2002, June 3), "Quitting Time," *Sports Illustrated, 96*(23).

95. Ibid.

96. Ryan (2000), op. cit., p. 23.

97. Ibid.

98. Ibid.

99. Ibid., p. 38.

100. Coakley (1998), op. cit., p. 153.

101. Ryan (2000), op. cit.

102. Ibid., p. 4.

103. Ibid.

104. Telander (1989), op. cit.

105. Ryan (2000), op. cit., p. 151.

106. Ibid., p. 21.

107. Ibid., p. 46.

108. Ibid.

109. Ibid., p. 204.

110. Ibid.

111. Fish et al. (2002), op. cit.

112. Frommer, F. (2004, September 9), "Ali Calls for U.S. Boxing Commission," *Associated Press.*

113. Howley, D. (2004, November 3), "No Foothold for Headgear; Soccer Community Slow to Adapt," *The Times Union*, p. C1.

114. Geiger, D. (2004, June 15), "Female Athletes Take a Hit: Girls at Greater Risk for Concussions, Studies Find," *Newsday*, p. B52.

115. Ryan (2000), op. cit.

116. Ibid., p. 234.

117. Ibid.

CHAPTER 4

1. Eitzen, D. S. (2002). In Holowchak, M. A. (Ed.). *Philosophy of Sport: Critical Readings, Crucial Issues.* Upper Saddle River, NJ: Prentice Hall, p. 236.

2. Callahan, D. (2004), *The Cheating Culture: Why More Americans are Doing Wrong to Get Ahead*, New York: Harcourt.

3. Ibid.

4. Gregorian, V. (2004, August 1), "Poor Sports Are as Old as the Games," *St. Louis Post-Dispatch*, p. A01.

5. *Austin American-Statesman* (2004, November 25), "Smackdown Culture Runs Amok, Fed by Anger . . . and Money."

6. Oppliger, P. (2004), *Wrestling and Hypermasculinity*, Jefferson, NC: McFarland.

7. Callahan, D. In Graney, E. (2004, June 11), "Games of Deceit," *The San Diego Union Tribune* (online version).

8. Ibid.

9. Gregorian (2004), op. cit.

10. Ibid.

11. Sage, G. (2000), *Power and Ideology in American Sport: A Critical Perspective*, Champaign, IL: Human Kinetics, p. 177.

12. Robertson, L. (2004, December 21), "Sportsmanship Is Taking a Beating," *Miami Herald*. (online version), www.miamiherald.com.

13. Callahan (2004), op. cit.

14. Ibid., p. 75.

15. Graney (2004), op. cit.

16. Atyeo, D. (1979), *Blood and Guts: Violence in Sports*, New York: Paddington, p. 11.

17. Walters, A. (2002, November 10), "Cheating in Sports," retrieved on December 4, 2004, from http://www.connectingwithkids.com/tipsheet/2004/202_nov10/cheat.html.

18. Ibid.

19. Aaseng, N. (1993), *The Locker Room Mirror: How Sports Reflect Society*, New York: Walker & Co., p. 51.

20. Rushin, S. (2003), "Our Cheatin' Hearts," *Sports Illustrated, 99*(2), p. 19.

21. Aaseng (1993), op. cit., p. 49.

22. *USA Today* (2003, June 5), "Cheating Not Limited to Putting Cork in Bat," p. 3C.

23. Kennedy, K., and Bechtel, M. (2003, June 16), "Much Ado about Corking," *Sports Illustrated, 98*(24), pp. 22–23.

24. McCallum, J. (1999, October 4), "Just For Kicks," *Sports Illustrated, 91*(13), pp. 56–60.

25. Ibid.

26. Taylor, P. (n.d.), "Food for Thought: Cheating Has Become Acceptable and Expected in All Sports," at http://www.CNNSI.com.

27. Eitzen, D. S. (2003), *Fair and Foul? Beyond the Myths and Paradoxes of Sport*, 2nd ed. Lanham, MD: Rowman & Littlefield.

28. Taylor (n.d.), op. cit.

29. Saunders, P. (2004, October 28), "Shanahan Rejects 'Dirty' Play," *The Denver Post*, p. D01.

30. Pells, E. (2004, November 4), "Lynch Injury Latest in Dirty-Play Debate," *The Associated Press.*

31. Eitzen (2003), op. cit.

32. Rushin (2003), op. cit.

33. Marthaler, J. (2004, April 5), "Unchecked Violence and Cheating Plagues NHL," *The Minnesota Daily* (online version).

34. Dixon, N. (2002), "On Winning and Athletic Superiority." In Holowchak, M. A. (Ed.), *Philosophy of Sport* (pp. 220–234), Upper Saddle River, NJ: Prentice Hall.

35. Jones, G. (2004, August 15), "Physical U.S. Team Blanks Brazil; Two Brazilian Players Go to the Hospital as Americans Advance to the Quarterfinals on Goals by Hamm and Wambach," *Los Angeles Times*, p. D15.

36. Shipnuk, A., and Eubanks, S. (2003), "Teed OFF," *Sports Illustrated, 99*(2), pp. 66–69.

37. Graney (2004), op. cit.

38. Aaseng (1993), op. cit.

39. Kennedy, K., Deitsch, R., and Lidz, F. (2002, September 2), "Gone Cheatin,'" *Sports Illustrated, 97*(9), p. 31.

40. Cook, K., and Mravic, M. (1999, April 26), "A Shocker in Arkansas," *Sports Illustrated, 90*(17), pp. 22–23.

41. Cashmore, E. (2000), *Making Sense of Sports*, London: Routledge, p. 222.

42. Rushin (2003), op. cit.

43. Aaseng (1993), op. cit., p. 23.

44. Herzog, B. (2004, December 17), "Histrionics Lesson: Eventful Chapters in the Pedro Martinez Story," *Newsday*, p. A88.

45. Walker, B. (2004, July 29), "Eight Suspended and/or Fined for Fighting in Yanks-Red Sox Game," *The Associated Press.*

46. Messner, M., and Sabo, D. (1994), *Sex, Violence, and Power in Sports," Rethinking Masculinity*, Freedom, CA: Crossing, p. 94.

47. McCallum, J. (1994, May 23), "Way Out of Control," *Sports Illustrated 80*(20), pp. 26–30.

48. Atyeo (1979), op. cit.

49. Leizman J. (1999), *Let's Kill 'Em*, Lanham, MD: University Press of America.

50. Oppliger (2004), op. cit.

51. Ibid.

52. Atyeo (1979), op. cit., p. 166.

53. Oppliger (2004), op. cit., p. 74.

54. Ibid.,

55. Ibid., p. 65.

56. Ibid.

57. Coakley, J. (1998), *Sport in Society: Issues and Controversies*, 6th ed. Boston, MA: Irwin-McGraw-Hill.

58. Atyeo (1979), op. cit.

59. Ibid.

60. Ibid., p. 168.

61. Ibid., p. 169.

62. Putnam, D. (1999), *Controversies in the Sports World*, Westport, CT: Greenwood.

63. Ibid.

64. Ibid., p. 191.

65. Atyeo (1979), op. cit., p. 178

66. Putnam (1999), op. cit., p. 189.

67. Atyeo (1979), op. cit., p. 212.

68. Ibid.

69. Ibid., p. 219.

70. Ibid., p. 220.

71. Telander, R. (1989), *The Hundred Yard Lie*, Urbana, IL: University of Illinois Press, p. 168.

72. Ibid., p. 173.

73. Rallo, C. (2004, November 20), "Dirty and Nasty; Purdue's Goldsberry: It's the Only Way," *South Bend Tribune*, p. W4.

74. Eitzen (2003), op. cit.

75. Telander (1989), op. cit., p. 170.

76. Eitzen (2003), op. cit.

77. Aaseng (1993), op. cit.

78. Atyeo (1979), op. cit., p. 209.

79. Telander (1989), op. cit., p. 168.

80. Atyeo (1979), op. cit., p. 228.

81. Allen, K. (2004, September 3), "NHL Fisticuffs Bring Out the Fury," *USA Today*, p. 3C.

82. Ibid.

83. Ibid.

84. Atyeo (1979), op. cit., p. 233.

85. Ibid., p. 233.

86. Ibid.

87. McCallum (1994), op. cit.

88. Allen (2004), op. cit.

89. Ibid.

90. Atyeo (1979), op. cit., p. 236.

91. *The Associated Press* (2004, December 17), "Report: Bertuzzi May Take Plea Deal in Assault Case."

92. Allen (2004), op. cit.

93. Atyeo (1979), op. cit., p. 237.

94. Feinstein, J. (2002), *The Punch*, Boston, MA: Little, Brown, & Co., p. 21.

95. Ibid.

96. Ibid., p. 5.

97. Ibid.

98. McCallum (1994), op. cit.

99. Brock, C. (2004, November 23), "Fortson the One Crying Foul; Seattle Forward Danny Fortson Says He's Being 'Singled Out' By Officials and that His Reputation for Dirty Play is Undeserved," *The News Tribune*, p. Co1.

100. Krieger, D. (2005, March 1), "Sports Becoming an Ethical Minefield," *Rocky Mountain News*, p. 2c.

101. Rushin (2003), op. cit.

102. Reilly, R. (1995, November 13), "Order on the Court," *Sports Illustrated, 83*(21), p. 136.

103. Zahn, P. (2004, November 22), "When Heroes Become Villains," CNN's *Paula Zahn Now.*

104. Ibid.

105. McCarron, A. (2005, April 2), "Fight Clubs: The History Decked Out in Red, Black, and White," *The Daily News*, p. 18.

106. Taylor (n.d.), op. cit.

107. Aaseng (1993), op. cit., p. 24.

108. Thorn, J. In Robertson (2004), op. cit.

109. Callahan (2004), op. cit.

110. Eitzen (2003), op. cit., p. 43.

111. Zahn (2004), op. cit.

112. Gregorian (2004), op. cit.

113. Ibid.

114. Walters (2004), op. cit.

115. Zahn (2004), op. cit.

116. Messner & Sabo (1994), op.cit.

117. Oppliger (2004), op. cit.

118. Aaseng (1993), op. cit., p. 39.

119. Ibid.

120. Putnam (1999), op. cit., p. 91.

121. Sage (2000), op. cit., p. 12.

122. Reilly, R. (2003, August 11), "Corrupting Our Utes," *Sports Illustrated, 99*(5), p. 154.

123. Jones, J. (2004, December 10), "Sports Fans Speak Out about Recent Controversies," *Gallup Poll News Service.*

CHAPTER 5

1. Harris, D. (2004, November 17), "Geiger, Tressel Defend Their Program; Athletic Director Rips Magazine, Says NCAA is Satisfied," *Dayton Daily News*, p. C1.

2. Ibid.

3. Judd, A. (2004, March 28), "UGA Ignored Clues on Harricks," *The Atlanta Journal-Constitution*, p. 1A.

4. Judd, A. (2004, March 12), "Harrick Jr: I Took 'Pride' in Teaching; Remember the No-Brainer Final Exam? Check out Ex-UGA Coach's Attendance Policy," *The Atlanta Journal-Constitution*, p. 1A.

5. Towers, C. (2004, August 6), "Bulldogs Slammed by NCAA; Georgia Loses Scholarships, 30 Wins in Fallout of Basketball Scandal," *The Atlanta Journal-Constitution*, p. 1A.

6. Rahn, A. (1996, November 7), "UCLA's Harrick Fired for Violations," *The Associated Press.*

7. Witz, B. (2003, March 11), "Harrick in Deep Trouble; Coach Suspended, Georgia Sanctions Itself amid Scandal," *The Daily News of Los Angeles,* p. S1.

8. Ibid.

9. Rahn (1996), op. cit.

10. Frias, C. (2003, March 22), "Harrick's Rhode Island Legacy; Success, Controversial Dealings, Current Probe," Cox News Service.

11. Witz (2003), op. cit.

12. Ibid.

13. Frias (2003), op. cit.

14. *USA Today* (2003, September 12), "Root for Sports Reforms."

15. Suggs, W. (2003, March 7), "Fresno State Faces Academic Scandal," *The Chronicle of Higher Education*, p. 43.

16. Telander, R. (1989), *The Hundred Yard Lie*, Urbana, IL: University of Illinois Press, p. 103.

17. Aaseng, N. (1993), *The Locker Room Mirror: How Sports Reflect Society*, New York: Walker & Co., p. 48.

18. O' Connor, I. (2004, May 3), "Some College Coaches Can't Be Trusted," *The Cincinatti Enquirer* (online version).

19. Miller, T. (2004, November 13), "NCAA Allows Cheaters to Win," *Seattle Post-Intelligencer* (online version).

20. Ibid.

21. Ibid.

22. Aaseng (1993), op. cit.

23. Ibid.

24. Putnam, D. (1999), *Controversies in the Sports World*, Westport, CT: Greenwood.

25. Ibid.

26. Telander (1989), op. cit.

27. Putnam (1999), op. cit.

28. Ibid.

29. Ibid.

30. Aaseng (1993), op. cit., p. 127.

31. Taylor, C., and Sonnerschein, S. (1990), *Down and Dirty: The Life and Crimes of Oklahoma Football*, New York: Carrol & Gief, p. 130.

32. Ibid.

33. Ibid., p. 205.

34. Ibid.

35. Switzer, B. (2003, December 29), "Feeding the Monster," *Sports Illustrated* (online version).

36. Ibid.

37. Green, B. (1997, August 6), "In Defense of Barry Switzer," http://www.wiseonly.com/themuse/Column17.htm.

38. Putnam (1999), op. cit.

39. Eitzen, D. S. (2003), *Fair and Foul? Beyond the Myths and Paradoxes of Sport*, 2nd edition, Lanham, MD: Rowman & Littlefield.

40. Gerdy, J. (2002), *Sport: The All-American Addiction*, Jackson, MS: University of Mississippi Press.

41. Ibid., p. 123.

42. Fosmoe, M. (2004, December 7), "Black Alumni Question Ty Firing," *South Bend Tribune*, p. A-1.

43. Benedict, J. (2004), *Out of Bounds: Inside the NBA's Culture of Rape, Violence, and Crime*, New York: HarperCollins, p. 151.

44. Ibid.

45. Wieberg, S., and Carey, J. (2004, February 11), "Miami Holds off on Recruit," *USA Today*, p. 6C.

46. Yaeger, D., and Wolff, A. (1997, July 7), "Troubling Questions," *Sports Illustrated*, *87*(1).

47. Ibid.

48. Ibid.

49. Degnan, S. (2005, November 30), "NCAA, Florida to Probe 'Diploma Mills,'" *The Herald*, pp. 1–2A.

50. Ibid.

51. Grimm, F. (2005, December 1), "Diploma Mills for Dumb Jocks: Wink-Wink," *The Herald*, p. B1.

52. Ibid.

53. Gregorian, V. (2004, December 15), "Grand Jury Indicts Ex-Coach at Barton," *St. Louis Post-Dispatch*, p. D01.

54. Gerdy (2002), op. cit., p. 95.

55. Ibid.

56. Telander (1989), op. cit., p. 110.

57. Gerdy (2002), op. cit., p. 84.

58. Telander (1989), op. cit.

59. Sailes, G. (2000), "The African American Athlete: Social Myths and Stereotypes." In Brooks, D., and Althouse, D. (Eds.), *Racism in College Athletics* (pp. 53–61). Morgantown, WV: Fitness Information Technology, Inc.,

60. Sperber, M. (2000), *Beer and Circus: How Big-Time College Sports is Crippling Undergraduate Education*, New York: Owl.

61. Stossel, J. (2004, November 19), "Clueless College Cheating," ABC *News Transcripts.*

62. Maxse, J. (2004, September 25), "More to Investigate at CSUl McFadden Says Associate AD Wrote Players' Papers," *Cleveland Plain Dealer*, p. D1.

63. Yaeger and Wolff (1997), op. cit.

64. Wetzel, D., and Yaeger, D. (2000), *Sole Influence: Basketball, Corporate Greed, and the Corruption of America's Youth*, New York: Warner.

65. Calkins, G. (2005, January 27), "Trial Testimony Indicts Dark Side of College Football," *The Rocky Mountain News*, p. 2C.

66. Joyner, J. (2006, April 11), Logan Young, key figure in Alabama scandal, murdered. *Outside the Beltway Sports.* Retrieved April 20, 2006, from http://sports.outsidethebeltway.com/2006/04/logan-young-key-figure-in-alabama-scandal/murdered/.

67. Yaeger and Wolff (1997), op. cit.

68. Sperber (2000), op. cit.

69. Ibid., p. 130.

70. Ibid., p. 132.

71. Auer, H., and Harrington, M. (2003, March 9), "What Went Wrong at St. Bonaventure," *The Buffalo News*, p. A1.

72. Ibid.

73. Watson, G. (2004, August 12), "NCAA Will Discuss Possible Sanctions with Missouri," *St. Louis Post-Dispatch*, p. D01.

74. Auer and Harrington (2003), op. cit.

75. Ibid.

76. Aaseng (1993), op. cit.

77. Sperber (2000), op. cit.

78. Bensel-Meyers, L. (2001, November 8), "The State of College Athletics." Paper presented to the Institute for International Sport, retrieved from http://www.internationalsport.cm.

79. Ibid.

80. Ibid.

81. Walker, T. (2005, February 11), "DU Professor: Stop 'Free Farm System,'" *The Rocky Mountain News*, p. 27C.

82. Sperber (2000), op. cit., p. 131.

83. Putnam (1999), op. cit., p. 8.

84. Miller (2004), op. cit.

85. Eitzen (2003), op. cit., p. 123.

86. Miller (2004), op. cit.

87. Walker, T. (2005, January 7), "NCAA Plan Would Monitor Athlete's Grades," *Associated Press Online.*

88. Ibid.

89. *The Associated Press* (2005, January 11), "NCAA Approves Initial Phase of Academic Reform," *Rocky Mountain News*, p. 44C.

90. Gerdy (2002), op. cit.

91. Watson, S. (2003, March 10), "Bona President Resigns; Basketball Scandal Prompts Action by University Trustees," *The Buffalo News*, p. A1.

92. Dobie, M., and Staple, A. (2004, December 4), "St. Johns; Taking Another Hit?" *Newsday*, p. B04.

93. Gerdy (2002), op. cit.

94. Watson (2003), op. cit.

95. Johnson, G. (2004, October), "NCAA Clears Neuheisel of Wrongdoing," *Xposed* (online version).

96. *News Wire Services* (March 8, 2005), "Neuheisel Settles Suit," *Rocky Mountain News*, p. 3C.

97. Miller (2004), op. cit.

CHAPTER 6

1. Oliff, H. (2002, April), "Lifting the Haze Around Hazing," *Education Digest, 67*(8), pp. 21–28, 22.

2. Nuwer, H. (2000), "Response to 'Praising Hazing,'" retrieved from http://www. stophazing.org.

3. Nuwer, H. (Ed.) (2004), *The Hazing Reader*, Bloomington, IN: Indiana University Press.

4. Ibid.

5. Nuwer, H. (1990), *Broken Pledges: The Deadly Rite of Hazing*, Atlanta, GA: Longstreet, p. 117.

6. Nuwer (2000), op. cit.

7. Nuwer (2004), op. cit.

8. Nuwer, H. (1999), *Wrongs of Passage: Fraternities, Sororities, Hazing, and Binge Drinking*, Bloomington, IN: Indiana University Press, p. 31.

9. Farrey, T. (2000, June 3), "Athletes Abusing Athletes," retrieved from http://www. espn.g.com/otl/hazing/monday.html.

10. Nuwer (2000), op. cit., p. 65.

11. Nuwer (2004), op. cit.

12. Ibid.

13. Nuwer (1999), op. cit.

14. Ibid.

15. Nuwer (2000), op. cit., p. 24.

16. Nuwer (1999), op. cit.

17. Nuwer (2000), op. cit.

18. Ibid.

19. Nuwer (1999), op. cit.

20. O'Hara, J. (2000, March 6), "The Hell of Hazing," *Macleans, 113*(10), pp. 50–53, 51.

21. Tiger, L. (2004), "Males Courting Males." In Nuwer, H. (Ed.), *The Hazing Reader* (pp. 14–18), Bloomington, IN: Indiana University Press.

22. Allan, E. (2004), "Hazing and Gender: Analyzing the Obvious." In Nuwer, H. (Ed.), *The Hazing Reader,* 9 (pp. 275–284), Bloomington, IN: Indiana University Press.

23. Tiger (2004), op. cit.

24. Allan (2004), op. cit.

25. Nuwer (2000), op. cit.

26. Nuwer (1999), op. cit.

27. Nuwer (2000), op. cit.

28. Nuwer (1999), op. cit.

29. Hoover N. (2000, August), "Initiation Rites in American High Schools: A National Survey," available at http://www.alfred.edu/hs_hazing.

30. Walsh, M. (2000, September 6), "Hazing is Widespread, Student Survey Shows," *Education Week, 20* (pp. 1, 14, 14–19).

31. Hoover (2000), op. cit.

32. O'Hara (2000), op. cit., p. 52.

33. Walsh (2000), op. cit.

34. Allan (2004), op. cit.

35. Nuwer (2000), op. cit., p. 30.

36. Crow, R., and Rosner, S. (2004). "Institutional Liability and Hazing—Mainly Athletics-Related." In Nuwer, H. (Ed.), *The Hazing Reader* (pp. 224–251), Bloomington, IN: Indiana University Press.

37. Ibid.

38. Ibid.

39. Finley, L., and Finley, P. (2006) "They're Just as Sadistic as Any Group of Boys! A Content Analysis of Gendered-Discourse of Sport-Related Hazing Incidents in High Schools." In Muraskin, R. (Ed.) *It's a Crime,* 4th ed.ition. Upper Saddle River, NJ: Prentice Hall. Unpublished manuscript.

40. Ibid.

41. Ibid.

42. Ibid.

43. Ibid.

44. Ibid.

45. Ibid.

46. Allan (2004), op. cit.

47. Ibid.

48. Suggs, W. (1999, September 3), "79% of College Athletes Experience Hazing, Survey Finds," *The Chronicle of Higher Education, 46*(2), p. A83.

49. Hoover, N. (1999, August 30), "National Survey: Initiation Rites and Athletics for NCAA Sport Teams," retrieved from http://www.stophazing.org.

50. Suggs (1999), op. cit.

51. Ibid.

52. Hoover (1999), op. cit.

53. Ibid.

54. Ibid.

55. Ibid.

56. Watson, S. (2004, September 6), "UB Hazing Illness Tied to Drinking Prune Juice; Soccer Suspensions Also Linked to Alcohol," *The Buffalo News,* p. B1.

57. Rosellini, L. (2000, September 11), "The Sordid Side of College Sports," *U.S. News & World Report, 129*(10), pp. 102–104.

58. Ibid.

59. Farrey (2000), op. cit.

60. Nuwer (2004), op. cit., p. 194.

61. Ibid.

62. Ibid., p. 196.

63. Ibid., p. 191.

64. Ibid., p. 195.

65. Ibid.

66. Ibid.

67. Sheahan, K. (2004, October 7), "Hazing Undermines Spirit of Sport," *The Cornell Daily Sun* (online version).

68. Finkel, M. (2004), "Traumatic Injuries Caused by Hazing." In Nuwer, H. (Ed.), *The Hazing Reader* (pp. 171–183), Bloomington, IN: Indiana University Press.

69. Farrey (2000), op. cit.

70. Rosselini (2000), op. cit.

71. Finkel (2004), op. cit.

72. Rosellini (2000), op. cit.

73. Mravic, M. (2000, January 31), "Vileness in Vermont," *Sports Illustrated, 92*(4), pp. 34–37.

74. O' Hara (2000), op. cit.

75. Rosselini (2000), op. cit.

76. Nuwer (1999), op. cit.

77. Farrey (2000), op. cit.

78. Crow, R., and Rosner, S. (2004), "Hazing and Sports and the Law." In Nuwer, H. (Ed.), *The Hazing Reader* (pp. 200–223). Bloomington, IN: Indiana University Press.

79. Ibid.

80. Ibid.

81. Armstrong, J. (2004, August 26), "Rookie Hazing Relevant to Raiders," *The Denver Post*, p. D02.

82. Ybarra, A. (2004, September 30), "Cleveland Pitcher Kyle Denney Shot in Calf while Riding on Team Bus," The Associated Press.

83. Nuwer (2000), op. cit.

84. Palmer, J. (2003, December 4), "Icers Will Face Niagara after EMU's Hazing Suspension," *The Penn State Collegian* (online version).

85. Nuwer (2000), op. cit., p. 76.

86. Ibid., p. 76.

87. O' Hara (2000), op. cit.

88. Crow and Rosner (2004), "Hazing and Sport and the Law," op. cit.

89. Ibid.

90. Finkel (2004), op. cit.

91. Crow and Rosner (2004), "Hazing and Sport and the Law," op. cit.

92. Ibid.

93. Crow and Rosner (2004), "Institutional Liability and Hazing—Mainly Athletics Related," op. cit.

94. Crow and Rosner (2004), "Hazing and Sport and the Law," op. cit.

95. Ibid.

96. Hoffer, R., and Cook, K. (1999, September 13), "Praising Hazing," *Sports Illustrated, 91*(10), p. 31.

97. Bias, K. (1997, November 10), "Hazy Memories," *Sports Illustrated, 87*(19), pp. 80–84.

98. Allan (2004), op. cit.

99. Hoover (1999), op. cit.

100. Nuwer (2004), op. cit.

101. Rosselini (2000), op. cit.

102. Allan (2004), op. cit.

103. Nuwer (2004), op. cit., p. xxi.

104. Ibid., p. xxi.

CHAPTER 7

1. Eitzen, D. S. (2003), *Fair and Foul: Beyond the Myths and Paradoxes of Sport*, 2nd ed. Lanham, MD: Rowman & Littlefield.

2. Ibid., p. 15.

3. Sage, G. (1998), *Power and Ideology in American Sport: A Critical Perspective*, 2nd ed. Champaign, IL: Human Kinetics, p. 47.

4. Gerdy, J. (2002), *Sport: The All-American Addiction*, Jackson, MS: University of Mississippi Press, p. 199.

5. Sage (1998), op. cit.

6. Telander, R. (1989), *The Hundred Yard Lie*, Urbana, IL: University of Chicago Press.

7. In Gerdy (2002), op. cit., p. 180.

8. Sage (1998), op. cit.

9. Walsh-Sarnecki, P., and Scott, M. (2004, August 16), "Rising School Expenses: Pay-to-Play Costs Hit Families Harder," *Detroit Free Press* (online version).

10. Coakley, J. (1998), *Sport in Society: Issues and Controversies*, 6th ed. Boston, MA: McGraw-Hill.

11. Walsh and Scott (2004), op. cit.

12. Wheeler, K. (2004, November 9), "Pay-to-Play: High School Sports Becoming Costly," retrieved on February 1, 2005, from http://www.wkyc.com/news.

13. Miller, S. (2004, September 2), "Parents, Coaches Rail against Increasing Pay-to-Play Fees," *The Christian Science Monitor*.

14. Ibid.

15. Sage (1998), op. cit.

16. Eitzen, D. S. (1999), *Fair and Foul: Beyond the Myths and Paradoxes of Sport*, Lanham, MD: Rowman & Littlefield.

17. Ibid., p. 137.

18. Gerdy (2002), op. cit., p. 68.

19. Harris, O. (2000), "African-American Predominance in Sport." In Brooks, D., and Althouse, D. (Eds.), *Racism in College Athletics* (pp. 37–52). Morgantown, WV: Fitness Information Technology, Inc., p. 48.

20. Eitzen (1999), op. cit.

21. Starling, K. (1998), "Why Stars Go Broke," *Ebony, 53*(7), pp. 58–61.

22. Putnam. D. (1999), *Controversies of the Sports World*, Westport, CT: Greenwood.

23. Starling (1998), op. cit.

24. Wertheim, J., Yaeger, D., and Schechter, B. (2000, May 29), "Web of Deceit," *Sports Illustrated, 92*(22), pp. 9–17.

25. Putnam (1999), op. cit.

26. Ibid.

27. Sage (1998), op. cit.

28. Coakley (1998), op. cit.

29. Ibid.

30. Sage (1998), op. cit., p. 236.

31. http://www.ncaa.org/grad_rates.html.

32. http://www.workers.org.

33. Harris (2000), op. cit.

34. Putnam (1999), op. cit.

35. Messner, M., and Sabo, D. (1994), "*Sex, Violence, and Power in Sports,*" *Rethinking Masculinity*, Freedom, CA: Crossing.

36. Ibid.

37. Gerdy (2002), op. cit.

38. Ibid., p. 177.

39. Eitzen (2003), op. cit.

40. Jenkins, C. (2003, October 22), "NASCAR Targets Diveristy," *USA Today*, p. 2C.

41. Perez, S. (2006, February 19).

42. Putnam (1999), op. cit.

43. Rosenstein, J. (1997), *In Whose Honor?* (motion picture), Newday films.

44. Eitzen (1999), op. cit., p. 33.

45. Williams, B. (2005, August 5), "NCAA Executive Committee Issues Guidelines for Use of Native American Mascots at Championship Events," available at http://www.2ncaa.org.

46. "NCAA American Indian Mascot Ban Will Begin Feb.1," (August 5, 2005), http://ESPN.com.

47. "Florida State Threatened to Sue over Postseason Ban," (August 23, 2005), http://ESPN.com.

48. Putnam (1999), op. cit., p. 25.

49. Ibid., p. 25.

50. Kennedy, K., and O' Brien, R. (1996, December 16), "The Sound, the Fury," *Sports Illustrated, 95*(25), pp. 22–24.

51. Putnam (1999), op. cit.

52. Kennedy, K., and Bechtel, M. (2003, December 13), "Welcome to Rush Week," *Sports Illustrated, 99*(14), pp. 22–24.

53. Ibid.

54. Lapchick, R. (2000), "Crime and Athletes: New Racial Stereotypes," *Society, 37*(3), pp. 14–21.

55. Messner and Sabo (1994), op. cit.

56. Wertheim, J. (2001, April 30), "King of Fools," *Sports Illustrated, 94*(18), p. 26.

57. Ibid.

58. Kozol, J. (2005), *The Shame of the Nation: Restoration of Apartheid Schooling in America*, New York: Crown.

59. Ley, B. (2000, June 4), "Football, Race, and the Power of the Word," *Outside the Lines*, retrieved from http://www.espn.com.

60. Eitzen (2003), op. cit.

61. Entine, J. (n.d). "Interview with John Entine," http://ESPN.com.

62. Ibid.

63. Ibid.

64. Sailes, G. (2000), "The African American Athlete: Social Myths and Stereotypes." In Brooks, D., and Althouse, A. (Eds.), *Racism in College Athletics* (pp. 53–64), Morgantown, WV: Fitness Information Technology, Inc.

65. Gonzales, E. L. (2001), "The Stacking of Latinos in Major League Baseball: A Forgotten Minority?" In Yiannakis, A., and Melnick, M. (Eds.), *Contemporary Issues in Sociology of Sport* (pp. 187–202), Champaign, IL: Human Kinetics.

66. Lopiano, D. (n.d.), "Gender Equity and the Black Female in Sport," *Women's Sports Foundation* (online version).

67. Lapchick (2000), op. cit.

68. Eitzen (2003), op. cit.

69. Lapchick (2000), op. cit.

70. Lapchick, R. (June 5, 2005), "The 2004 Race and Gender Report Card: College Sports." *Northeastern University Center for the Study of Sport and Society.* Available from: www.northeastern.edu/csss/rgrc2004.html.

71. Gerdy (2002), op. cit.

72. *Black Issues in Higher Education* (2003, March 13), "Report: Minorities Hold Few Top College Sports Jobs in Michigan," pp. 15–20.

73. Sage (1998), op. cit.

74. Marot, M. (November 9, 2005), "S.C., Utah Flunk on Minority Hiring Report Card," available at http://www.mercurynews.com.

75. Madden, J. (2004), "Difference in the Success of NFL Coaches by Race, 1990–2002," *Journal of Sports Economics, 5*(1), pp. 6–19.

76. Gerdy (2002), op. cit.

77. Madden (2004), op. cit.

78. Ibid., p. 16.

79. Lapchick (2000), op. cit.

80. Lopiano (2000), op. cit.

81. Orton, K. (March 16, 2005), "Black Female Coaches Few and Far between," http://*Washingtonpost.com*.

82. Krawczynski, J. (July 9, 2005), "Vikings All Business under New Ownership," *The Associated Press.*

83. Franke, G. (2003, October 14.), "Quotas Undermine NFL's Colorblind Tradition." *Free Republic.* Available at http://www.freerepublic.com.

84. Saraceno, J. (2002, October 10), "NFL Needs Black Owners, Not Suits," *USA Today,* p. 3C.

85. Putnam (1999), op. cit., p. 27.

86. Sage (1998), op. cit., p. 93.

87. Coakley (1998), op. cit.

88. Eitzen (1999), op. cit.

89. Entine (n.d.), op. cit.

90. Coakley (1998), op. cit.

91. ESPN (1999, November 10), "The Native American Sports Experience," available at http://www.espn.com.

92. Ibid., p.127.

93. Evans, A. (2001), "Blacks as Key Functionaries: A Study of Racial Stratification in Professional Sport." In Yiannakis, A., and Melnick, M. (Eds.), *Contemporary Issues in Sociology of Sport* (pp. 211–218), Champaign, IL: Human Kinetics.

94. Adams (2004, December 9), "Sharpe Dispute Worked in Past," *The Rocky Mountain News*, p. 2C.

95. Putnam (1999), op. cit., p. 90.

96. Ibid.

97. Coakley (1998), op. cit.

98. Putnam (1999), op. cit.

99. Boxill, J. (2002), "Title IX and Gender Equity." In Holowchuk, M.A. (Ed.), *Philosophy of Sport* (pp. 395–402), Upper Saddle River, NJ: Prentice Hall.

100. Eitzen (2003), op. cit.

101. Ibid.

102. Ibid.

103. Ibid.

104. Ibid.

105. Ibid.

106. Messner, M., Dunbar, M., and Hunt, D. (2000), "The Televised Sports Manhood Formula," *Journal of Sport & Social Issues, 24*(4), pp. 380–394.

107. Lopiano (2000), op. cit.

108. Messner et al. (2000), op. cit.

109. Ibid.

110. Ibid., p. 392.

111. Anderson, K. (2001), "Snowboarding: The Construction of Gender in an Emerging Sport." In Yiannakis, A., and Melnick, M. (Eds.), *Contemporary Issues in Sociology of Sport* (pp. 275–290), Champaign, IL: Human Kinetics.

112. Coakley (1998), op. cit.

113. Knight, J., and Guiliano, T. (2003), "Blood, Sweat, and Jeers: The Impact of the Media's Heterosexist Portrayals on Perceptions of Male and Female Athletes," *Journal of Sport Behavior, 26*(3), pp. 272–285.

114. Boxill (2002), op. cit.

115. Ibid.

116. Knight and Guiliano (2003), op. cit.

117. McCallum, J. (2000, August 16), "Topless Thompson: Empowering or Enraging?" *Sports Illustrated* (online version).

118. Messner and Sabo (1994), op. cit.

119. Eitzen (2003), op. cit.

120. *The Economist* (n.d.), "Kiss My Ass."

121. Pratt, M. (n.d.), "Sexism & Sports: The Playing Field of Profit," *Workers World* (online version), retrieved on February 1, 2005, from http://www.workers.org.

122. Messner and Sabo (1994), op. cit.

123. Eitzen (1999), op. cit., p. 25.

124. Coakley (1998), op. cit.

125. Bloomberg (2002, September 6), "Pros Club Together to Back Augusta's No-Women Stance," retrieved on February 1, 2005, from http://www.smh.com.au.

126. Coakley (1998), op. cit.

127. Eitzen (2003), op. cit.

128. Ibid.

129. Lapchick, R. (2003), "Long Way to Go for Racial and Gender Equality in Sports Hiring Practices: Major League Soccer Lags Then Leads," available at http://www.sportinsciety.org.

130. Coakley (1998), op. cit., p. 226.

131. Suggs, W. (2000, March 17), "An Old-School Athletics Director and Title IX in the Deep South," *The Chronicle of Higher Education, 46*(28), p. A53.

132. Ibid.

CHAPTER 8

1. Howard, D., and Crompton, J. (2004), *Financing Sport*, 2nd ed. Morgantown, WV: Fitness Information Technology, Inc.

2. Delaney, K., and Eckstein, R. (2003), *Public Dollars, Private Stadiums*, New Brunswick, NJ: Rutgers University Press.

3. Ibid.

4. Schwarz, A. (May 9, 2005), "Not Just Peanuts: Minor-League Baseball is More than Quaint Stadiums and Dancing Umpires," *Newsweek, 36*.

5. Spirou, C., and Bennett, L. (2003), *It's Hardly Sportin': Stadiums, Neighborhoods, and the New Chicago*, Dekalb, IL: Northern Illinois University Press.

6. Keating, R. (April 5, 1999), "Sports Pork: The Costly Relationship between Major League Sports and Government," *Policy Analysis # 39*. NY: The Cato Institute.

7. Delaney and Eckstein (2003), op. cit.

8. Howard and Crompton (2004), op. cit.

9. Delaney and Eckstein (2003), op. cit.

10. Ibid.

11. Cagan, J., and deMause N. (1998), *Field of Schemes*, Monroe, ME: Common Courage Press.

12. Delaney and Eckstein (2003), op. cit.

13. Ibid.

14. Cagan and deMause (1998), op. cit.

15. Delaney and Eckstein (2003), op. cit.

16. Noll, R., and Zimbalist, A. (1997), "Sports, Jobs, and Taxes: The Real Connection." In Noll, R., and Zimbalist, A. (Eds.), *Sports, Jobs, and Taxes* (pp. 494–508), Washington, DC: The Brookings Institute.

17. Cagan and deMause (1998), op. cit.

18. Ibid.

19. Ibid.

20. Howard and Crompton (2004), op. cit.

21. Ibid.

22. Cagan and deMause (1998), op. cit.

23. Ibid.

24. Delaney and Eckstein (2003), op. cit.

25. Ibid.

26. Ibid.

27. Cagan and deMause (1998), op. cit.

28. Delaney and Eckstein (2003), op. cit.

29. Cagan and deMause (1998), op. cit.

30. Delaney and Eckstein (2003), op. cit.

31. Ibid.

32. Ibid.

33. Euchner, C. (1993), *Playing the Field: Why Sports Teams Move and Cities Fight to Keep Them*, Baltimore, MD: Johns Hopkins University Press, p. 55

34. Cagan and deMause (1998), op. cit.

35. Weiner, J. (2000), *Stadium Games*, Minneapolis, MN: University of Minnesota Press.

36. Cagan and deMause (1998), op. cit.

37. McGraw, D. (May 2005), "Demolishing Sports Welfare," *Reason.*

38. Cagan and deMause (1998), op. cit.

39. Ibid.

40. Ibid.

41. Howard and Crompton (2004), op. cit.

42. Cagan and deMause (1998), op. cit.

43. Ibid.

44. Delaney and Eckstein (2003), op. cit.

45. Cagan and deMause (1998), op. cit.

46. Delaney and Eckstein (2003), op. cit.

47. Cagan and deMause (1998), op. cit.

48. Spirou and Bennett (2003), op. cit.

49. Baade, R., and Dye, R. (1990), "The Impact of Stadiums and Professional Sports on Metropolitan Area Development," *Growth and Change, 21*(2), pp. 1–14.

50. Baade, R. (1990), "Stadiums, Sports and Economic Development: Assessing the Reality," *Heartland Policy Study no. 62*, Chicago, IL: Heartland Institute.

51. Spirou and Bennett (2003), op. cit.

52. Howard and Crompton (2004), op. cit.

53. Rosentraub, M. (1997), *Major League Losers: The Real Cost of Sports and Who's Paying for It*, New York: Basic.

54. Euchner (1993), op. cit.

55. Cagan and deMause (1998), op. cit.

56. Delaney and Eckstein (2003), op. cit., p. 31.

57. Zirin, D. (2005), *What's My Name, Fool?* Chicago, IL: Haymarket Press.

58. Cagan and deMause (1998), op. cit.

59. Ibid.

60. Delaney and Eckstein (2003), op. cit., p. 34.

61. Clarke, L. (1999), *Mission Impossible: Using Fantasy Documents to Tame Disasters*, Chicago, IL: University of Chicago Press.

62. Cagan and deMause (1998), op. cit.

63. Delaney and Eckstein (2003), op. cit.

64. Ibid.

65. Spirou and Bennett (2003), op. cit.

66. Cagan and deMause (1998), op. cit.

67. Weiner (2000), op. cit.

68. Zirin (2005), op. cit.

69. Delaney and Eckstein (2003), op. cit.

70. Cagan and deMause (1998), op. cit.

71. Ibid.

72. Ibid.

73. Spirou and Bennett (2003), op. cit.

74. Howard and Crompton (2004), op. cit.

75. Cagan and deMause (1998), op. cit.

76. Ibid.

77. Ibid.

78. Weiner (2000), op. cit.

79. Ibid.

80. Cagan and deMause (1998), op. cit.

81. Ibid.

82. Ibid.

83. Ibid.

84. Ibid.

85. Delaney and Eckstein (2003), op. cit., p. 41.

86. Ibid.

87. Noll and Zimbalist (1997), op. cit.

88. Howard and Crompton (2004), op. cit.

89. Ibid.

90. Cagan and deMause (1998), op. cit.

91. Ibid.

92. Weiner (2000), op. cit.

93. Ibid., p. 333.

94. Howard and Crompton (2004), op. cit.

95. Ibid.

96. Cagan and deMause (1998), op. cit.

97. Pastier, J. (1996, July 31), "Diamonds in the Rough," *Slate.*

98. Cagan and deMause (1998), op. cit.

99. Ibid.

100. Schwartz (2005), op. cit.

101. "How Much Does It Really Cost?" (February 1997), *Critique.*

102. Lewin, T. (1997, May 21), "Seeking to Shield Schools from Tax Breaks," *New York Times.*

103. Zirin (2005), op. cit.

104. Ibid.

105. Weiner (2000), op. cit.

106. Frank Rahid, in Cagan and deMause (1998), op. cit., p. 84.

107. Zirin (2005), op. cit., p. 224.

108. Delaney and Eckstein (2003), op. cit.

109. Cagan and deMause (1998), op. cit.

110. Ibid.

111. Tully, M. (2005, May 1), "Smaller NFL Markets Pay More for New Stadiums," *Detroit News.*

112. Delaney and Eckstein (2003), op. cit.

113. Spirou and Bennett (2003), op. cit.

114. Siegfried, J., and Zimbalist, A. (2000), "The Economics of Sports Facilities and Their Communities," *Journal of Economic Perspectives, 14*(3), pp. 95–114.

115. Delaney and Eckstein (2003), op. cit.

116. Ibid.

117. Cagan and deMause (1998), op. cit.

118. Delaney and Eckstein (2003), op. cit.

119. Cagan and deMause (1998), op. cit.

120. Ibid.

121. Weiner (2000), op. cit.

122. Crompton and Howard (2004), op. cit.

123. Weiner (2000), op. cit.

124. Cagan and deMause (1998), op. cit.

125. Tibbetts, T. (May 4, 2005), "U Officials Contemplate Stadium Fee," *Minnesota Daily*, available at http://www.mndaily.com/articles/2005/05/04.

126. Crompton and Howard (2004), op. cit.

127. Menninger, B. (1999, May 3–9), "Byproduct of Success: Money," *Sports Business Journal*, *21*, 30–31.

128. Crompton and Howard (2004), op. cit.

129. Campbell, B. (2001, August 8), "Big Money on Campus," *The Bryan-College Station Eagle, 1*, 5.

130. Menninger (1999), op. cit.

131. Menez, G. (May 16, 2005), "The $20 Million Stadium Boom," *Sports Illustrated, 102*(20), p. 67.

132. Ibid.

133. Ibid.

134. Ibid.

135. Ibid.

136. Weiner (2000), op. cit.

137. Cagan and deMause (2003), op. cit., p. 159.

138. Delaney and Eckstein (2003), op. cit.

139. Huxtable, A. (1992), *The Unreal America: Architecture and Illusion*, New York: The New Press.

140. Delaney and Eckstein (2003), p. 196.

141. Ibid.

142. Cagan and deMause (1998), op. cit.

143. Ibid.

144. Ibid.

145. McGraw (2005), op. cit.

146. Ibid.

147. Ibid.

CHAPTER 9

1. McCarthy, M. (2003, May 22), "Reebock Signs Talented Kids Up," *USA Today*, p. 2B.

2. *Denver Post* (2005, February 19), p. 2C.

3. Patrick, D. (2002, July 26), "Let the Kids Play," *USA Today*, p. 1C.

4. Cary, P., Dotinga, R., and Comarow, A. (2004, June 7), "Fixing Kids' Sports," *U.S. News & World Report, 136*(20), pp. 44–52.

5. Patrick (2002), op. cit.

6. Coakley, J. (1998), *Sport in Society: Issues and Controversies*, 6th ed. Boston, MA: MCGraw-Hill.

7. Cary et al. (2004), op. cit.

8. Powell, R. (2003), *We Own This Game*, New York: Atlantic Monthly Press.

9. Cary et al. (2004), op. cit.

10. In Gerdy, J. (2002), *Sport: The All-American Addiction*, Jackson, MS: University of Mississippi Press, p. 31.

11. Ibid.

12. Ibid.

13. Telander, R. (1989), *The Hundred Yard Lie*, Urbana, IL: University of Illinois Press.

14. Gerdy (2002), op. cit.

15. Cary et al. (2004), op. cit.

16. Gerdy (2002), op. cit.

17. Cary et al. (2004), op. cit.

18. Ibid., p. 36.

19. Gerdy (2002), op. cit., p. 195.

20. Cary et al. (2004), op. cit.

21. Ibid.

22. Wolff, A., and Menez, G. (2003, October 6), "The American Athlete Age 10," *Sports Illustrated, 99*(13), pp. 59–68.

23. Ibid.

24. Gerdy (2002), op. cit.

25. Ibid., pp. 22–23.

26. Ibid.

27. Ibid., p. 115.

28. Ibid., p. 23.

29. Eitzen, D.S. (1999), *Fair and Foul: Beyond the Myths and Paradoxes of Sport*, Lanham, MD: Rowman & Littlefield.

30. Ibid.

31. Gerdy (2002), op. cit.

32. Jay, K. (2004, December 12), "Athletes We Deserve; We Built That Pedestal, and We Can Tear It Down," *The Washington Post*, p. Bo1.

33. Gerdy (2002), op. cit.

34. Ibid.

35. Patrick (2002), op. cit.

36. Devereaux, E. (2001), "Backyard versus Little League Baseball: Some Observations on the Impoverishment of Children's Games in Contemporary America." In Yiannakis, A., and Melnick, M. (Eds.), *Contemporary Issues in Sociology of Sport* (pp. 63–72), Champaign, IL: Human Kinetics.

37. Ibid.

38. Ryan, J. (2000), *Little Girls in Pretty Boxes*, New York: Warner.

39. Cary et al. (2004), op. cit.

40. Cary et al. (2004), op. cit.

41. Telander (1989), op. cit., p. 213.

42. Gerdy (2002), op. cit., p. 227.

43. Ibid.

44. Sperber, M. (2000), *Beer and Circus: How Big-Time College Sports is Crippling Undergraduate Education*, New York: Owl.

45. Sperber, M. (1998), *Onward to Victory: The Crises That Shaped College Sports*, New York: Henry Holt.

46. Sperber (2000), op. cit.

47. Telander (1989), op. cit., p. 56.

48. Gerdy (2002), op. cit.

49. Brosnan, J. (2004, September 14), "Bloom Rips NCAA at Congressional Hearing," *Scripps Howard News Service.*

50. Eitzen (1999), op. cit.

51. Ibid.

52. Ibid.

53. Ibid.

54. Gerdy (2002), op. cit.

55. Sperber (2000), op. cit., p. 24.

56. Ibid.

57. Gerdy (2002), op. cit.

58. Eitzen (1999), op. cit.

59. Petkofsky, A. (2004, November 28), "Fees Boosting Sports Don't Get Much Play; What Students Pay to Aid Athletics Programs Often Is Unpublicized," *Richmond Times-Dispatch*, p. A-1.

60. Eitzen (1999), op. cit.

61. Ibid.

62. Renck, T. (2004, December 5), "Incident Could Cost Neagle $19 Million," *The Denver Post*, pp. 1B, 20B.

63. Benedict, J. (1998).

64. Ibid., pp. 223–224.

65. Ibid.

66. Kohn, A. (1986), *No Contest: The Case against Competition*, Boston, MA: Houghton-Mifflin, p. 2.

67. Ibid.

68. Jay (2004), op. cit.

69. Kohn (1986), op. cit., pp. 84–85.

70. Ibid.

71. Ibid.

72. Telander (1989), op. cit., p. 84.

73. Sage (1998), op. cit.

74. Gerdy (2002), op. cit., p. 57.

75. Eitzen (1999), op. cit., p. 38.

Index

About the Author

PETER FINLEY is Assistant Professor of Sport and Recreation Management in the H. Wayne Huizenga School of Business and Entrepreneurship at Nova Southeastern University, where he specializes in sociology of sport and sport ethics. He is the author of several publications about sport-related issues, including use of the Web for recruiting, privacy rights, and a variety of other sociology of sport topics. The Finleys are co-authors of *Piss Off! How Drug Testing and Other Privacy Violations are Alienating America's Youth.*

LAURA FINLEY is Professor of Sociology at Florida Atlantic University, where she teaches a variety of sociology topics. She is the author of numerous journal articles about such topics as peace education, crime in the media, school violence, and privacy rights.